FEDERAL COURTS IN THE EARLY REPUBLIC

KENTUCKY 1789-1816

FEDERAL COURTS IN THE EARLY REPUBLIC

KENTUCKY 1789-1816

MARY K. BONSTEEL TACHAU

PRINCETON UNIVERSITY PRESS
PRINCETON, NEW JERSEY

Library of Congress Cataloging in Publication Data will be
found on the last printed page of this book

Publication of this book has been aided by a grant from the
Paul Mellon Fund of Princeton University Press
This book has been composed in Linotype Caledonia

Clothbound editions of Princeton University Press books
are printed on acid-free paper, and binding materials are
chosen for strength and durability.

Printed in the United States of America by
Princeton University Press, Princeton, New Jersey

To Eric

Contents

TABLES

Acknowledgments

T HE greatest pleasure in finishing a work of this kind lies in remembering the friends, colleagues, and family whose generosity is reflected in the pages. Without the help of some of them, the book might never have been written; without the help of others it would certainly have been poorer. It is a pleasure to acknowledge publicly the gratitude that I hope I have already conveyed privately to these people:

Mary E. Young, for years of sustaining encouragement; Robert M. Ireland, for suggesting the topic; Kermit L. Hall, for thorough criticism; Patricia Watlington, James R. Broussard, and Richard H. Kohn, for enlightening insights; Stanley I. Kutler and Arthur J. Slavin, for useful advice; Kathryn T. Preyer, Harold M. Hyman, Stanley N. Katz, and Melvin I. Urofsky, for timely suggestions; William E. Read, James R. Merritt, and Patrick A. Lovell, for guidance through the labyrinthine mysteries of law and legal history; James R. Bentley, and the staffs of The Filson Club, the Kentucky Historical Society, the University of Louisville Libraries, the Special Collections Department of the Margaret I. King Library of the University of Kentucky, the Connecticut Historical Society, the Massachusetts Historical Society, the Historical Society of Pennsylvania, the Manuscript Division of the Library of Congress, and the National Archives, for true professionalism and many personal kindnesses; The Board of Trustees of the University of Louisville, for special leave to accomplish the research, and the Research Committee of the College of Arts and Sciences, for typing and travel assistance; Patricia R. Bonsteel and William E. Bonsteel, for hospitality during extended research trips; Katherine H. Tachau-Auerbach and Susan McKee Tachau, for their confidence; David Brandeis Tachau, for sharing his stylistic gifts; and Eric S. Tachau, for his uncommon wisdom.

FEDERAL COURTS IN THE EARLY REPUBLIC

KENTUCKY 1789-1816

I N 1922, Charles Warren published *The Supreme Court in United States History*, a pioneering work concerned with the impact of the Supreme Court and the federal judiciary on American history from 1789 to 1918.[1] The book was immediately recognized as an important contribution toward understanding the third, and often neglected, branch of government. Among the complimentary letters Warren received was one from United States Supreme Court Justice Louis D. Brandeis. He wrote that Warren had "performed an important public service," because "a better understanding of the function of our Court is an essential of political and social health." Like many other readers, Justice Brandeis found that the book inspired ideas for further research. He suggested in the conclusion of his letter: "Much having makes me hunger more. Have you ever thought of writing on the lower Federal Courts? A consideration of their functioning in the past would be interesting."[2] But Warren's investigations led him in other directions, and Brandeis's casual remark lay forgotten among Warren's correspondence.

Six years later, the suggestion was repeated from another source. In response to the public interest generated by passage of the Judiciary Act of 1925, Felix Frankfurter and James M. Landis wrote *The Business of the Supreme Court*.[3] Their book was intended to explain "the surface technicalities governing the jurisdiction of the Federal Courts." It also evaluated the role played by the judiciary in the balances of power between the states and the national government, and between "growingly divergent economic interests."[4] In a passage describing the problems of the circuits and the caseload of the Supreme Court, the authors repeated the Brandeis suggestion, which was probably unknown to them:

> Our national history will not have been adequately written until the history of our judicial systems can be adequately told through monograph studies of individual courts. . . . Nor shall we be able to know

[1] Charles Warren, *The Supreme Court in United States History, 1789-1918* (Boston, 1922). References hereafter are to rev. ed. (Boston, 1926).
[2] Louis D. Brandeis to Charles Warren, June 23, 1922, Charles Warren Papers, Box 1, Manuscript Division, Library of Congress.
[3] Felix Frankfurter and James M. Landis, *The Business of the Supreme Court: A Study in the Federal Judicial System* (New York, 1928).
[4] *Ibid.*, vi.

how our courts function until an effective system of judicial statistics becomes part of our tradition. . . . What is needed is an annual detailed analysis of litigation, the courts whence cases come, the dispositions made of them, the nature of the questions involved, etc., etc., etc.[5]

Although the suggestion was here made publicly rather than privately, it too has been largely overlooked.[6] Three recent books have examined different aspects of lower federal courts, but none has been as comprehensive or as methodically analytical as Frankfurter and Landis proposed.[7]

It is the purpose of the present study to pursue their suggestion by a systematic examination of the lower federal courts of one state during the first generation after the adoption of the Constitution. It is not an investigation to test any particular hypothesis, but an inquiry, as in the original etymological meaning of the word *history*. In the course of the research many tantalizing tangents have been explored, ranging from technical legal problems to the relationships between the court and its personnel and important events and persons in national history. But the findings that are reported are sharply limited to those which affected the federal courts in Kentucky. This is, therefore, an institutional history with an intentional focus upon the courts themselves. Although legal scholars interested in substantive and juris-

[5] *Ibid.*, 52.
[6] Two recent exceptions are: R. Kent Newmyer, "Justice Joseph Story on Circuit and a Neglected Phase of American Legal History," *American Journal of Legal History*, xiv (1970), 112-135, and Bradley T. Johnson, *Reports of Cases Decided by Chief Justice Chase in the Circuit Court of the United States Fourth Circuit 1865-1869*, introd. Ferne B. Hyman and Harold M. Hyman (New York, 1972 [orig. publ. New York, 1876]), v-xxvii.
[7] Julius Goebel, Jr., *Antecedents and Beginnings to 1800*, in Paul A. Freund, ed., *The Oliver Wendell Holmes Devise History of the Supreme Court*, i (New York, 1971). (Hereafter cited as *Antecedents and Beginnings*.) However, Goebel was principally interested in the lower courts as they related to the United States Supreme Court, and his analyses of cases were directed toward illustrating questions of substantive law. A survey of the numbers and kinds of cases docketed in the federal district and circuit courts is included in Dwight F. Henderson's *Courts For a New Nation* (Washington, 1971). Henderson's purpose was to evaluate the need for those courts, and he did not systematically examine the disposition of the cases. Marvin Schick's *Learned Hand's Court* (Baltimore, 1970) is a study of the United States Court of Appeals for the Second Circuit from 1941 to 1951. As the author pointed out in his preface, the contextual limitation of a single decade distorts the work of the court because it overlooks the court's previous history and does not pursue the ultimate disposition of all the cases arising during that decade.

4

dictional questions may find some useful information, I wrote this study for historians and others without formal training in law.[8]

Source material for this subject is abundant. All the essential federal court records are still housed in the old Federal Building in Frankfort, Kentucky. The most important of these, the Order Books of the courts, have been made more accessible by a microfilming project conducted by the Church of Jesus Christ of Latter-Day Saints. They have also microfilmed the Complete Record of the Seventh Circuit Court, an incomplete collection of case papers containing illuminating material. (Copies of the microfilm are in the Special Collections Department of the Margaret I. King Library of the University of Kentucky, Lexington.) Other court records were made available by the clerk of the United States Court for the Eastern District of Kentucky at Lexington.

The chronological limits of the study were determined by the tenure of the first judge of the United States Court for the District of Kentucky, Harry Innes. Innes kept an astonishing number and variety of his personal papers. His descendants deposited them in the Manuscript Division of the Library of Congress, where they fill twenty-eight volumes, capriciously numbered and arranged. Additional Innes papers are held by the Filson Club in Louisville, Kentucky, and by the Kentucky Historical Society in Frankfort. During the years while he sat alone on the Kentucky federal bench, Innes copied ninety-two of his opinions (which, according to custom, were not included in the court records) in a small leather-bound book that was found by chance in the office of the clerk of the United States Court for the Western District of Kentucky at Louisville. An important body of related government records is held by the National Archives in Washington. Supplemental material is in the manuscript collections of the Massachusetts Historical Society, Boston; the Connecticut Historical Society in Hartford; and in the Historical Society of Pennsylvania in Philadelphia.

In order to discover what happened in the federal courts in Kentucky, my fundamental research technique was to transpose these scattered sources into more manageable form by virtually reconstructing the cases in a card file. This involved copying the work of the courts recorded in the Order Books and then setting up a separate card for each case. All of the significant actions taken on a case were

[8] The distinction between institutional legal history and legal history emphasizing substantive law is described by Herbert Alan Johnson, "American Colonial Legal History: A Historiographical Interpretation," in Alden T. Vaughan and George Athan Billias, eds., *Perspectives on Early American History: Essays in Honor of Richard B. Morris* (New York, 1973), 262-269.

noted on each card. The technique thus invented produced a kind of evidence heretofore absent from legal history: the disposition of each case and, collectively, the day in, day out work of the courts. With eleven Order Books completed during the period under examination, containing 4,689 pages of notations on 2,290 cases, this system made possible quantitative as well as qualitative evaluation.

Because of the time limitations involved in working with microfilm borrowed through interlibrary loan, the collection of evidence was well under way before the background reading was completed. While this reversal of the usual procedure resulted in some initial disorientation, it had a fortuitous consequence. I had very few preconceived ideas about what conclusions to expect, and the evidence was gathered without commitment to a particular frame of reference. By the time I had fully assimilated the theses of other writers, I had compiled a large body of evidence against which their generalizations could be tested.

The unique opportunity provided by immediate and constant reference to the concrete evidence of the courts' own records led me, in many instances, to conclusions which differ from those of other students of American legal and constitutional history. The data, in fact, so frequently contradict so much of the conventional wisdom that a reexamination of many popular assumptions may be in order. It is, of course, possible that the Kentucky federal courts were atypical. Whether that proves to be the case can only be known after a research design similar to the one used in this study is applied to the records of other contemporaneous courts. With the growing availability and accessibility of early court records, one hopes that they will be used to seek comparisons with the findings presented here and to gain a more comprehensive understanding of this segment of the national past.[9]

Ever since the Works Progress Administration surveyed federal records in the states in the 1930s, it has been known that federal court records were available even where they were not easily accessible. It seems now somewhat surprising that they have not been used. Ap-

[9] A convenient listing of the location of many federal district and circuit court papers is in Goebel, *Antecedents and Beginnings*, 815. Some federal court records have been inventoried and microfilmed by the National Archives. An example of the potential for reevaluation may be seen in an article based upon the federal circuit court records for the District of Georgia, which presents a significant revision of the circumstances relating to the case that prompted the Eleventh Amendment. Doyle Mathis, "*Chisholm* v. *Georgia*: Background and Settlement," *Journal of American History*, LIV (1967), 19-29.

parently, most scholars, if they thought about the lower federal courts, assumed that they already knew in general terms what went on in them. If mentioned at all, they are described as inferior courts in every sense of that word. It was in the early federal circuit courts that the travesties of the Sedition Act of 1798 were carried out; it was in an early federal district court that Judge John Pickering so misbehaved that he was later impeached. Not until Robert Trimble of Kentucky was appointed to the Supreme Court in 1826 was any judge of a lower federal court elevated to the high court. This fact suggests that the lower federal courts were not seen as useful training grounds for judicial eminence.

Almost all the courts of the new nation are believed to have been so anti-British that they ignored the proprieties of their English legal traditions. Lawyers are said to have been poorly trained and unpopular.[10] A recent study suggests that courts were governed more by politics than by law.[11] When, to these impressions, are added Charles Warren's assertions that the people of at least five states were at war with the federal judiciary during this time, it has seemed reasonable to conclude that the lower federal courts are best forgotten.[12] If the third branch of government made any contribution toward the permanence and stability of the new republic, it has seemed that only the court of John Marshall did so. American historians interested in the early federal judiciary have, therefore, tended to concentrate on the United States Supreme Court, its members, and its most significant cases.

In doing so, they have been aided by the Court itself, which recognized from the beginning that its decisions must be understandable if they were to be acceptable to the citizenry. Supreme Court opinions are written in terms that any interested literate person can comprehend, and sometimes are truly eloquent. That public interest of which the Court has always been mindful has been well served by historians who have expanded the language of the court to explain the policy issues and the public consequences of what were, at heart, legal questions.

But to move from the Supreme Court to the lower federal courts means to move from constitutional history to legal history, and that is another world altogether. It is a world into which a nonlawyer ven-

[10] Charles Warren, A History of the American Bar (Boston, 1911), 212-214. Maxwell Bloomfield, American Lawyers in a Changing Society, 1776-1876 (Cambridge, Mass., 1976), 39-58.
[11] Richard E. Ellis, The Jeffersonian Crisis: Courts and Politics in the Young Republic (New York, 1971).
[12] Warren, Supreme Court, I, 366-400; 541-565; 633-652.

tures cautiously. Many historians have doubtless been chastened, at least vicariously, by the reprimands delivered by Julius Goebel, Jr. A lawyer-historian of stature and candor, Goebel scathingly denounced what he considered the presumptuousness of historians who attempted to deal with matters that he thought were better left to lawyers. So contemptuously did he dismiss several such pioneering efforts by people trained in history that his words have doubtless had a chilling effect on many others.[13]

Even historians who have never heard of Goebel are easily deterred from working in early lower court records. They are unlike any other official American documents. The law then had a language all its own, a highly stylized English interspersed with Latin. The English was not like spoken or literary English, and the Latin was not the Latin of Cicero or Caesar. Together they formed a strange tongue that had been brewed out of the melting pot of English history to mark the guideposts of English law as it was understood (and misunderstood) in these former English colonies. Until the reforms of the codification movement of the mid-nineteenth century, all court cases at the trial level were pursued in forms of action that have since been superseded and largely forgotten. Not only is the nature of a grievance obscured by language barriers, but also the methods of resolving it seem almost incomprehensibly ritualistic. There are no adequate guidebooks, ancient or modern, to help one through this most unfamiliar terrain. What was once so obvious and elementary that it did not seem worth writing down and explaining is now elusive and abstruse to a conventionally trained historian. Everyone confronting such obstacles understands and shares the lament of a law clerk of that era: "How many hours have I hunted, how many books turned up, for what three minutes of explanation from any tolerable lawyer would have made clear to me."[14]

But those who have some acquaintance with these archaic procedures and practices do not ask the questions for which historians need the answers. Lawyers with training in legal history are not particularly

---

[13] Julius Goebel, Jr. and T. Raymond Naughton, *Law Enforcement in Colonial New York: A Study in Criminal Procedure (1664-1776)* (Montclair, N.J., 1970), xxxii-xxxvi. See also, Goebel's review of Dorothy S. Towle, ed., *Records of the Vice-Admiralty Court of Rhode Island, 1716-1752*, in *American Historical Review*, XLIII (1938), 403-406.

[14] Henry C. Van Schaack, *Life of Peter Van Schaack, LL.D.* (New York, 1842), 9. The problems and significance of early court records are described by Elizabeth Gaspar Brown, "Frontier Justice: Wayne County 1796-1836," *Am. J. Legal Hist.*, XVI (1972), 126-153.

8

interested in how law affected the general population, or how the work of the courts interacted with other institutions. Legal training emphasizes precedent, the isolation of topical issues, and the development of legal doctrines. The analytic skills of lawyer-historians have therefore been principally devoted to discovering the history of American law rather than the legal history of the American people. For example, many lawyers have responded to the challenge of Chancellor James Kent's undocumented assertion that when he became a judge of the New York Supreme Court in 1798, "we had no law of our own, and nobody knew what it was."[15] One group of legal historians joined Dean Roscoe Pound in his belief that a rejection of English common law, the departure of leading Loyalist attorneys, and an undeveloped reporting system in the post-Revolutionary period, together led to a noticeable break from the past.[16] Another group has concentrated on the colonial period in order to discover whether the significant antecedents of American law derived from English local courts or from the central courts in London.[17] Both groups have been concerned with questions of substantive law and the development of legal principles rather than with the place of law in the lives of ordinary people.

Legal research has ranged from bench to bar to legislative chambers. Scholars have collected, calendared, and edited the papers of prominent predecessors.[18] Even the notebooks of obscure attorneys practicing in a local court have been mined for clues.[19] Legislative debates have been examined to discover intention, statutes to determine implementation, and judges' opinions to find legal perception.[20] Members

[15] William Kent, *Memoirs and Letters of James Kent, LL.D.* (Boston, 1898), 117.

[16] Roscoe Pound, *The Formative Era of American Law* (Boston, 1938); Francis R. Aumann, "Some Problems of Growth and Development in the Formative Period of the American Legal System, 1775-1866," *University of Cincinnati Law Review*, XIII (1939), 382-445; Anton-Hermann Chroust, "The American Legal Profession: Its Agony and Ecstacy," *Notre Dame Lawyer*, XLVI (1971), 487-525.

[17] A particularly useful collection of these studies is David H. Flaherty, ed., *Essays in the History of Early American Law* (Chapel Hill, N.C., 1969).

[18] Julius Goebel, Jr., *et al.*, eds., *The Law Practice of Alexander Hamilton* (New York, 1964-1969); L. Kinvin Wroth and Hiller B. Zobel, eds., *Legal Papers of John Adams* (Cambridge, Mass., 1965); Irwin S. Rhodes, *The Papers of John Marshall: A Descriptive Calendar* (Norman, Okla., 1969); David John Mays, ed., *The Letters and Papers of Edmund Pendleton, 1734-1803* (Charlottesville, Va., 1967); Herbert A. Johnson, *et al.*, eds., *The Papers of John Marshall* (Chapel Hill, N.C., 1974-   ).

[19] Daniel J. Boorstin, ed., *Delaware Cases 1792-1830* (St. Paul, Minn., 1943).

[20] Morton J. Horwitz, "The Emergence of an Instrumental Conception of American Law, 1780-1820," in Donald Fleming and Bernard Bailyn, eds., *Law in American History*, Perspectives in American History, V (Cambridge, Mass., 1971), 287-326.

of the bar in at least two states have been scrutinized.[21] A variety of evidence has been gathered from widely scattered sources. As a result, the legal history of the young nation has been reconstructed from fragments of information and interpretation that are often unrelated to each other, and generalists have been forced to rely upon such disparate bits and pieces in the absence of more comprehensive knowledge.[22]

There have been few systematic studies of the total caseloads of any courts and fewer still that have analyzed the disposition of all the cases.[23] Sampling techniques have dominated research. Yet the comprehensive study of any court's records yields both a quantity and a quality of evidence not found elsewhere. While debates and statutes suggest possibilities, and private papers indicate probabilities, only court records provide certainties. And the court itself provides a focus for otherwise disconnected facts.

Court records, especially contemporaneous ones, also facilitate comparisons not otherwise feasible. It may prove to be impossible to develop a body of knowledge based upon state court records because they seem often to have been lost or destroyed. But the most essential records of the lower federal courts, the Order Books (or Minute Books) have been preserved for many if not all of the jurisdictions. Their records reveal actual legal practice. They show how national laws,

[21] Donald M. Roper, "The Elite of the New York Bar as Seen from the Bench; James Kent's Necrologies," *New-York Historical Society Quarterly*, LVI (1972), 199-237; Gerard W. Gawalt, "Massachusetts Lawyers: A Historical Analysis of the Process of Professionalization, 1760-1840" (Ph.D. diss., Clark University, 1969).

[22] The first general history of American law is Lawrence M. Friedman, *A History of American Law* (New York, 1973). The author describes the limitations of existing knowledge throughout his book. See, e.g., 9, 83, 110, 144, 596-601.

[23] Francis W. Laurent's study of the circuit court of Chippewa County, Wisconsin, from 1855 to 1954, *The Business of a Trial Court: 100 Years of Cases* (Madison, 1959) received only one thoughtful review, by Lawrence M. Friedman in *St. Louis Law Review*, v (1959), 454-466. One of the rare examples of published court records for this period is William Wirt Blume, ed., *Transactions of the Supreme Court of the Territory of Michigan 1805-1814* (Ann Arbor, 1935). Even colonial court records, which have received greater attention, are seldom published in their entirety. A convenient guide to these is Michael G. Kammen, "Colonial Court Records and the Study of Early American History: A Bibliographic Review," *American Historical Review*, LXX (1965), 732-739. Analyses of post-Revolutionary legal history based upon court records are: William Wirt Blume, "Civil Procedure on the American Frontier: A Study of the Records of a Court of Common Pleas of the Northwest and Indiana Territories (1796-1805)," *Michigan Law Review*, LVI (1957), 161-224; M. Leigh Harrison, "A Study of the Earliest Reported Decisions of the South Carolina Courts of Law," *Am. J. Legal Hist.*, XVI (1972), 51-70; Brown, "Frontier Justice," *ibid.*, 126-153.

constitutional interpretations, and federal authority were, in fact, applied to the citizens and the circumstances of the nation.

It is important to remember that the federal judiciary encompasses much more than the United States Supreme Court. Certainly the appellate function of that court gives it a unique status. But the presumption that a court of last resort is the most (or only) important court in the legal system should be qualified, especially for the early national period. Most cases originate and terminate in the trial courts; it is there that most people have their only contact with the judicial system. The traditional emphasis upon the Supreme Court may have distorted our understanding of the importance of the federal judiciary. Systematic investigations into the work of the early inferior courts may show that their impact was much greater than has been assumed.

In the beginning of the national experience, it was generally thought that state courts could handle most of the cases that would be docketed in the federal district and circuit courts. These lower courts were believed to be needed, not to share the burden of volume (which was expected to be slight), but to protect nonresidents from possible local prejudices, and to assure uniformity where a single national practice was considered necessary, as in admiralty and maritime law.[24] Local variations in legal practice were expected and accepted as long as the right of appeal to the Supreme Court was preserved. The original district and circuit courts were considered useful more for political purposes than because they were needed for the administration of private or public law.

From the passage of the Judiciary Act of 1789 to the present, no evidence has been presented to challenge these assumptions. But an examination of the records of the federal courts in Kentucky suggests that they may need reevaluation. The most striking discovery is the number of cases. During a period when the United States Supreme Court handed down 457 decisions, the federal courts in Kentucky acted on 2,290 causes. Constitutional and legal questions were decided much more frequently by these inferior courts than by the Supreme Court, and for 98 percent of the litigants, those decisions were final.

Only forty-nine cases were carried to the Supreme Court, where they appear in the early Reports (although the case files are incomplete in the Supreme Court's records).[25] The remaining 2,241 cases have been

[24] Charles Warren, "New Light on the History of the Federal Judiciary Act of 1789," *Harvard Law Review*, xxxvii (1923), 49-132.

[25] Appellate Case Files of the Supreme Court of the United States, 1792-1831, M-214, Records of the Supreme Court of the United States, Record Group 267, National Archives.

11

completely overlooked by the compilers of federal and state digests and do not appear in any published records. Only two Kentucky cases from this period have ever received any public attention at all, and even that has been limited to specialists.[26]

This hitherto hidden litigation provides a wealth of illuminating material. Its usefulness for legal history is obvious. Some of the information yields insights into social and economic history. Other data are important in political history. For example, one-third of the cases were brought by officers of the government. Most of this litigation came about because of the internal revenue laws and it illustrates the difficulties of enforcing unpopular statutes among a population determined to resist them. The remaining cases were private civil suits between individuals. The volume alone indicates that in Kentucky the federal courts were perceived as essential in the adjudication of private controversies.

Thousands of people were directly affected by the proceedings in these courts. And because the influence of a lawsuit may extend beyond the nominal litigants, it is likely that thousands more were affected indirectly. It seems clear that the federal courts in Kentucky must have been much more important than has been assumed, and in a different way from that described by Charles Warren. It is doubtful whether any other branch of the federal government acted so directly upon so many people in Kentucky as did this segment of the federal judiciary. Probably only the government's policies on the Indians and on navigation of the Mississippi River were of greater significance to these citizens in the interior. During a period when the executive and legislative branches so often seemed "at a distance and out of sight," and the United States Supreme Court was available only to a tiny, privileged minority, the courts of Harry Innes were accessible, visible, and deeply involved in the concerns of the population.[27]

Because contact with the federal courts was so extensive, these institutions may well have exercised considerable influence on the attitudes of Kentuckians toward their central government. It has, therefore, seemed important to evaluate the kind of law practiced in the

[26] The better known is the charge of treason unsuccessfully brought against Aaron Burr, described in Chapter Six. *Green* v. *Biddle* was discovered in the Supreme Court Reports by Paul W. Gates, who described its progress there in "Tenants of the Log Cabin," *Mississippi Valley Historical Review*, XLIX (1962), 3-31.

[27] The quotation from *The Federalist*, No. 27, by Alexander Hamilton, illustrates James Sterling Young's description of the alienation of citizens from their government in *The Washington Community 1800-1828* (New York, 1966), 13-37.

courts to determine what kind of image they projected to the people. Did these courts aspire to that equal justice which is consonant with political equality? Were the procedures of the courts new ones that were devised in response to the requirements of the frontier, or were they the familiar English procedures as they had been modified by the colonial experience? What kind of men were identified with the courts? Did they enhance the prestige of the judiciary, or did they dissipate its potential authority? What was the range of power available to the lower courts?

This study attempts to answer these questions. Whether the experience of Kentucky was unique or was typical will not be known until similar studies are made of other federal and state courts of this period. The difficulties of transportation and communication may have superseded a common tradition, the perceptions and convictions of certain key individuals may have been uncommon, and the expense of carrying cases to the Supreme Court may have prevented challenges to the practices of the Kentucky courts and inhibited the development of a uniform federal practice. But what happened in the Kentucky federal courts from 1789 until 1816 is revealed in an unusually rich combination of records. They provide the evidence for this examination of the jurisdiction of those courts, the judges and other personnel who served in them, the procedures followed, and the disposition of cases according to categories. Taken together, these findings illustrate one segment of our judicial history—and raise questions about the remainder.

CHAPTER ONE

The Style, Structure, and Jurisdiction
of the Courts

K ENTUCKY acquired a federal court in 1789, two and one-half years
before it achieved statehood. What was then the western district
of Virginia was a wilderness, only recently vacated by Indians who
frequently recrossed the Ohio River to attack the Anglo-Americans
who had taken their hunting and farming lands.[1] It was a forested and
fertile land which promised great productivity and wealth to those
who could hold and exploit it, but it was a land that could be reached
only after hazardous journeys along primitive trails or along the rivers.
No stagecoaches penetrated the region, and the unimproved Wilderness Road, recently carved through the mountains, was too rugged
for wagons.[2] There was no mail service: even letters from President
Washington and his secretary of war were carried in the packs and
saddlebags of private citizens.[3] Communications within and away from
the area were exceedingly irregular.

Yet despite the primitive environment, the federal court in Kentucky
soon became very busy, in part because the law practiced there did not
yield the crude justice generally associated with the frontier.[4] This

---

[1] Harry Innes to John Brown, Dec. 7, 1787, Harry Innes File, Manuscript
Collection, Kentucky Historical Society, Frankfort, Ky.; William Elsey Connelley
and E[llis] M[erton] Coulter, *History of Kentucky*, ed. Charles Kerr, I (Chicago,
1922), 239-307, *passim*.

[2] Thomas Todd to Charles S. Todd, Aug. 23, 1808, Todd Family Papers, Manuscript Dept., Filson Club, Louisville, Ky.; Thomas Speed, *The Wilderness Road*
(Louisville, 1886), 30; Robert L. Kincaid, *The Wilderness Road* (Harrogate, Tenn.,
1955), 184.

[3] George Washington (by Tobias Lear) to John Brown, Oct. 2, 1789, Miscellaneous Letters of the Department of State, 1789-1906, M-179, roll 2, General
Records of the Department of State, Record Group 59, National Archives. (Hereafter cited as Misc. Letters, Dept. of State, M-179); Henry Knox to Beverly
Randolph, Dec. 17, 1789, W. P. Palmer *et al.*, eds., *Calendar of Virginia State
Papers and Other Manuscripts . . . Preserved . . . at Richmond (1652-1869)*,
v (Richmond, Va., 1875-1893), 82.

[4] Writers who accept the thesis that English common law was rejected during
this period often conclude that English procedures also were proscribed, and that
frontier courts were crude and undignified. E.g., Charles Warren, *A History of
the American Bar* (Boston, 1911), 212-214; Roscoe Pound, "The Pioneers and
the Common Law," *West Virginia Law Quarterly*, XXVII (1920), 1; Richard E.
Ellis, *The Jeffersonian Crisis: Courts and Politics in the Young Republic* (New
York, 1971), 115-117; Anton-Hermann Chroust, "The American Legal Profession: Its Agony and Ecstasy," *Notre Dame Lawyer*, XLVI (1971), 487-525; Charles

court and its immediate successors upheld the traditions of centuries of English experience, modified in the colonial period and now applied to a new political and judicial experiment. Some of that law was very old, developed in a different political and socioeconomic environment, but applicable in many of its forms and procedures to this sparsely settled and crudely surveyed land. Some of the law was an adaptation of familiar principles to the requirements of the new Constitution, which was founded on the unprecedented ideal of political and legal equality for all white men. Some of the law evolved in Kentucky in response to the competitiveness and land hunger of the population. Always it was law characterized by a time-consuming concern for due process and by an avoidance of arbitrary judgments and summary methods.

There are several reasons for the sophisticated nature of the legal practice in these courts. First, it was part of the expectations of the settlers themselves, many of whom came from Virginia where they had known a well-trained bar and bench, conservatively dedicated to English legal traditions.[5] Second in importance is the fact that Harry Innes served as district judge for the courts' first twenty-seven years. Innes was a man of strong character, firm convictions, and excellent legal education who was well aware both of the precedents he had to follow and the importance of those he would establish. The third reason lies in the qualifications of the other officers of the courts. All were remarkably well trained for their generation. Many were men whose families or whose own reputations were known personally to

---

M. Haar, ed., *The Golden Age of American Law* (New York, 1965), 4. Most of the evidence for this conclusion comes from lawyers' memoirs. Such sources should be treated with skepticism, for they may be colored by self-interest, political and legal prejudices, and (especially in an age of circuit riding) the temptation to tell good stories whether or not they are true. While irregularities doubtless occurred, their prevalence has probably been exaggerated, as scholars who have studied court records assert. See Zechariah Chafee, Jr., "Colonial Courts and the Common Law," in David H. Flaherty, ed., *Essays in the History of Early American Law* (Chapel Hill, N.C., 1969), 69; William Wirt Blume, "Civil Procedure on the American Frontier: A Study of the Records of a Court of Common Pleas of the Northwest and Indiana Territories (1796-1805)," *Michigan Law Review*, LVI (1957), 209; Julius Goebel, Jr., *et al.*, *The Law Practice of Alexander Hamilton*, I (New York, 1964), 7-10, 33; Elizabeth Gaspar Brown, "Frontier Justice: Wayne County 1796-1836," *American Journal of Legal History*, XVI (1972), 126-128, 152.

[5] David H. Flaherty, "An Introduction to Early American Legal History," in Flaherty, ed., *Essays in the History of Early American Law*, 25; Charles Warren, *The Supreme Court in United States History*, I (Boston, 1926), 37; Ellis, *Jeffersonian Crisis*, 121; Herbert A. Johnson *et al.*, *The Papers of John Marshall*, I (Chapel Hill, N.C., 1974).

the presidents who appointed them. The clerks, who served at the pleasure of the judges, were lawyers who could meet their exacting standards. Finally, there was no lay bar in Kentucky's federal courts. Counsel were admitted only upon presentation of credentials indicating that they had been licensed to practice in the state courts or upon motion of attorneys already accepted by the court.[6]

Tradition and stability were, however, only part of the nature of these courts. An equally important characteristic was their experimental quality. In Kentucky, as throughout the nation, the judiciary was involved in a legal experiment that paralleled (as it proceeded from) the contemporaneous political experiment in federalism. The new Constitution had created a federal system that divided authority between the national government and the states. Although in certain areas it was supreme, the national government was one of limited powers. The states had rights and jurisdictions reserved to them which were not always clearly specified. Any concentration of power was generally feared, yet the central government had to be strong enough that it might hope to achieve the purposes expressed in the Preamble to the Constitution.

The principal function of the federal judiciary was to resolve conflicts: those between the states, between citizens of different states, and between the states and their citizens and the national government. These conflicts had to be resolved without infringing the recently won and jealously guarded liberties of the people, and they had to be resolved in states that were competing not only with each other but also with the federal government. To the degree that the powers, rights, and liberties claimed in these conflicts were defined in legal as well as in political terms, it was the responsibility of the judiciary to guide the experiment in federalism by declaring what the law was.

For federal judges, especially, the assignment was a challenging and ironic one. They had been reared in a legal system that had provided a measure of justice to a remarkably high proportion of the population through its emphasis upon custom and precedent. They belonged to a generation that had violently resisted what had been construed as arbitrary departures from these. They had defied legal authority themselves and were now engaged in justifying a government based upon revolution. Yet they had to draw upon their knowledge of English law and history to find the legal mechanisms needed to stabilize and rationalize an American government. It was the particular obligation of

---

[6] United States Court for the District of Kentucky, "Rules of the Court," Order Book A, Apr. 1, 1790, ix. (Hereafter cited as DC OB).

16

federal judges to discover traditional principles that would provide sufficient continuity with the past to give the new legal system the predictability and prestige needed for its survival.

Specifically, this meant that every federal judge needed to be familiar with English common law, English statutes, and English chancery procedures and decisions. All of these then had to be interpreted in the spirit of the new American Constitution, in conformity with the statutes passed by Congress, and with a responsible awareness of political realities. In addition, the Judiciary Act of 1789 required federal judges to be expert interpreters of the individual constitutions and laws of the states in which their federal courts were situated. Section 34 stated: "The laws of the several States, except where the Constitution, treaties, or statutes of the United States shall otherwise require or provide, shall be regarded as rules of decision in trials at common law in the courts of the United States in cases where they apply."[7]

But following the laws of the states was difficult because the states themselves were nascent political bodies. Their laws were not uniform. They were unclear, uncodified, and unsystematically recorded if recorded at all. Even where there were no conflicts between state practices and national principles, it was hard for federal judges to determine whether their decisions would be consistent with those of other federal courts because a nationwide reporting system had not yet been developed.

And so declaring the law in the new federal judiciary was a complicated and subjective process. The Kentucky court records illustrate that the concept of a clear and simple "rule of law" upon which all could agree was a myth believed only by laymen. Conflicting traditions, decisions, and statutes had to be weighed. Discovering "the law" for a particular case was often a delicate matter requiring a high degree of selectivity and interpretation. Sometimes it was difficult to fathom the intentions of the Congress; occasionally it seemed inexpedient to press those intentions too vigorously. Often the administration of the housekeeping details of the court was a formidable task, and always it was troublesome to obtain law books and court reports. The distances and the procedures prevented any rapid termination of most causes. The day in and day out work of the court was a tedious process of moving cases slowly and cautiously toward judgment.

During their first generation, the Kentucky federal courts developed an identifiable style that was manifested in their proceedings and in

[7] Richard Peters, ed., *The Public Statutes at Large of the United States of America, 1789-1873* (Boston, 1850-1873), i, 73. (Hereafter cited as i Stat.)

the disposition of the caseload. Some of the determinants of this style were unique to Kentucky, such as the location of the court and the judges' points of view. Others were shared by certain other courts, like the response of the people to controversial congressional statutes and the applicability of particular land laws. Still other determinants were common to all federal courts, including the constitutional and statutory provisions that empowered and at the same time limited the judiciary. In order to evaluate the work of the Kentucky federal courts it may be useful to examine these provisions first, because they provided the boundaries within which the courts could operate.

All federal courts were established under two constitutional provisions, one in section 1 of Article III, the other in section 8 of Article I. These provisions stated:

> The judicial Power of the United States, shall be vested in one supreme Court, and in such inferior Courts as the Congress may from time to time ordain and establish.

> The Congress shall have Power . . . [t]o constitute Tribunals inferior to the supreme Court.

Only the Supreme Court itself was required by the Constitution, and only the Supreme Court had an original jurisdiction specified in the Constitution. Other federal courts were created at the discretion of Congress, and Congress could distribute the federal jurisdiction of these courts. The range of judicial power was potentially great, as may be seen in the following clauses from section 2 of Article III:

> The judicial Power shall extend to all Cases, in Law and Equity, arising under this Constitution, the Laws of the United States, and Treaties made, or which shall be made, under their Authority; . . . to all Cases of admiralty and maritime Jurisdiction;—to Controversies to which the United States shall be a Party; . . . between Citizens of different States,—between Citizens of the same State claiming Lands under Grants of different States, and between a State, or the Citizens thereof, and foreign States, Citizens or Subjects.

During the early years of the republic, Congress frequently exercised its authority over the structure and jurisdiction of the judicial branch. It experimented with the size of the Supreme Court, the numbers of circuit and district courts, the procedures and processes to be followed in those courts, and the extent of their jurisdiction. In fact, eighty-six statutes relating to the judiciary were passed during the time covered

by this study. Many of these laws were not applicable to the Kentucky courts, and others were not of lasting significance. But the Judiciary Acts of 1789, 1801, 1802, and 1807, which dealt with structure and jurisdiction, immediately affected the Kentucky federal courts in important ways.

The United States Court for the District of Kentucky was established by the Judiciary Act of 1789. In that first judiciary act, Congress devised a three-part federal court system, made up of district courts, circuit courts, and the United States Supreme Court. Although the names of these courts have been retained, their functions have changed over time. In this respect, the Supreme Court has changed less than the original lower courts, which were quite different from their modern counterparts because of the different division of federal jurisdiction. In the modern federal system, the district courts are the courts of general original jurisdiction. They hear by far the greatest proportion of federal cases. Only a minority of those are appealed to what are now called the circuit courts of appeal, and a still smaller number of those cases are carried to the United States Supreme Court. Together, the federal courts today resemble a three-tiered layer cake, with the lowest layer, the district courts, having the largest caseload.

In the original system, however, it was the circuit courts that were the courts of general original jurisdiction and had the largest number of cases. The division of the federal caseload between the circuit courts and the district courts was then like a pie, with the district courts having a very small slice and the circuit courts having the larger share. Although there were minor changes, this proportional distribution remained constant throughout the early years of the republic. Initially there were three circuit courts and thirteen district courts: one district court for each of the eleven states that had already ratified the Constitution, and one for each of the remote Districts of Maine and Kentucky.[8] The districts of the seaboard states were fitted into a system of circuit courts who heard their appeals. Circuit courts were held by the judge of the district and by Supreme Court justices assigned to the circuit. The distinctions between the inferior courts can be seen in sections 9 and 11 of the Judiciary Act of 1789:

[T]he district courts shall have, exclusively of the courts of the several States, cognizance of all crimes and offenses that shall be cognizable under the authority of the United States, committed

[8] *Ibid.*, secs. 1-3. Maine was then a part of Massachusetts, as Kentucky was a part of Virginia. Congress created an additional district court for each of the other states as they entered the union.

within their respective districts, or upon the high seas; where no other punishment than whipping, not exceeding thirty stripes, a fine not exceeding one hundred dollars, or a term of imprisonment not exceeding six months, is to be inflicted; and shall also have exclusive original cognizance of all civil causes of admiralty and maritime jurisdiction . . . and shall also have exclusive original cognizance of all seizures on land, or other waters than as aforesaid, made, and of all suits for penalties and forfeitures incurred, under the laws of the United States.

And shall also have cognizance, concurrent as last mentioned, of all suits at common law where the United States sue, and the matter in dispute amounts, exclusive of costs, to the sum or value of one hundred dollars. . . . And . . . of all suits against consuls or vice-consuls.

Circuit court jurisdiction included:

[O]riginal cognizance, concurrent with the courts of the several States, of all suits of a civil nature at common law or in equity, where the matter in dispute exceeds, exclusive of costs, the sum or value of five hundred dollars, and the United States are plaintiffs, or petitioners; or an alien is a party, or the suit is between a citizen of the State where the suit is brought, and a citizen of another State.[9]

If the Kentucky District Court had been like other district courts, it would have had very little to do.[10] There were then few petty crimes defined as federal crimes and no admiralty or maritime cases on the inland waters. Rarely did consuls or vice-consuls go to Kentucky, and never did aliens sue there for wrongs or injuries committed against them. (There were, however, federal suits at common law brought in connection with the internal revenue acts.)

But the early federal court in Kentucky was unlike other inferior federal courts because it had both district court and circuit court jurisdiction until 1807. Congress did change the name of the court twice before then, which lent a superficial confusion to its records. The district court established in 1789 was supplanted by the Sixth Circuit Court in 1801, which was in turn replaced by the district court again in 1802. Yet whatever it was called, there was only one court for the first eighteen years, and it had this unusual combined caseload. (It

---

[9] *Ibid.*, sec. 9; sec. 11.
[10] Dwight F. Henderson, *Courts for a New Nation* (Washington, D.C., 1971), 55-63, 105-114.

could not, however, under its circuit court jurisdiction hear appeals or writs of error from its district court because such cases went directly to the United States Supreme Court.)[11] Finally, in 1807, Congress divided the jurisdictions and created two courts. The district court kept the cases that came under district court jurisdiction, and the cases that came under circuit jurisdiction went to a new United States Court for the Seventh Circuit in the District of Kentucky. After that, the two courts met separately and kept separate records, just like the federal courts in other states.

Even with its combined jurisdictions, the federal court in Kentucky did not appear to be much of an asset to the national government during its first decade. Its private caseload was small: not until March 1799 were more than twenty new suits docketed in a single term.[12] Its government caseload was disappointing, especially to Treasury officials.[13] They were intent upon enforcing the internal revenue acts of the period, but most Kentuckians were determined to avoid them, and the federal judge in Kentucky clearly sympathized with the citizens. Government officers could only watch helplessly from afar.

Although there was a flurry of activity in the court in 1779 and 1800, the results were uncertain as the Federalist era approached its end. The revenue cases got bogged down in technicalities, and almost half the private cases (149 of a total of 338 docketed) were still pending.[14] After the Republicans won the election of 1800, the Federalists decided that the time had come to preserve the judiciary from those whom they viewed as irresponsible, and to stamp a Federalist imprint on the court in Kentucky.

Although some aspects of the Judiciary Acts of 1801 embodied reforms that had long been under discussion, other aspects were clearly political.[15] Whatever may have been intended by the Federalists, the impact of their program on Kentucky was clearly partisan. Congress

[11] I Stat. 73, sec. 10. As other federal courts were established on the frontier, they, too, were given this combined caseload and direct appeal to the Supreme Court. (Under sec. 4, district judges in the coastal circuit courts were denied a vote in cases of appeal or error arising from their own decision.)

[12] Appendix A shows the private cases docketed by terms of the court.

[13] Appendix C shows the government's civil and criminal cases by terms of the court.

[14] Appendix B shows the judgments of the court in private cases by terms of the court.

[15] There were two important statutes: one passed Feb. 13, 1801 (II Stat. 89), and one passed Mar. 3, 1801 (II Stat. 121). The reform aspects of the former are described in Kathryn Turner, "Federalist Policy and the Judiciary Act of 1801," *William and Mary Quarterly*, 3d Ser., xxII (1965), 3-32.

21

abolished the district court with its single judge and replaced it with a circuit court having three judges, two of whom knew little about Kentucky laws. If it was hoped that augmenting the bench would diminish the pending caseload, the experience in Kentucky proved otherwise. On the contrary, the number of judgments decreased during the effective period of the statute and increased after its repeal.

The political ramifications of the Federalist plan are more obvious when one compares the new Kentucky circuit court with the five others elsewhere in the nation. Each of them was assigned three circuit judges. But the Sixth Circuit, made up of the districts of Kentucky, East Tennessee, West Tennessee, and Ohio, was to have one circuit judge and two district judges.[16] These two were men who had served in recently eliminated district courts in Kentucky and Tennessee.[17] Both were experienced federal judges, but neither was promoted to circuit judge. (Section 7 of the act even specified that "[w]henever the office of District Judge in Kentucky or Tennessee becomes vacant, circuit judges are to be appointed.") It was doubtless no coincidence that the judges in those states were Jeffersonians. It was also no coincidence that a Federalist named William McClung, who had no judicial background, was named circuit judge and made senior to his more experienced colleagues. Whatever deficiencies he may have had as a lawyer or jurist were apparently outweighed by the fact that he was a brother-in-law of Secretary of State and Chief Justice John Marshall.

Furthermore, although the Kentucky federal court had docketed the fourth highest number of cases in the nation, the three judges in the Sixth Circuit were to be paid an annual salary of only $1,500.[18] This

[16] II Stat. 89, sec. 7. Ohio was not yet a state. The district of Ohio, described in sec. 4, included "the territory of the United States northwest of the Ohio, and the Indiana territory," which meant the entire Northwest Territory. The court met at Cincinnati in December 1801, but Innes did not attend because of illness. He wrote that "the circuit is too large for three Judges—2 Circuits in the year amounts to 1640 miles, thro' bad roads—bad lodgings and intolerable living—the fair thro' the Ky. wilderness is the best part of it. There ought to be another Judge and his residence on the north side of the Ohio." Harry Innes to John Breckinridge, Dec. 27, 1801, Breckinridge Family Papers, Manuscript Division, Library of Congress, xxi, 3559.

[17] It should be noted that by shifting these district judges to the circuit court, the Federalists avoided a constitutional problem encountered by the Jeffersonians in 1802, when abolition of the circuit judgeships terminated the appointments of federal judges who, under Art. iii, can expect permanent tenure.

[18] Walter Lowrie and Walter S. Franklin, eds., *American State Papers, Miscellaneous: Documents, Legislative and Executive of the Congress of the United States*, i (Washington, 1834), 302, 320, 325; ii Stat. 89, sec. 41.

was $500 more than had been paid to the former district judges of Kentucky and Tennessee, but it was $100 to $300 less than was allotted to seven of the new district judges, and $500 less than the salaries of the judges serving the other circuits.[19] The salary provisions seemed designed to add insult to injury.[20]

The Federalists also tried to change the site of the court in Kentucky. Originally it had met at Harrodsburg, which was then the center of political activity in the district. Two years after Kentucky became a state and established its capital at Frankfort, the federal court moved to that city. But the new circuit court was to meet at "Bairdstown" (Bardstown), which in 1801 was chiefly notable as the center of opposition to the Jeffersonian political establishment in Kentucky. Bardstown also happened to be the largest town near the home of the new circuit judge.[21] Apparently, however, the convenience of the circuit judge was soon overridden by the convenience of the lawyers and litigants who would appear before the court. The law was changed a month later, and the Sixth Circuit Court, like its predecessor, held its terms in Frankfort.[22]

To many Kentuckians, these Federalist judiciary acts were further evidence of what they perceived to be inattention and even disregard by the distant federal government of the problems of the people beyond the mountains.[23] During Washington's administration they had bitterly resented the whiskey tax, Jay's Treaty with England, the delay in securing navigation of the Mississippi and a grant of deposit at the river's mouth from the Spanish, and several mismanaged and poorly supported expeditions against the Indians that preceded the Battle of Fallen Timbers. (That victory was made possible, in Kentuckians' eyes,

[19] I Stat. 72; II Stat. 121, sec. 1.

[20] And so they appeared to Judge Innes, who complained to Senator John Breckinridge. Innes to Breckinridge, Dec. 27, 1801, Breckinridge Family Papers, xxi, 3559.

[21] II Stat. 89, sec. 7; Connelley and Coulter, *History of Kentucky*, i, 488; W[illiam] M[cClung] Paxton, *The Marshall Family* (Cincinnati, 1885), 72.

[22] II Stat. 121, sec. 6; United States Court for the Sixth Circuit, in DC OB C, May 15, 1801, 50; Nov. 16, 1801, 66; May 15, 1802, 188.

[23] James Sterling Young has described the attitude of the citizenry toward the federal government as generally one of indifference in his *The Washington Community 1800-1828* (New York, 1966), 27-36 and *passim*. During the earlier, Federalist era, a significant body of opinion in Kentucky was decidedly resentful toward the central administration and manifested itself in widespread opposition to legislative and executive actions of that period. This hostility abated with Jefferson's accession to the presidency. The indifference suggested by Young might be thought of as a relatively positive attitude, in that it implied a tolerant acceptance of the government that had formerly been lacking.

only by the wise employment of Kentucky men and horses.)[24] But Washington was at least a Virginian; Adams with his New England heritage and conscious Federalism had no such redeeming feature. He continued an "outsider" as United States attorney who then harassed the distillers; he supported a stamp act in order to fund an unwanted and undeclared war against France, despite the negative association of the tax with British policies in the pre-Revolutionary period; he signed a sedition act aimed at the supporters of Jefferson; and, finally, he appointed two federal judges who were unsophisticated about the peculiarly complicated land laws of Kentucky and might change the established pattern of decisions.

Many Kentuckians expressed their resentment of the Adams administration in a variety of ways. They evaded the whiskey tax and blocked the efforts of the United States attorney so effectively that he was finally relieved of his appointment. They acquitted the two persons who were charged by his successor with violating the stamp act.[25] They answered the sedition act with the Kentucky Resolutions.[26] And when the Republican-dominated Seventh Congress convened in December 1801, many urged Senator John Breckinridge to lead the repeal of the Federalists' judiciary acts and congratulated him after he had done so.[27]

[24] These matters and others mentioned in the following paragraph are described in greater detail in succeeding chapters in connection with their impact upon the work of the court and its personnel.

[25] U.S. v. Hart, DC OB C, Nov. 18, 1801, 117; May 17, 1802, 194; U.S. v. Robinson, ibid., Nov. 18, 1801, 116; May 17, 1802, 192; Nov. 24, 1802, 385; 1 Stat. 536.

[26] 1 Stat. 596; Kentucky Gazette (Lexington), Nov. 14, 1798; Nov. 28, 1799.

[27] Breckinridge Family Papers, xx, 3515; xxi, 3559, 3563, 3581, 3585, 3587, 3641, 3647, 3651, 3655, 3674, 3676, 3688. The misinterpretation of this correspondence by Charles Warren was a major factor in his misunderstanding the stature of the federal courts in Kentucky. He thought that these letters showed "that the Kentuckians were adverse to all Federal Courts" and that the "correspondence presents such affirmative proof of the reasons for hostility to the Federal Courts." He concluded, "that these fears had some justification was seen, twenty years later, when the Supreme Court of the United States in Green v. Biddle overturned the most important land-claimant laws of Kentucky on the ground of unconstitutionality." Charles Warren, Supreme Court, i, 220-222. Although some writers complained about the federal court because it was finally effectively enforcing the ten-year-old internal revenue laws and others worried about the expense of appeals to the United States Supreme Court, most criticized the Sixth Circuit Court with its "foreign" judges, and supported instead the single-judge court of Harry Innes, who was familiar with Kentucky and Virginia land laws. A striking example of Warren's misconstruction is seen in a letter from Thomas Todd: the "one Judge" whom Todd preferred to "the additional Judges" was Innes; the others were McClung and McNairy, appointed under the terms of the Judiciary Act of 1801. Warren's misunderstanding apparently stemmed

The Jeffersonian Congress reestablished the district court with Harry Innes as its single judge.[28] The circuit judges' positions were eliminated and the Federalist incumbent thereby deprived of his post. A Republican replaced a Federalist as marshal. But Federalist Joseph Hamilton Daveiss, a midnight appointment as United States attorney, was retained. So was James Morrison, the internal revenue supervisor who had earlier been appointed by Adams. Together they secured the first effective enforcement of the decade-old internal revenue laws—after Jefferson became president and repeal was promised. Their retention suggests that in Kentucky, Jefferson's patronage policy may not have been as "thoroughly partisan" during his first term as has recently been suggested.[29] On the contrary, the president appears to have been satisfied with Daveiss and fired the attorney in 1807 only after he had repeatedly criticized Jefferson in public for his earlier handling of the Burr affair. Morrison, as supervisor, glad to see the internal revenue laws repealed, conscientiously wound up his work and retained his office until it was finally abolished in 1808 by a general administrative reorganization.[30]

---

partly from his reliance upon the condemnation of Innes found in the *History of Kentucky* written by Innes's lifelong political enemy Humphrey Marshall, and partly from his belief that the attacks upon the federal courts following the *Green* v. *Biddle* decision marked the culmination of a generation's continuous resentment of federal judicial authority. However, that decision was denounced because it *overturned* earlier precedents established by Innes upholding the occupying claimants' statutes. Similarly, the other circumstances pitting what Warren called "Kentucky Against the Court" in 1821-1825 represented major divergences from earlier practices. Warren listed these as the "usurpation" of admiralty jurisdiction over Kentucky's inland waters, the federal courts' protection of the Bank of the United States from state taxation after *McCulloch* v. *Maryland*, and an alleged disregard by the Kentucky federal courts of state statutes protecting judgment debtors (pp. 633-651). The court records show that it is anachronistic to apply these criticisms to the courts during Innes's lifetime. There were no admiralty cases docketed during these years, and no suits involving the Bank of the United States (except criminal charges brought against suspected thieves and counterfeiters). From 1789 to 1816, the court rigorously upheld Kentucky statutes of all kinds, according to the requirement of sec. 34 of the Judiciary Act of 1789, including laws applying to judgment debtors. The misunderstanding about the Kentucky federal court, perhaps inevitable in a pioneer work of such broad scope, gained greater significance because it was combined with similar conclusions about an alleged hostility toward the United States Supreme Court by the people of Pennsylvania, Georgia, and Virginia, and led to the assumption that the federal judiciary was generally feared or despised in the early republic.

[28] II Stat. 132.
[29] Carl E. Prince, "The Passing of the Aristocracy: Jefferson's Removal of the Federalists, 1801-1805," *Journal of American History*, LVII (1970), 565.
[30] II Stat. 148; James Morrison to John Breckinridge, Feb. 27, 1802, Breckinridge Family Papers, XXI, 3688; Albert Gallatin to President Jefferson, Sept. 3,

The caseload of the court did change after 1802. With the repeal of the whiskey tax, there were few new cases against distillers, but there were an astonishing number of government suits against former revenue collectors, who seem to have been almost universally delinquent.[31] In addition, the number of private suits continued to grow steadily, a circumstance that may have been unique to the Kentucky federal court. It experienced none of that "decline of business . . . during Jefferson's administrations" ascribed to the federal courts.[32] As a matter of fact, the caseload grew more rapidly from 1801 to 1807 than it had before or would for some time afterwards, because Innes even accepted cases below the jurisdictional minima of the period.[33]

This singular interpretation of jurisdiction ended in 1807, when the structure of the federal court in Kentucky was brought in line with those of other states. The Jeffersonians' judiciary acts were perhaps as political as the Federalists', but were much more popular in the West. Just as the Judiciary Acts of 1801 climaxed years of inattention and apparent discrimination against people beyond the mountains, so the Judiciary Act of 1807 climaxed Republican efforts to placate the interior and bind it more firmly to the Union. Jefferson's administration had first repealed the Federalist judiciary acts and the internal revenue taxes, and then purchased Louisiana, securing forever the Mississippi River and New Orleans. The president sympathized with the land hunger of frontiersmen and encouraged territorial organization and cessions from the Indians.[34] And when it came to the judiciary, he pro-

1808, Internal Revenue Direct Tax, Correspondence 1807-1829, file 11713, General Records of the Department of the Treasury, Record Group 56, National Archives; Gallatin to Morrison, Oct. 20, 1808, *ibid.*

[31] Carl E. Prince considered that Jefferson's failure to define misconduct or delinquency in his records was evidence that the many dismissals during his administration were made for political reasons. The records of the Treasury Department as well as of the Kentucky federal court provide abundant evidence of misconduct and delinquency. This is discussed in Chapter Five; cf. Prince, "Passing of the Aristocracy," 570.

[32] Ellis, *Jeffersonian Crisis*, 233.

[33] These were debt cases brought by British merchants. They are described in Chapter Seven. The jurisdictional amount required for such cases by the Judiciary Act of 1789 was $500. This was lowered to $400 in 1801, and then restored to $500 in the Repeal Act of 1802. I Stat. 73, sec. 11; II Stat. 89, sec. 11; II Stat. 132, sec. 3.

[34] Jefferson's policy was to support settlement that would "gradually circumscribe and approach the Indians, and they will in time either incorporate with us as citizens of the US. or remove beyond the Missisipi," a plan congenial to those on the frontier. Thomas Jefferson to Governor [William Henry] Harrison, Feb. 27, 1803, Clarence Edwin Carter, ed., *The Territorial Papers of the United States*, VII, *The Territory of Indiana 1800-1810* (Washington, D.C., 1939), 91.

posed an additional seat on the Supreme Court to be filled by a resident of one of the newly admitted states of the West.[35]

After consulting with their congressional delegations, Jefferson chose Thomas Todd of Kentucky as the new justice. Todd was respected and popular in Kentucky, and because he had been associated with the state Court of Appeals for fifteen years he was an expert on the land laws that would be interpreted in the federal court.[36] Furthermore, Todd was a younger cousin of Judge Innes and had been his student and protégé. Sitting together on the circuit bench, they could be expected to retain the line of decision that Innes had established over the preceding eighteen years and thereby to reinforce the stability and prestige of the federal court.

The Jeffersonians retained the interdependence of the Supreme Court and the circuit courts, even beyond the mountains. But the new Seventh Circuit was far from Washington and the difficulty of traveling through his circuit and to the nation's capital would prove to be an almost unbearable burden to Justice Todd.[37] Although an 1802 statute had provided that district judges could hold circuit courts in the absence of the Supreme Court justice assigned to the circuit, Todd tried to make the rounds from Kentucky to Tennessee to Ohio twice a year, as well as the arduous journey to the East.[38] Evidently Judge Innes believed that the Seventh Circuit Court was only truly constituted when Justice Todd was present, because in his absence the Order Books sometimes recorded "Pleas before Judge Innes" rather than "At the Circuit Court for the District of Kentucky." Innes announced judgments at terms when Justice Todd was not present, but only on cases that had been under consideration for some time, which suggests that the judges had reached their decision together.

The docket of the new circuit court demonstrated how great a proportion of the caseload of the district court had been carried under its circuit court jurisdiction. Most cases were transferred to the Seventh

[35] A later statute, passed in 1812, required that all district and territorial judges must be residents of the state or territory to whose federal courts they were appointed. II Stat. 788.

[36] Todd was said to have been either the first or second choice of all the members of Congress from Kentucky, Tennessee, and Ohio. Warren, *Supreme Court*, I, 301. Surprisingly, there are no letters about Todd in Letters of Application and Recommendation During the Administration of Thomas Jefferson, 1801-1809, M-418, General Records of the Department of State, Record Group 59, National Archives.

[37] II Stat. 420; Thomas Todd to Charles S. Todd, Aug. 23, 1808, Mar. 1, 1810, and Feb. 17, 1811, Todd Family Papers, MS Dept., Filson Club.

[38] II Stat. 156.

Circuit, and the work of the district court abruptly diminished. Only a handful of suits in which the government was plaintiff remained there, a reflection of the continuing but often futile effort of the United States to collect its money from delinquent postmasters, army contractors, and revenue officers. The business of the district court fell off so sharply that no new cases were docketed in 1809, 1811, or 1812. Only one pending suit was heard in 1811 and 1812, and no terms were held at all in 1813. Not until after the passage of a new series of revenue laws (to pay for the War of 1812) did the district court revive, in 1815. By the end of the period under examination, these measures once again gave the district court an active docket.[39]

The addition of a second judge to its bench did not substantially change the character of the Kentucky federal court. Procedures remained the same, and cases still moved slowly toward termination. The number of judgments did not increase materially. Where Judge Innes had averaged 32.4 judgments on private cases per term from November 1802 (when the district court was reestablished after the dissolution of the Sixth Circuit Court) through 1806, Judges Innes and Todd together averaged 32.8 judgments per term from May 1807 through the November 1815 term. The number of cases technically still pending remained high. By 1816, 520 private cases and 95 government suits remained open. Many had been inactive for years and were probably terminated, although this is not indicated in the Order Books.

The most obvious difference between the Seventh Circuit Court and its predecessor was in the number of cases dismissed for want of jurisdiction. This disposition was rarely made earlier, but in the seven terms immediately following the creation of the new circuit court, ninety causes were dismissed for that reason. (There had been only five cases dismissed before 1801, and forty-nine from 1801 through 1806. The reasons for these dismissals were usually not given in the Order Books.) Apparently Justice Todd did not share Judge Innes's expansive interpretation of federal jurisdiction, especially where jurisdictional minima were concerned. It was probably this stricter interpretation that was responsible for the decline in the number of new cases docketed. In the nineteen terms from 1807 to 1816, the circuit court aver-

[39] The lower third of the last 50 pages of District Court Order Book G, containing entries for the 1809-1815 terms, have been badly damaged by fire or water, and are among the very few sections of this substantial collection of records that are illegible. The upper portions of these pages are clear, however, and indicate the work of the court. So few judgments were rendered during these terms that this circumstance does not seriously distort the statistical analyses.

aged 31.5 new causes, a measurable difference from the average of 40 per term for the preceding thirteen district court terms.

But the judges' interpretations of federal jurisdiction did not insure the caseload of their court. The Constitution and federal statutes made jurisdiction possible but not inevitable. Virtually all of the jurisdiction exercised by the district and circuit courts in Kentucky was a concurrent jurisdiction that could also be exercised by the state courts. Plaintiffs could choose between these courts, and it might have been expected that they would prefer their state courts. Kentucky judges were appointed by governors who were immediately responsible to the electorate, and state court procedures could be changed by the legislature. But federal judges were appointed by a president who might have a limited local constituency, and the duties of federal courts were prescribed by a distant Congress. The people of any given region or state might withhold their cooperation from the federal judiciary, but they could not control it, because they were a small minority of the whole. And where, as in Kentucky, federal courts were preferred over state courts, it must have been because the former had a reputation that was in some way superior to the latter: the opportunity for redress was the same in both.

Modern federal courts derive much of their prestige from their identification with the United States Supreme Court and from the importance of a powerful national government. But during the period under discussion, both the Supreme Court and the national government were seen in a very different light. Before 1801, the high court was relatively unimportant, and after that date it was led by Chief Justice John Marshall, a man whose politics and principles were shared by few Kentuckians. The central government was much less powerful in its early years than it later became. Moreover, it was often a source of frustration and anxiety to its citizens in the interior. The national government as the embodiment of the union of all the states did not then have the stature it subsequently gained; in fact, the whole concept of the nation developed very gradually. The indexes to the Order Books of the Kentucky federal courts provide an illuminating example of this distinctively different attitude: when the United States was plaintiff, the cases are not indexed under "U" for the United States, but under "S" with the designation "States, United."[40]

[40] This attitude was not unique to Kentucky. In the sections of the Judiciary Act of 1789 quoted above, "the United States" is treated as a plural subject requiring a plural verb.

29

The reasons why 2,290 causes were docketed in the federal courts in Kentucky between 1789 and 1816 are not, therefore, entirely explained by the national character of the courts or by the constitutional and statutory provisions that have been described. When Kentuckians so often chose their federal over their state courts, it must have been because the federal courts had something to offer that the state courts did not. The reputation of a federal court was shaped by its officers, and especially its judges, who set its style and guided the disposition of its cases. These men created a sophisticated judiciary despite the frontier environment of early Kentucky, and maintained the predictability of the law in a world that was otherwise so often uncertain. Understanding who they were, and how they fulfilled their responsibilities, are essential components of understanding the history of the federal courts in Kentucky.

CHAPTER TWO

Judge Harry Innes

A MERICANS take great pride and comfort in the belief that theirs is a government of laws and not of men. This shibboleth is generally understood to mean that the laws are superior to all men regardless of their station. It also carries an implication that laws, once enacted or discovered, go into effect automatically. But the records of the early federal courts in Kentucky indicate that there, at least, men decided which laws would be enforced, how they would be interpreted, and to whom they would be applied. While Kentucky was, for the most part, a law-respecting community, the laws did not operate there in a mechanical way. The human element was crucial. A review of the personnel of these courts may illustrate how important a determinant it was.

The most important individual in the Kentucky federal courts from 1789 until 1816 was Harry Innes, judge of the United States Court for the District of Kentucky throughout these years. Innes was born in 1752 in Caroline County, Virginia to the former Catherine Richards, a woman of English ancestry, and Robert Innes, a clergyman who had emigrated from Scotland. The family was comfortably well off, although not wealthy, and Innes was educated at Donald Robertson's school and at William and Mary College. He read law under George Wythe and numbered among his friends the sons of many prominent Virginia families.

Innes was admitted to the bar in 1773 and practiced law in Bedford County, in western Virginia. Three years later he began his public career administering lead and powder mines for the Virginia Committee of Public Safety in the foothills of the Blue Ridge Mountains.[1] In 1779 Governor Thomas Jefferson appointed Innes to adjust and settle land claims in the western Montgomery and Washington districts.[2] In 1780 he became escheator and later commissioner of the specific tax (a direct tax imposed by the state). Governor Benjamin Harrison promoted him in 1782 to the post of district commissioner of the specific tax for six western counties: Charlotte, Halifax, Pitsylvania, Henry,

---

[1] Statement of Otto A. Rothert, Feb. 27, 1925, Otto A. Rothert, Collector, Papers Relating to Harry Innes, Manuscript Dept., Filson Club, Louisville, Ky. (Hereafter cited as Rothert-Innes Papers, Filson Club.)

[2] Julian P. Boyd *et al.*, eds., *The Papers of Thomas Jefferson* (Princeton, N.J., 1950-   ), xv, 583.

31

Bedford, and Campbell.[3] Later in that year he was appointed assistant judge of the newly established Supreme Court of Judicature for the Kentucky District of Virginia.[4] Innes moved to Kentucky in 1783.[5]

Despite its impressive name, the new court met in a log cabin at Crow's Station, a tiny settlement between Harrodsburg and what soon became Danville.[6] The court had full civil and criminal jurisdiction, but it was chiefly occupied trying to settle land claims, which were already in a state of incredible confusion. It was staffed by a chief judge, two assistant judges, a clerk, and an attorney. When the first attorney was killed by Indians in 1784, Innes resigned his judgeship to take up the vacant post, preferring the fees of that office to those available to the judges.[7]

The duties of the court did not fill his days, and once in Kentucky, Innes did as other Kentuckians did: he speculated in land. He also farmed, practiced law, and reared six daughters (four by his first marriage; another and a stepdaughter by his second). He became a trustee of Transylvania University and the most honored charter member of the Political Club of Danville.[8] He was soon recognized as a leading member of his new community: a strong-minded, competent, and responsible person. He borrowed money, bought land and slaves, paid his bills, and prospered.[9] He ordered trunk loads of books from England and built a distinguished library.[10] He got involved in a variety of mercantile and commercial ventures and often acted as agent for his

[3] Harry Innes Papers, Manuscript Division, Library of Congress, xvi, Pt. i, 18, 19; Harry Innes to Col. Davies, July 21, 1782, *ibid.*, Pt. ii, 234. (Hereafter cited as Innes Papers, Library of Congress.)

[4] The certificate of appointment is in the Rothert-Innes Papers, Filson Club.

[5] Innes to Henry Knox, July 7, 1790, Innes Papers, Library of Congress, xix, 40.

[6] Thomas Speed, *The Political Club, Danville, Kentucky 1786-1790* (Louisville, Ky., 1894), 20.

[7] Robert S. Cotterill, *History of Pioneer Kentucky* (Cincinnati, 1917), 241; Patricia Watlington, *The Partisan Spirit: Kentucky Politics, 1779-1792* (New York, 1972), 54-58; John Marshall to George Muter, Jan. 7, 1785, Herbert A. Johnson, *et al.*, eds., *The Papers of John Marshall*, i (Chapel Hill, N.C., 1974), 134.

[8] The Political Club, Danville, Kentucky, Records, 1786-1790, ms Dept., Filson Club, Louisville, Ky.

[9] Innes Papers, Library of Congress, *passim* but especially xvi; Harry Innes Papers, 1750-1810, ms Dept., Filson Club, Louisville, Ky. (Hereafter cited as Innes Papers, Filson Club.)

[10] A book order of 1785 which included works of fiction and the classics, as well as law books, is given in Appendix D. The importance of studying the holdings in private libraries to evaluate the intellectual sophistication of frontier lawyers is shown in Michael H. Harris, "The Frontier Lawyer's Library; Southern Indiana, 1800-1850, as a Test Case," *American Journal of Legal History*, xvi (1972), 239-251.

friends when they traveled and as executor when they died.[11] He made a lifelong enemy of Humphrey Marshall and a permanent friend of John Brown. He also found time to teach law to Thomas Todd, a younger first cousin who would become his senior associate a generation later.

Innes soon became convinced that Kentucky's destiny could not be successfully realized within the confines of Virginia. The decisions of the district court were not final, and appeals had to be carried over the mountains to Richmond. There was no executive authority in Kentucky. Nor was there anyone in the district with authority to call out the militia to retaliate against the Indians who frequently attacked isolated settlements. (Virginia laws empowered Kentuckians to take defensive action, but not to engage in activities that could be construed as offensive.)[12] It seemed to the settlers that many Virginians (like other easterners) were not aware that Kentucky had a separate destiny from that of her parent state. Impatient with what he construed as Virginia's indifference, Innes quickly joined the movement for immediate and unconditional separation from Virginia. It would take eight years and ten conventions before Virginia, the United States, and Kentucky could agree upon terms and before an acceptable constitution was finally written for the new state. Innes was a member of at least eight of these conventions.[13]

Innes was not only opposed to the connection with Virginia, he was also doubtful about the value of the national government provided by the Articles of Confederation. Like other westerners, he was convinced that Congress was insensitive to the needs of the interior and he was angered when it contemplated surrendering for twenty-five years the navigation of the Mississippi River, "the first and greatest blessing of the Western Country."[14] Furthermore, he believed that government

[11] Innes's most controversial client was his friend General James Wilkinson. Innes was careful to avoid conflicts of interest, and after he became federal judge he declined agencies and executorships from which litigation might arise that would be tried in his court. He continued to practice law in the state courts, however. Innes Papers, Library of Congress, xx, Pt. ii, 3-285 to 3-288; Joseph Jones to Innes, Jan. 20, 1796, ibid., xxvi, Pt. ii, 7-158.

[12] Innes to John Brown, Apr. 4, 1788, Innes Papers, Library of Congress, xix, 10.

[13] The conventions' records are incomplete, but the thread of continuity in the conventions, and Innes's participation, are traced in Watlington, Partisan Spirit, 98, 101, 103, 117, 123, 129, 159, 174, 184, 197. See also William Elsey Connelley and E[llis] M[erton] Coulter, History of Kentucky, ed. Charles Kerr, i (Chicago, 1922), 226-285.

[14] Innes to Brown, Apr. 4, 1788, Innes Papers, Library of Congress, xix, 10. John Jay's willingness to cede navigation of the Mississippi in his negotiations with

troops stationed at forts along the Ohio River were not there to protect Kentucky settlers from the Indians, but to prevent settlement on the national domain of the Northwest Territory. (He was partly correct: the troops had the dual mission of preventing settlement on unopened Indian lands and preventing Indian raids across the river.)[15] And when Kentuckians were authorized to conduct expeditions against the Indians, the government failed to reimburse them.[16] Letters, petitions, and protests on all these matters were unavailing. To Innes, "such unequivocal proofs of the inattention paid to their repeated solicitations" justified a serious search for some other alternative.[17] An alliance with Spain might be more useful than membership in the weak Confederation, because Spain held the Mississippi and exerted great influence among the southern Indians.

Innes did not think that the proposed federal Constitution offered satisfactory solutions to Kentucky's problems, and he opposed its ratification. He feared the broad grant over commerce given to Congress because he expected that it would be dominated by the seaboard states and that they would continue to sacrifice navigation of the Mississippi for commercial agreements benefiting only the East. He complained to John Brown that "we shall be the mere vassals of the Congress and the consequences to me are horrible and dreadful."[18] Ironically, in light of his later career, he also feared the power of the federal judiciary. He especially disliked the provisions in Article III for federal jurisdiction in diversity cases (those between citizens of different states) because he thought that suits would be brought against Kentuckians in a distant federal court and his countrymen would lose nine times out of ten. (He did not anticipate the geographically dispersed lower court system that the Judiciary Act of 1789 later provided.)

Many Kentuckians shared Innes's insistence upon immediate separation from Virginia and his rejection of the Constitution, although these

---

Diego de Gardoqui was universally condemned by Kentuckians and by sympathetic Virginians. Marshall to Muter, Feb. 11, 1787, Johnson et al., eds., Marshall Papers, I, 204; Watlington, Partisan Spirit, 118.

[15] Malcolm J. Rohrbough, The Land Office Business: The Settlement and Administration of American Public Lands, 1789-1837 (New York, 1968), 14-17.

[16] Eight years later, Kentuckians were still seeking payment for a 1785 expedition. Christopher Greenup to Thomas Jefferson, Jan. 28, 1793, Miscellaneous Letters of the Department of State, 1789-1906, M-179, roll 9, General Records of the Department of State, Record Group 59, National Archives. (Hereafter cited as Misc. Letters, Dept. of State, M-179).

[17] Innes to Brown, Apr. 4, 1788, Innes Papers, Library of Congress, xix, 10.

[18] Innes to Brown, Feb. 20, 1788 (typed transcript), ibid., xxviii, 9-204.

views were not unchallenged. (Only three of the fourteen Kentucky delegates to the Virginia convention supported ratification, and the opposition of its western district contributed greatly to doubt about Virginia's decision.)[19] These disagreements over the wisdom of ratifying the Constitution and the timing and terms of separation from Virginia brought about the first political groupings in Kentucky. Each group accused the other of being a mere faction, but well before 1790 both groups possessed major characteristics of political parties: stability of membership and ideology, organizational structure, popular support, and conscious identification with national issues and personages.[20] The immediacy and clarity of the alternatives and the presence of sophisticated leaders stimulated the development of parties earlier in Kentucky than in many other parts of the new nation.[21]

Most of those who wanted immediate and unconditional separation from Virginia were Antifederalists, and they sometimes considered Spain a more useful ally than Great Britain.[22] Innes, Brown, and Todd were soon joined in Kentucky by George Nicholas, John Breckinridge, and Henry Clay. Together they considered themselves Republicans and looked to Thomas Jefferson for leadership in the emerging national party structure.[23] Over the following generation they retained a remarkable consistency in membership despite the emergence of new issues and programs at both the local and national levels.

The challenge to this group came initially from the Marshall family, headed by Colonel Thomas Marshall. Although outnumbered, the Marshalls were not insignificant opponents. Colonel Marshall had a particularly vocal nephew and fifteen children, including the future

[19] Connelley and Coulter, *History of Kentucky*, I, 252; Broadus Mitchell and Louise Pearson Mitchell, *A Biography of the Constitution of the United States* (New York, 1964), 169; Watlington, *Partisan Spirit*, 155.

[20] The Kentucky data has not yet been quantified, but available evidence supports both a substantive and a structural definition of party. This finding may be seen in a larger context described by H. James Henderson, "The First Party System," in Alden T. Vaughan and George Athan Billias, eds., *Perspectives on Early American History* (New York, 1973), 325-371.

[21] A third factor, more difficult to measure but unquestionably present in Kentucky, was the degree of animosity engendered by such flamboyant personalities as James Wilkinson and Humphrey Marshall, whose activities tended to diminish the number of political neutrals.

[22] There were some ideological inconsistencies in both groups, but personal allegiances were unwavering (except, perhaps, those of George Muter).

[23] Jefferson, in turn, had a more comprehensive and sympathetic appreciation of the grievances of these Kentuckians than did most easterners. A full discussion of the issues involved and the positions held by participants in both sections is found in an editorial note, "Threat of Disunion in the West," Boyd *et al.*, eds., *Jefferson Papers*, XIX, 429-518.

chief justice (who had remained in Virginia when most of the rest of the family migrated to Kentucky). The Marshalls—the colonel, his sons and sons-in-law, and his nephew Humphrey Marshall—constituted the heart of the group opposing what they considered precipitate separation from Virginia. They supported the Constitution before and during ratification; they were Anglophiliac; and they considered that dealing with Spain was potentially if not actually treasonous. Colonel Marshall was an old friend of George Washington and his land agent in the West, and in time the loyalty Washington evoked was extended to Alexander Hamilton and John Adams and their policies. The Marshall kin became the nucleus of the Federalist party in Kentucky and provided an organized core for any other dissident groups who opposed the dominant Jeffersonian political establishment in the state.[24]

Humphrey Marshall, Colonel Marshall's son-in-law as well as his nephew, was the most intemperate member of the family. He seems to have believed that opponents of ratification remained Irreconcilables forever, somewhat like Royalists in the French Republic. However, Innes and Brown and their political allies pragmatically accepted the Constitution once ratification was assured. Brown was elected to represent the Kentucky District of Virginia in the House of Representatives and was United States senator from Kentucky from 1792 until 1805. While in New York for the convening of the First Congress, he used his considerable influence with the Virginians in the new government to secure federal positions for his friends. On September 28, 1789, he wrote to Innes:

> The Act establishing the Judicial Courts of the United States passed a few days ago and has rec^d the approbation of the President . . . and it is with pleasure I add you are appointed Judge for the District of Kentucke. I was induced to take the liberty to recommend you to the President for this office from a confidence that the appoint-

[24] Watlington argues in *Partisan Spirit* that in the 1780s there was also a third identifiable party which she calls the Partisans. Its membership was made up chiefly of settlers from Pennsylvania and North Carolina who had no land claims deriving from Virginia and were more liberal, democratic, and antislavery than were the Virginia-born leaders of the other two parties. The point is persuasively presented and may give a more accurate picture of the Kentucky political situation than the traditional one, which identifies only two parties and emphasizes Kentucky's Republican heritage. The power inherent in numbers may have made the Partisans important enough to have affected the policies of the federal court, but this influence cannot be identified through existing records or correspondence. The significant polarities for the present study remain those between Harry Innes and his Jeffersonian associates on one side, and Humphrey Marshall and the Federalists on the other.

ment would meet with the unanimous approbation of the District, and from a conviction that you were better qualified to fill it than any other we could hope to obtain. The Salary is 1000 Dollars . . . I could not at present get it raised beyond that sum as an opinion prevailed that the Business in that Court would be inconsiderable. . . . I flatter myself . . . that you will consent to accept the appo[int-ment] e[spec]ially as the Law does not prohibit you f[rom continuing?] your present Docket.[25]

Innes evidently found no inconsistency between his antifederalism and his appointment as judge of the United States Court for the District of Kentucky. He promptly took the oath of office and he conscientiously interpreted the Constitution whose ratification he had opposed. His lifestyle did not change once he went on the bench: it is obvious that he considered it as proper to continue to practice politics as it was to continue to practice law. Innes was apparently particularly useful to the Republican cause as a writer of broadsides and position papers, and only once showed embarrassment when his support for a candidate became publicly known.[26] He avoided public association with the Democratic Society when it was organized by John Breckinridge in 1793 and later stated that he had never attended any of its meetings, although papers among his collection indicate that he had been an interested observer of its activities even if he was not a participant.[27] Innes's political sympathies were not secret because he occasionally published partisan statements in the *Kentucky Gazette* un-

[25] Brown to Innes, Sept. 28, 1789, Innes Papers, Library of Congress, XIX, 18. Federal judges were permitted to practice law privately until 1812, as indicated by II Stat. 788. Innes had many clients and maintained a large practice in the state courts, as accounts and other memoranda among his papers prove. Innes Papers, Library of Congress; Innes Papers, Filson Club; Innes File, Manuscript Collection, Kentucky Historical Society, Frankfort, Ky.; Autographs File no. 25, *ibid.* Brown's role in securing the appointment of Innes as judge and George Nicholas as attorney is confirmed by a letter from Washington's secretary to Brown, enclosing the two commissions of office with the suggestion that he had better means of conveyance than did the president. George Washington (by Tobias Lear) to John Brown, Oct. 2, 1789, Misc. Letters, Dept. of State, M-179, roll 2. The first post road to Kentucky was not begun until 1792 when one was authorized from Richmond, Va. to Danville, Ky. The mail was irregular and slow for years after that, as letters from Thomas Todd to Innes in 1807 demonstrate. I Stat. 232, sec. 1; Todd to Innes, Sept. 23, 1807, Innes Papers, Library of Congress, XVIII, 2-92; Todd to Innes, Sept. 27, 1807, *ibid.*, 2-93.

[26] Statement on the candidacy of John Jouett, July 21, 1807, Innes Papers, Library of Congress, XVIII, 2-91.

[27] Statement of Jan. 29, 1808, *ibid.*, XIX, 196, 114, 124.

der his well-known pseudonym, "A Farmer."[28] Whether it was superior
leadership or a surer manipulation of popular issues that was responsible—or both—the Innes-Brown-Nicholas group were even more
successful politically after the adoption of the Constitution than they
had been earlier. The irony of their achievement was not appreciated
by Colonel Marshall, who complained bitterly to George Washington
that they had gotten "almost every post of power or proffit in the state
fill'd by their friends and adherents."[29]

The correspondence with John Brown and other Kentuckians in
Congress and occasional letters from Jefferson show that Innes was
kept well informed on national and international events. But his involvement in these matters seems to have been limited to their impact
on the local concerns of Kentuckians. Innes's interests were almost
strictly parochial: he was first a Kentuckian and only distantly and
secondly an American. The strength of his political convictions owed
more to his uncompromising antifederalism than to any positive adoption of Jeffersonian principles. What Innes shared most spontaneously
with Jefferson was a common interest in grape culture, moldboard
plows, merino sheep, shepherd dogs, and Indian artifacts.[30] The judge
had little of Jefferson's eighteenth-century optimism or his faith in the
virtue and wisdom of the people. Innes felt dismayed and threatened
by political equality, and his response to universal manhood suffrage
was decidedly elitist:

> The people of Kentucky are all turned Politicians from the highest
> in Office to the Peasant. The Peasantry are perfectly mad. Extraor-
> dinary prejudices and without foundation have arisen against the
> present Officers of Government, the Lawyers and the Men of For-
> tune. They say plain honest Farmers are the only men who ought to
> be elected to form our [state] Constitution. What will be the end of
> these prejudices it is difficult to say, they have given a very serious
> alarm to every thinking man, who is determined to watch and court
> the temper of the people.[31]

[28] See, for examples, the partisan analyses of Kentucky politics and candid electioneering written by "A Farmer" which was "published at the request of a pure
Democratic Society," Kentucky Gazette (Lexington), Mar. 1, 1794; Mar. 8, 1794.
[29] Thomas Marshall to George Washington, Sept. 7, 1792, George Washington
Papers, Library of Congress (microfilm), reel 102.
[30] Thomas Jefferson to Innes, June 20, 1806, Innes Papers, Library of Congress,
xxi, Pt. ii, 1-189; Jefferson to Innes, May 23, 1793, ibid., xxi, Pt. i, 1-15; Jefferson
to Innes, Sept. 18, 1813, ibid., Pt. ii, 1-271; Innes to Jefferson, July 8, 1790, Papers
of Thomas Jefferson, Manuscript Division, Library of Congress (microfilm), reel
20. (Hereafter cited as Jefferson Papers.)
[31] Innes to Jefferson, Aug. 27, 1791, Jefferson Papers (microfilm), reel 23.

Grand jury addresses provided a convenient opportunity to express his philosophy, and Innes sometimes repeated favorite observations, such as that of "the depravity of the manners of mankind increasing with their numbers."[32] He considered his convictions to be self-evident and confirmed by common experience:

It being a received opinion that Man is of so depraved a Nature as not to be trusted to himself, and that the Commission or Omission of certain Acts are prejudicial to the Community, it is absolutely necessary that there should be a punishment inflicted on Offenders, otherwise we should soon fall into a state of Savage Barbarity, for the allurements of Vice are so pleasing that we are apt to be caught in the mesh before we are aware of danger; for in a general sense of things, most of our Actions which are termed pleasure are more or less Vicious, and so corrupt are the manners of our Citizens that their conduct may be termed Licentiousness. . . . It is an undeniable fact. Vice and immorality daily increases among us, and every Evil which can possibly arise is to be [avoid]ed: Profanity, Lust, Avarice, Intemperance, and Cruelty are the usual attendants on a Vicious Mind.[33]

Innes sometimes sounded like a seventeenth-century Puritan magistrate in his concern with private behavior. Portions of his addresses were indistinguishable from sermons, as when he wrote:

Blasphemy, Profane cursing and swearing, Adultery, Fornication, Breaking of the Sabbath and Drunkenness, are offensive to the Devine and Human Laws, these are Crimes which too many think of a very light and trivial Nature . . . but every person must on reflection admit . . . that the Guilty are threatened with the severest denunciations of God's wrath, and it must be acknowledged, that the commission of those Crimes, open a Door to Offences of the most pernicious consequences to Society.[34]

If Innes had little confidence in humanity in general, he was even more skeptical about women in particular. In a lawsuit challenging a conveyance of land by a preacher to his landlady, the judge was convinced that the donor had been "entrapped by the smiles and artifices of a subtle artful woman into an excess of passion too powerful for his reason to correct." The "snares [which] were extended to catch and

[32] Grand Jury Address, n.d. (1784?), Innes Papers, Library of Congress, xviii, 2-25.
[33] Grand jury address, n.d., but apparently before 1789, ibid., 2-120.
[34] Ibid.

bind" him were not, in Innes's opinion, uncommon: "The influence which the fair sex has over the mind of man has been fatal to many, there are I presume very few men who have not at some period of their lives experienced in greater or lesser degree this influence."[35]

Innes's attitudes did not diminish his reputation or responsibilities. In 1790 Secretary of War Henry Knox authorized him to organize Kentucky's defense against the Indians. Innes had discretionary power to employ and equip scouts—who were more expensive but more effective than militia—and shared responsibility for planning strategy.[36] (He then spent five years trying to collect the promised compensation from the War Department, which made the honor of having had "superintending power over the Business" seem an empty one, and increased his frustration with the national government.)[37] Outspokenly critical of St. Clair's defeat in 1791, Innes continued to demand more efficient organization and more effective leadership of American forces. He had a typical frontiersman's opinion of Indians and considered them to be savages with inferior claims to the land. But he condemned settlers who violated treaties or committed outrages on peaceful Indians and thereby invited retaliation.[38]

Innes's local duties included spearheading the effort to improve the Wilderness Road, which in the early 1790s was only a trail over the mountains. This route was sometimes safer from Indians than travel down the Ohio River, but it was too narrow and steep to permit transport of goods or families easily. With Levi Todd, Innes raised money for the project, purchased supplies, found workers, and supervised construction.[39]

Innes was also involved in both of the Kentucky constitutional conventions held during the state's first decade. The first constitution (1792) was based in large part on ideas that had been discussed and debated in the Political Club and was drafted by Innes's close friend, George Nicholas.[40] One of its provisions gave the state supreme court

[35] *Montgomery* v. *Viers and Wife*, "Cases in the Court of the United States for the District of Kentucky, from its first Organization to the year 1806 Inclusive," 329-334, United States Court for the Western District of Kentucky, Louisville. (Hereafter cited as Innes Opinions.)

[36] Knox to Innes, Apr. 13, 1790, Innes Papers, Library of Congress, xix, 31.

[37] Brown to Innes, Apr. 27, 1790, *ibid.*, 33; Innes to War Dept., May 13, 1795, *ibid.*, 142.

[38] Innes to the secretary of war [Henry Dearborn], Oct. 14, 1802, Innes Papers, Library of Congress, xxi, Pt. ii, 1-145.

[39] Account Book of John Logan, Innes Papers, Filson Club; Robert L. Kincaid, *The Wilderness Road* (Harrogate, Tenn., 1955), 185.

[40] Political Club Records, Filson Club. The role of the Political Club, many of whose members participated in the first convention, has been largely overlooked

original and final jurisdiction over land cases. The measure has some-times been cited as evidence of local resentment of the federal court, which had concurrent authority in many of the land cases. But this interpretation overlooks the facts that the Kentucky constitution did not assert exclusive jurisdiction in land cases, and that Innes partici-pated in the convention and apparently expressed no opposition to the clause. Furthermore, whatever Nicholas's role in the framing of the document, it is highly unlikely that he would have tried to diminish the jurisdiction of the court presided over by Innes, who was his po-litical ally. What did concern them and other Kentuckians was that under the Virginia land law, a competing claimant to Kentucky lands could prevent issuance of a patent by filing a Caveat in a Virginia court. This tended to favor nonresidents because it required Kentuck-ians to endure the inconvenience and expense of defending their claims in Richmond, and was one of the principal reasons why statehood was desired by the people of the western district.[41]

After the work of the convention was completed and the new state government went into operation, Innes was selected chief judge of the state Court of Appeals. He declined the appointment, preferring the federal judgeship, apparently because Kentucky provided only meager salaries for the officers of its highest court.[42]

Innes's refusal of the state position did not mean that he was unin-terested in the problems of local government. By the time of the second constitutional convention in 1799, he was a prominent person whose judgment was sought and he played a leading role in formulating the

and the significance of Nicholas's important contribution has been correspondingly exaggerated. Part of the reason for this is that Humphrey Marshall ascribed the first constitution "if to any one man, to Nicholas." Humphrey Marshall, *History of Kentucky* (1812; rev. ed. in 2 vols., Frankfort, 1824), I, 414. This statement has been gradually expanded to a recent assertion that "he [Nicholas] prepared assiduously for the convention, and, when it met, immediately obtained control of it." Richard E. Ellis, *The Jeffersonian Crisis: Courts and Politics in the Young Republic* (New York, 1971), 128. Marshall did not mention the preparatory role of the Political Club, perhaps because he was for a time blackballed from member-ship. Political Club Records, Filson Club.

[41] The provision is found in Art. v, sec. 3, first constitution of Kentucky (1792). Disagreement over its possible conflict with the supremacy clause in Article vi of the United States Constitution was argued in *Wilson v. Mason*, 1 Cranch 45 (1801) and is discussed in Chapter Eight. The present interpretation of its purpose is shared by Watlington, in *Partisan Spirit*, 16, 219. The proceedings of the con-vention and Innes's participation may be traced in *Journal of the First Constitu-tional Convention of Kentucky, Held in Danville, Kentucky, April 2 to 19, 1792* (Lexington, Ky., 1942 [orig. publ. 1792]).

[42] *Ky. Gaz.*, June 30, 1792; Brown to Innes, Apr. 13, 1792, Innes Papers, Library of Congress, XIX, 91.

41

new Kentucky constitution. Elected as a delegate from Franklin County, he was chosen on the second day to be honorary chairman of the proceedings and was also one of the twelve-member committee on privileges and elections. This second constitutional convention operated daily by resolving itself into a committee of the whole and considering revision of specific sections of the existing constitution. Innes was on the drafting committee that met after each day's debates to formulate the new provisions, which would then be presented to the convention the following morning. He voted with the majority on fifteen of twenty-five recorded ballots; significantly, he was among the minority who proposed amendments designed to protect the independence of the state judiciary.[43]

Judicial, legal, and political commitments did not consume all of Innes's intellect and energy: every aspect of his public and private life was colored by his unremitting contempt for Humphrey Marshall. It was a passion that was matched and returned by its object. There is scarcely a year during the last quarter-century of Innes's life for which his papers do not reflect his hatred for a man who was generally recognized as an unrelenting opponent. It is even possible that the emotional content of the judge's inflexible antifederalism was due to Marshall's association with the opposition party and its most obstructive policies. As early as 1792, Innes publicly dismissed Marshall in a newspaper statement: "If he was a man of character, I would adopt proper measures to punish him for insolence. . . . But as Coriolanus [Marshall's pseudonym] is that abandoned man Humphrey Marshall, of Woodford County, I shall take no further notice of him."[44]

It was a vain hope. No one was able to ignore Humphrey Marshall. He was a formidable antagonist—suspicious, sharp-tongued, and tenacious. His invective created such passages as this, written about Innes eight years after his death:

> Nevertheless, to this day, it is a matter of doubt, whether the head, or the heart, of this man, is most to be pitied, censured, or despised. Some suppose him not only weak in reasoning, and in judgment, but corrupt and debased in principle; while others think, that the imbe-

[43] *Journal of the Convention, Begun and Held at the Capitol in the Town of Frankfort on Monday the Twenty-Second Day of July, in the Year of Our Lord One Thousand, Seven Hundred and Ninety-Nine* (n.p., [1799]), MS Coll., Kentucky Historical Society.
[44] *Ky. Gaz.*, Dec. 1, 1792. A clipping is in Innes Papers, Library of Congress, XVIII, 2-42.

cility of his intellect, the prevalence of his vanity, and the importance of his office as criminal prosecutor, exposed him to flattery.[45]

Because Marshall wrote the most popular of the early histories of Kentucky, such passages have doubtless contributed to clouding the reputation of Judge Innes and to obscuring the positive work accomplished in the early federal courts. No attempt at revision has yet been able to compete successfully with Marshall's uninhibited and colorful attacks upon Innes and numerous other adversaries. John Brown, a more temperate man than Innes, referred to Marshall's "insensibility and meanness."[46] Thomas Todd called him "that abandoned and profligate villain."[47] Henry Clay, who was less restrained, eventually fought a duel with him.[48] Even Marshall's great-nephew, who wrote the genealogy of the family and praised every other member of it, said that he was "violent, profane and irreligious. He had but little respect for God or man."[49]

Any friend of Innes was an enemy of Marshall, who assailed them all for their political convictions, private behavior, and professional incompetence. His attacks were returned in kind, and the charges and countercharges echoed for generations afterwards.[50] The intensity, duration, and mutual belligerence of their conflict was truly remarkable, even in a state noted for its feuds.

The climax of their warfare began in July 1806 after an advisory jury in Innes's court noted evidence of fraud in a land case and Marshall was generally believed to have been responsible. Marshall bitterly criticized Innes's custom of relying upon the advice of juries in chancery cases, but the damage to Marshall's cause had been done, and

[45] Marshall, *History of Kentucky*, i, 311.

[46] Brown to Innes, Dec. 29, 1792, Innes Papers, Library of Congress, xix, 98.

[47] Todd to Innes, Sept. 27, 1807, *ibid.*, xviii, 2-93.

[48] Henry Clay to James Clark, Jan. 19, 1809, James F. Hopkins and Mary W. M. Hargreaves, eds., *The Papers of Henry Clay*, i (Lexington, Ky., 1959), 400.

[49] W[illiam] M[cClung] Paxton, *The Marshall Family* (Cincinnati, 1885), 81. Marshall's irreligious diatribes are believed to have been so offensive to his Victorian descendants that they burned his papers.

[50] John Mason Brown, *The Political Beginnings of Kentucky* (Louisville, Ky., 1889); Thomas Marshall Green, *The Spanish Conspiracy* (Cincinnati, 1891); Temple Bodley, "Introduction," in [William Littell], *Reprints of Littell's Political Transactions In and Concerning Kentucky and Letter of George Nicholas To his friend in Virginia also General Wilkinson's Memorial* (Louisville, Ky., 1926 [orig. publ. Frankfort, Ky., 1806]); Temple Bodley, *History of Kentucky*, i (Chicago, 1928); John Mason Brown to Harry Innes Todd, Sept. 5, 1884, John Mason Brown File, ms Coll., Kentucky Historical Society.

Innes dismissed the suit in November.[51] Thomas Bodley, the husband of Innes's stepdaughter, then began a campaign in the Kentucky House of Representatives to censure Marshall and expel him from his seat in that body. The campaign was successful in 1808, but Marshall was re-elected in 1809.[52]

Meanwhile, in the summer of 1806, Marshall directed a newspaper crusade through the Frankfort *Western World* against Court of Appeals Judge Benjamin Sebastian, a friend of Innes. Sebastian was accused of receiving a pension from the Spanish to promote the separation of Kentucky from the Union. Marshall's cries of treason were not new, but for the first time there appeared to be substance to his charges. A select committee of the Kentucky House of Representatives began an investigation and called Judge Innes as a witness, who admitted that he had learned a few months earlier that Sebastian was receiving a pension from Spain.[53] He then went on to volunteer the information that in November 1795 he, George Nicholas, and William Murray had encouraged Sebastian to investigate an overture made by Baron Francisco de Carondelet, Spanish governor of Louisiana. While Sebastian was in New Orleans, news of the Treaty of San Lorenzo, granting free navigation of the Mississippi to Americans, reached the governor. Sebastian's mission was rendered moot. But de Carondelet delayed putting the treaty into effect and once again the Kentuckians questioned the efficacy of the national government.

Furthermore, Innes disclosed that in 1797 de Carondelet sent another agent to Kentucky who offered a bribe of $100,000 to Sebastian, Nicholas, Murray, Innes, and their allies in return for their efforts to separate the western country from the Union and establish a government that would treat independently with Spain. Innes reported that he and Nicholas had immediately and indignantly refused the bribe and, through Colonel James Morrison, had informed James Ross, a Federalist United States senator from Pennsylvania who was then visiting Kentucky. Innes insisted that they did not make the offer pub-

[51] The suit involved a 6,666⅔-acre tract originally claimed both by Levi Todd and Prettyman Merry. Marshall, claiming under Todd's entry, was thought to have mutilated the margin of the land office records so that a subsequent withdrawal from entry of 6,276⅔ acres could not be proven, and Marshall could gain the entire area.

[52] *Report of the Select Committee Appointed to Investigate Certain Charges against Humphrey Marshall, Feb. 19, 1808*, Innes Papers, Library of Congress, XVIII, 2-96.

[53] Bodley, "Introduction," in *Reprints of Littell's Political Transactions*, xcvii-cx; Green, *Spanish Conspiracy*, 336-383; *Annals of Congress*, 10th Cong., 1 sess., 2759-2790.

lic or inform President John Adams because they believed that the administration would use the incident as a pretext to send troops into Kentucky.[54] Their fears may have been justified, because as everyone knew, Kentucky was still suffering from what Colonel Thomas Marshall had earlier called "Monongalia fever"—continued evasion of the six-year-old whiskey tax.[55] Troops had been sent to Pennsylvania: they might well be sent to Kentucky. And Innes and his friends believed that if they were, Kentuckians would not submit as tamely as their allies up the river. Instead, a federal army "could only excite resentment and disgust, and might produce what it was meant to prevent [i.e., a rebellion]."[56]

Marshall rejected Innes's explanation. But Innes was so confident that he could convince objective observers of his innocence and rectitude that he asked the Kentucky representatives in Washington to request the Speaker of the House to appoint a committee to investigate his conduct. It happened, however, that Congress was then distracted by a separate matter with which Innes had been involved, and Henry Clay advised the judge that the times were "inauspicious to an investigation, by Congress, into your Conduct, if at any time it would be proper."[57] That other matter was the affair of Aaron Burr. It was only a matter of weeks since two successive grand juries in Innes's court had refused to indict Burr for treason, despite the strenuous efforts of the federal district attorney in Kentucky, Joseph Hamilton Daveiss.[58] In January it appeared that Daveiss had been right, and the judge's interpretation of due process might have facilitated Burr's escape down the Mississippi. Further complicating the situation was the fact that

[54] The mechanism was not unfamiliar to Innes. In 1788 he had reported to George Washington on the activities of a British agent who was trying to organize Kentuckians for a British-supported attack on New Orleans, and in 1794 he had warned Thomas Jefferson about preparations for a French-supported expedition against New Orleans. Innes to Washington, Dec. 18, 1788, Misc. Letters, Dept. of State, M-179, roll 2. A copy of the letter is in Innes Papers, Library of Congress, XXVI, Pt. ii, 7-297. The reply is Washington to Innes, Mar. 2, 1789, John C. Fitzpatrick, ed., *The Writings of George Washington from the Original Manuscript Sources, 1745-1799* (Washington, D.C., 1939-1944), XXX, 214. Innes to Jefferson, Jan. 21, 1794, Jefferson Papers (microfilm), reel 32.

[55] See Chapter Five.

[56] Caleb Wallace to Innes, June 6, 1807, copied in Innes to Wilson Cary Nicholas, June 10, 1807, Papers of Thomas Jefferson in the Collections of the Massachusetts Historical Society, Boston, given by Thomas Jefferson Coolidge. (Hereafter cited as Jefferson-Coolidge Papers, MS Coll., Massachusetts Historical Society.)

[57] Clay to Innes, Jan. 24, 1807, Hopkins and Hargreaves, eds., *Clay Papers*, I, 270.

[58] See Chapter Six.

Daveiss was Humphrey Marshall's brother-in-law and his closest political ally. The remarkable coincidence of the Sebastian investigation and the Burr affair proved most unfortunate for Innes.

While Daveiss attacked Innes about the Burr affair, Marshall attacked Innes about the stunning revelations of the Sebastian investigation. Securing the resignation of Sebastian was only a first step: Marshall hoped to remove all the Kentucky Republican leaders from power. His suspicions converged on the charge that they had been conspiring with the Spanish for twenty years.[59] While General James Wilkinson, John Brown, Thomas Todd, and George Nicholas (who had died in 1799) were among those also accused, the point of the attack was focused upon Innes. Marshall exploited his long-awaited opportunity to discredit Innes once and for all and began a drive to impeach him through the pages of the *Western World* which soon reached the Kentucky General Assembly. A resolution strongly supported by Marshall condemning Innes and calling for an impeachment inquiry passed the House of Representatives. The Kentucky Senate, however, was willing only to ask for an investigation without an accusation of guilt. The Senate resolution was eventually accepted by the House by the slim margin of one vote, that of Innes's ally, Henry Clay, who as Speaker broke the tie.[60]

Innes, of course, knew that an impeachment inquiry would have an entirely different tone from an inquiry conducted in response to his own request. He began a four-pronged counteroffensive: he initiated one libel suit against Humphrey Marshall and another against the publisher of the *Western World*, he subsidized publication of an alternative version of events, and he wrote to Wilson Cary Nicholas, the surviving brother of George Nicholas, to head off impeachment.[61] In a

[59] Humphrey Marshall's suspicions evidently derived from those of Colonel Thomas Marshall, which were first aroused when John Brown wrote to George Muter in 1788 describing an overture made by Diego de Gardoqui. Brown's innocence is suggested by his report to James Madison that it was "not only improper but impracticable." Brown to Madison, Nov. 23, 1788, James Madison Papers, Library of Congress (microfilm), reel 3. For a discussion of the evidence relating to the Spanish conspiracy and the subsequent historiographical literature, see Boyd *et al.*, eds., *Jefferson Papers*, xix, 469-478; Watlington, *Partisan Spirit*, 253-260.

[60] "Resolutions Relating to Judge Innes," Hopkins and Hargreaves, eds., *Clay Papers*, I, 319.

[61] Innes, Todd, Brown, and Caleb Wallace (a judge of the Kentucky Court of Appeals) paid for William Littell's *Political Transactions In and Concerning Kentucky, From The First Settlement Thereof, Until It Became An Independent State, in June, 1792* (Frankfort, 1806), which was intended to contradict Marshall's accusations.

46

remarkable series of letters he recounted the events that had been disclosed during the Sebastian investigation, described the mood of Kentuckians a decade earlier, and encouraged Nicholas to use his influence to save his deceased brother's reputation—and, of course, Innes's own.[62] For his part, Nicholas forwarded the correspondence to the president, and Jefferson then weighed the evidence for and against an acquaintance with whom he had shared political and agricultural information for twenty-five years.[63] He could not have failed to appreciate the fact that the campaign against the Republican federal judge in Kentucky was led by the Federalist cousin and brother-in-law of Chief Justice John Marshall, Jefferson's own political adversary.

Fortunately for Innes and for the president, Humphrey Marshall did not have access to the Spanish archives in Seville and Madrid. Two letters found there were published in 1928 and show that in 1794 Innes had been sufficiently interested in a Spanish connection to write to the Spanish governor at Natchez, Colonel Manuel Gayoso de Lemos, asking about concrete proposals and assurances of indemnity, and requesting answers in code.[64] Innes clearly had not been as innocent as he claimed.

These Innes letters were written on February 14, 1794 and December 11, 1794, dates that bracketed a critical period for Kentucky. It was during those ten months that the bonds holding Kentucky in the Union were severely strained. When Innes wrote his first letter, the statehood for which Kentuckians had so long struggled seemed of little value: the national government appeared unwilling or unable to help solve the problems of the West and, on the contrary, was attempting to tax its most liquid asset. It seemed to have given up negotiations with Spain for the free navigation of the Mississippi. Kentuckians expected another Indian war in the summer, but if Secretary of War Henry Knox still advocated economizing by fighting Indians with regular troops armed with muskets, many thought it would result in a defeat as disastrous as those of Harmar and St. Clair.[65] Kentuckians

[62] Innes to Wilson Cary Nicholas, June 9, 1807; June 10, 1807; July 6, 1807; Oct. 18, 1807; Edmund Randolph to Cary Nicholas, Oct. 19, 1807 (copy in Innes's handwriting); Innes to Wilson Cary Nicholas, Nov. 16, 1807; Jan. 12, 1808; Feb. 25, 1808 (two letters); Nov. 18, 1808; Jefferson-Coolidge Papers, MS Coll., Massachusetts Historical Society.

[63] The letters are labeled in Jefferson's handwriting, apparently for filing among his papers.

[64] Arthur Preston Whitaker, "Harry Innes and the Spanish Intrigue: 1794-1795," *Mississippi Valley Historical Review*, xv (1928), 236-248.

[65] Boyd *et al.*, eds., *Jefferson Papers*, xix, 436-442. In May, Knox suggested recruiting mounted volunteers from Kentucky in order to divert them from at-

knew from mortal experience that successful Indian warfare required a more expensive system of scouts and rangers backed by mounted militia armed with rifles.

While Innes awaited an answer from Gayoso to his first letter, relations with the Washington administration got worse. Kentuckians learned in May that John Jay, who was widely distrusted because of his earlier willingness to barter away navigation of the Mississippi, had gone to London to negotiate with the British, and they feared the concessions he might make. They learned in July of still another revenue act. They learned in September that the president had called up 15,000 troops and moved them into Pennsylvania to end the resistance to the whiskey tax. The only bright spot in the year was the news of Anthony Wayne's victory at the Battle of Fallen Timbers, where mounted Kentucky riflemen vindicated the westerners' military judgment.[66] But no Indian cession was immediately forthcoming: the Treaty of Greenville was not concluded until a year later, in August 1795. Thus, until the government of the United States negotiated successfully with the Indians and the Spanish, it seemed to be of little use to Kentucky. Some concluded that an alliance with Spain, instead, was a prerequisite to survival. Furthermore, many who had survived the Revolution thought that negotiating with Spain was much more patriotic than negotiating with Great Britain.

During the year when other Kentuckians expressed their dissatisfaction by adopting "A Remonstrance to the President and Congress" at mass meetings throughout the state and by refusing to register their stills or pay duties on their whiskey, Innes expressed his discontent by asking the Spanish what they specifically had to offer. However curious or tempted he may have been, his taste for intrigue ended abruptly by Christmas time, when the coincidental timing of three unrelated events put an end to his unilateral inquiries.

The first threatened his professional position. A man named Owen who was traveling upriver was murdered near Evansville. The victim was said to have been carrying $6,000 from Governor de Carondelet to General Wilkinson at Fort Washington (Cincinnati). Owen's oarsmen were suspected of the murder and subsequent theft; three of them were captured in Kentucky and brought before Judge Innes at Frank-

tacking Spanish territories. Knox to Washington, May 12, 1794, Washington Papers (microfilm), reel 105.

[66] *Ky. Gaz.*, May 31, 1794; July 26, 1794; Sept. 27, 1794; Nov. 29, 1794; Jan. 3, 1795.

fort. Innes obviously wanted nothing to do with the whole affair. He hastily denied jurisdiction on the grounds that the men were Spanish subjects and sent them under guard to Wilkinson, who eventually had them returned to New Madrid.[67]

The second event threatened his reputation. Despite Innes's insistence upon discretion and the use of a code, Gayoso answered in English and entrusted his letter to a garrulous agent who wandered through Kentucky freely announcing that he carried a message from the Spanish governor for Judge Innes. Furthermore, Gayoso promised nothing but required that Kentucky must establish its independence before negotiations could be pursued. Innes was indignant, and replied on December 11 that unless "real and substantial advantages" and "unequivocal assurances of indemnity" were guaranteed, "no change can ever be expected." He again stressed the importance of secrecy and ciphers.[68]

The third event was perhaps the most effective deterrent of all, an appeal based upon family loyalty. On Christmas Day, the judge's brother James paid him a timely visit. James Innes was a leader of the Virginia bar and a close friend of President Washington, but was ill and so huge that travel of any kind was exceedingly difficult for him. Only something of extraordinary importance could have inspired the long and arduous journey from Virginia. Innes's charge, it turned out, was to bring a personal message from the president informing Kentuckians that he was making a new and major effort to secure free navigation of the Mississippi.

For although Kentuckians had not then known it, the administration had realized during the summer the seriousness of the disaffection of the West. During the same weeks that the cabinet debated and finally determined to end the rebelliousness in Pennsylvania by force, Secretary of State Edmund Randolph persuaded Washington to employ a different strategy for Kentucky. That strategy, which took months to

[67] Thomas P. Abernethy, *The South in the New Nation, 1789-1819*, in Wendell H. Stephenson and E. Merton Coulter, eds., *A History of the South*, IV (Baton Rouge, La., 1961), 197-199. Abernethy believed the money was to pay Wilkinson a Spanish pension and to compensate him for expenses incurred in thwarting George Rogers Clark's French-supported proposed expedition against New Orleans. It is possible, however, that the money was to pay Wilkinson for goods earlier shipped downriver. Wilkinson's business ventures are described *ibid.*, 47-48; 63-69. As late as 1813, Innes apparently thought Wilkinson innocent of illicit dealings with the Spanish. Innes to Madison, Apr. 25, 1813, Madison Papers (microfilm), reel 15.

[68] Whitaker, "Harry Innes," *MVHR*, xv (1928), 239.

implement, was to send one emissary to Spain and another to Kentucky.[69]

And so James Innes was chosen to do what an army could never accomplish—convince the people of Kentucky, including his own brother, of the good will and the commitment of the national government. James Innes brought details of William Carmichael's preliminary negotiations and Thomas Pinckney's appointment as envoy extraordinary and commissioner plenipotentiary to settle all matters of navigation, boundaries, and commerce with the Spanish government. (Innes was also instructed to explore the local response to the insurrection in Pennsylvania and an effective method to secure compliance with the revenue laws in Kentucky.)[70] The negotiations with the Spanish court were to be given the widest possible publicity. Since the Kentucky General Assembly had just adjourned and that forum was unavailable, the Innes brothers encouraged Governor Isaac Shelby to publicize the Carmichael-Pinckney mission through the newspapers.[71]

The news and the conciliatory approach bought time for the government, but barely enough. In 1795 its promises were made good in the Treaties of Greenville (concluded in August) and San Lorenzo (October). In the former, the Indians ceded the southeastern corner of the Northwest Territory, making the Ohio River safe as far west as the mouth of the Kentucky River; in the latter, the Spanish gave the

[69] Edmund Randolph to William Bradford, Alexander Hamilton, and Henry Knox, July 11, 1794, Harold C. Syrett et al., eds., The Papers of Alexander Hamilton (New York, 1961-   ), xvi, 588; Randolph to Washington, Aug. 7, 1794, Domestic Letters of the Department of State, M-40, roll 7 (hereafter cited as Domestic Letters, Dept. of State, M-40); Randolph to James Innes, Aug. 22, 1794, ibid.; Randolph to the governor of Kentucky [Isaac Shelby], Aug. 15, 1794, Aug. 25, 1794, and Nov. 16, 1794, ibid. Randolph, on Washington's behalf, asked Jefferson to go to Spain as commissioner plenipotentiary and, when he refused, asked Patrick Henry. Randolph to Jefferson, Aug. 28, 1794, ibid. When Henry also refused, Randolph turned to Pinckney who was minister to the Court of St. James but was then playing a subordinate role to John Jay while he was in London as envoy extraordinary and minister plenipotentiary. Samuel Flagg Bemis, Pinckney's Treaty: America's Advantage from Europe's Distress, 1783-1800 (New Haven, Conn., 1960 [orig. publ. 1926]), 247. It was almost as difficult to get Innes's mission underway: he became ill shortly after accepting the appointment and Randolph, citing the beneficent effects of "easy journies" and "northern air," urged him "betake yourself to the road, even before your strength is absolutely re-established." Randolph to Innes, Sept. 5, 1794, Domestic Letters, Dept. of State, M-40, roll 7. Cf. Richard H. Kohn, "The Washington Administration's Decision to Crush the Whiskey Rebellion," Journal of American History, LIX (1972), 567-584.

[70] "Instructions for Col. James Innes," Nov. 11, 1794, Domestic Letters, Dept. of State, M-40, roll 7.

[71] Innes to Shelby, Jan. 17, 1795, Isaac Shelby Papers, MS Dept., Filson Club. A full report covered more than three pages in Ky. Gaz., Mar. 14, 1795.

Americans a renewable three-year right to navigate the Mississippi and a grant of deposit at New Orleans. The administration also concluded a less public treaty with leading Kentucky distillers by which duties that had accrued before July 1794 were forgiven in return for a promise to comply with the internal revenue acts after that date.[72] If the news of Pinckney's treaty had reached Kentucky sooner, and if the Spanish had immediately complied with its provisions, presumably Innes would not have reopened negotiations in 1795 through Sebastian, and would have been spared the later embarrassment of that association.[73]

Of course Innes was not one to offer evidence of his own culpability, and when Marshall accused him in 1806 of participating in a Spanish conspiracy, the judge never mentioned the 1794 letters to Gayoso. Innes gambled on revealing some while concealing the rest, and continued to assert the patriotism of his motives. Marshall was not assuaged. Nor was John Rowan, Marshall's ally from Louisville, Kentucky, who led the fight for Innes's impeachment in the federal House of Representatives.[74] In the spring of 1808 Rowan secured the appointment of a select committee:

> to inquire into the conduct of Harry Innes, District Judge of the United States for the District of Kentucky, relative to his having, while in the tenure of his office as aforesaid, been party or privy to a project, on the part of Spain, or her subjects, to dismember these United States, or to the seduction of the State of Kentucky from this Union; or relative to his having been party or privy, during the time aforesaid, to a project of France, or her citizens, to embroil these United States in a war with Spain; or relative to his having illicitly corresponded with both or either of the Governments aforesaid, or their subjects or citizens, upon one or both projects aforesaid, or relative to his having known and concealed from this Government one or both the said projects.[75]

The seven-member committee which considered the depositions of the Sebastian investigation and Innes's copies of the correspondence

[72] See Chapter Five.

[73] Innes was not alone in his impatience and apparent skepticism. On Nov. 19, 1795, the Kentucky House of Representatives passed a resolution instructing the state's United States senators to find out what was going on in the negotiations with Spain. Statement by Thomas Todd, then clerk of the Kentucky House of Representatives, Innes Papers, Library of Congress, XIX, 148.

[74] Rowan is usually associated with Bardstown because the home he built there, named Federal Hill, was made famous by Stephen Foster as "My Old Kentucky Home."

[75] *Annals of Congress*, 10th Cong., 1 sess., 2757.

of 1795-1797 included Rowan. He insisted that the evidence was sufficient to impeach, but after three weeks a majority reported that Innes "had not so acted as to require the interposition of the Constitutional powers of this House." Rowan demanded an immediate decision, but the House would not be hurried. On a roll call vote of forty-eight to twenty-five it committed the report to a committee of the whole, which required each member to consider the facts and thereby created further delay.[76]

Time was running out in the session, and Rowan wanted another select committee to continue the investigation during adjournment. But a majority of the House believed other matters were more important than allegations of an earlier Spanish conspiracy and ancient dangers of secession of the West. In 1808 it was England and France who challenged national survival, and New England that then threatened to leave the Union. Furthermore, the House had lost its earlier enthusiasm for removing federal judges, possibly because this one was a Republican. Rowan was declared out of order and the matter remained in the committee of the whole, never again to be reconsidered.[77]

Innes's position was saved, but his vindication awaited. Back in Kentucky, two years later, he won his libel suit against *Western World* publisher Joseph Street. The Jessamine County jury who heard the case assessed damages which Innes, on Henry Clay's advice, refused to forgive. Street was forced to transfer all his property to the judge and leave the state.[78]

The suit against Humphrey Marshall, however, dragged on for years, and did not go to trial until 1815. What happened then, like many things in the Innes-Marshall feud, is a matter of dispute between the descendants of these remarkable protagonists. Whether the case was dismissed, the jury was hung, or the prosecution discontinued is unclear.[79] Evidently a juror was withdrawn to avert a verdict while a

[76] *Ibid.*, 1886, 2197, 2247-2250. Not all members of the House can be identified by party affiliation, but apparently only four Federalists voted with the Republican majority, suggesting that the political ramifications were recognized. However, half of the nays appear to have been Republicans.

[77] *Ibid.*, 2273.

[78] Innes's evidence for the trials against Street and Marshall is scattered throughout the Innes Papers, Library of Congress, but most of the relevant papers are in xviii, xix, and xxii, Pts. i, ii. Clay to Innes, Apr. 21, 1812, is also in Hopkins and Hargreaves, eds., *Clay Papers*, i, 648. Thomas Todd, too, sued Street for libel. The suit was dismissed in 1810 with the defendant assuming all costs. Todd to Clay, May 23, 1807, *ibid.*, 295.

[79] E.g., compare Green, *Spanish Conspiracy*, 375-379, with Bodley, "Introduction," in *Reprints of Littell's Political Transactions*, cix-cxii.

compromise was arranged. It is a matter of record that a mutual acquaintance of these two ancient enemies induced them both to sign a public statement. In it they pledged "themselves each to the other that they will not write or publish or cause to be written or published any matter or thing of and concerning the other which shall be disrespectful of the character of the other on any subject existing prior to the compromise."[80]

Innes, who lived seven months longer, seems to have lived up to his pledge. Humphrey Marshall did not. The second edition of his *History of Kentucky*, published in 1824, was sharply critical of his opponent. Marshall repeated the charges against Innes, including an accusation that he was "a weak and partial judge, an enemy to his government."[81] Yet Harry Innes may have had the last word after all—for the records of the federal court in Kentucky reveal a man whose competence, conscientiousness, and devotion to due process made his court a respected institution in the life of his state. Perhaps not least among his achievements, he may even have reconciled his skeptical countrymen to the authority of a government "at a distance and out of sight."[82]

[80] Copies of this agreement of Feb. 17, 1816 are in Innes Papers, Filson Club; Innes File, MS Coll., Kentucky Historical Society; and Innes Papers, Library of Congress, XXII, Pt. ii, 6-161.
[81] Marshall, *History of Kentucky*, II, 452.
[82] Alexander Hamilton, *The Federalist*, No. 27.

CHAPTER THREE

The Personnel of the Courts

ALTHOUGH the federal courts in Kentucky from 1789 until 1816 were identified in the public mind most closely with Harry Innes, he was not alone in determining their destiny. During the twenty-seven years he sat as judge, twenty other men were appointed to serve with him in various capacities. By their service (and sometimes by their refusal to serve) these men, too, contributed to the history of those courts. The roster of judges, clerks, marshals, and federal attorneys includes men of prominence and others who have rarely been chronicled. Among them were Federalists and Republicans who had little in common beyond their Revolutionary War heritage and their appointments to the courts. For some that appointment defined their careers; for others it was a matter of little importance. Yet collectively these appointments furnish insight into the political as well as the legal history of the era, and show how this small part of the federal judiciary contributed to the history of Kentucky and of the nation.

The three men of potentially greatest importance to the Kentucky federal courts were those who shared the bench with Innes: John McNairy, William McClung, and Thomas Todd. McNairy and McClung were appointed to serve during the brief tenure of the Federalist judiciary act, in 1801 and 1802. Todd was appointed in 1807 and remained on the court until his death in 1826.

Innes had been the only federal judge in Kentucky for almost twelve years when the Judiciary Act of 1801 abolished the Kentucky District Court and reassigned him to the new Sixth Circuit Court, comprised of Ohio, Kentucky, and Tennessee. Joining him on that bench were a newly appointed circuit judge and the district judge of Tennessee, whose district court also was abolished. This second man was John McNairy. He had little impact on the new court in Kentucky because he came to Frankfort only for the brief three-day term in May 1801, when no decisions were rendered. (He did not attend the two later terms in November 1801 and May 1802.) But if his fame in Kentucky is slight, McNairy ought to be remembered in Tennessee as a man who feuded with Andrew Jackson, but with whom Jackson declined to duel.

McNairy and Jackson were once close friends who read law together in North Carolina. In the winter of 1787-1788 they set out for its western Mero District, where they worked in the recently established state and federal territorial courts.[1] But McNairy became a supporter of Jackson's principal political opponent, Governor John Sevier. By 1797 they were sufficiently estranged that Jackson wrote McNairy and referred to their "once intimate friendship."[2] Jackson also wrote to President Washington and recommended another man, as well as McNairy, for the expected federal district court.[3] McNairy felt that their earlier friendship had been compromised and wrote letters that Jackson might have construed as challenges. That he did not is perhaps more significant than if he had, considering Jackson's reputation as an almost indiscriminate dueler.

Washington did appoint McNairy as judge of the Tennessee District Court. He served in that court until it was supplanted by the United States Court for the Sixth Circuit in Tennessee, and then again in the district court when it was reestablished in 1802. He and Jackson were eventually reconciled.[4] McNairy became a substantial citizen of sufficient distinction (or political power) that when the part of Hardin County west of the Tennessee River was separated in 1823, the new county was named in his honor. He served thirty-seven years as a

[1] McNairy was judge of the Superior Court of Law and Equity for the Mero district of North Carolina; Jackson was the district attorney. In 1790, McNairy was appointed judge of the United States Court for the Territory South of the River Ohio, which included the area later organized as Tennessee and the northern thirds of what would become the states of Mississippi and Alabama. McNairy was a member of the state constitutional convention, and when Tennessee gained statehood in 1796, was judge of its supreme court. J. Louis Adams, "Old Purdy," West Tennessee Historical Society, *Papers*, vi (1952), 5-33; "Hugh Lawson White, Frontiersman, Lawyer, and Judge," East Tennessee Historical Society, *Publications*, xix (1947), 3-25; Samuel C. Williams, "Moses Fisk," *ibid.*, xx (1948), 16-36; Miriam L. Fink, "Judicial Activities in Early East Tennessee," *ibid.*, vii (1935), 38-50; A[lbigence] W[aldo] Putnam, *History of Middle Tennessee, or Life and Times of Gen. James Robertson* (Knoxville, Tenn., 1971 [orig. publ. 1859]), 533. The continuing importance of the Spanish in the West is shown by the name of the district: Estaban Miro was de Carondelet's predecessor as governor of Louisiana. Thomas P. Abernethy, *The South in the New Nation, 1789-1819*, in Wendell H. Stephenson and E[llis] Merton Coulter, eds., *A History of the South*, iv (Baton Rouge, La., 1961), 49.

[2] Andrew Jackson to John McNairy, May 12, 1797, John Spencer Bassett, ed., *The Correspondence of Andrew Jackson* (Washington, 1926), i, 37.

[3] McNairy may not have known that Jackson also recommended him but qualified the recommendation with the comment that he was state judge. Andrew Jackson to the president [George Washington], Feb. 8, 1797, Miscellaneous Letters of the Department of State, 1789-1906, M-179, roll 15, General Records of the Department of State, Record Group 59, National Archives. (Hereafter cited as Misc. Letters, Dept. of State, M-179.)

[4] Bassett, ed., *Jackson Correspondence*, i, 5-29; *ibid.*, iii, 205-209; *ibid.*, vi, 417-422.

federal judge in Tennessee and resigned in 1834, four years before his death.[5]

In 1801, when the Sixth Circuit Court replaced the district courts of Kentucky and Tennessee, McNairy and Innes were both experienced federal judges, and they were both Jeffersonians. They also shared the distinction of being the only two of the eighteen judges in the new circuit courts who were not elevated to circuit judgeships. William McClung, who was appointed circuit judge of the Sixth Circuit and was therefore nominally superior to Innes and McNairy, had no judicial experience. At the time, Innes stated flatly that McClung was not qualified. Innes considered him "void of candour," "a mere creature to party and faction," and a failure at the bar.[6] Thomas Todd thought that he added neither "talent, learning nor dignity to the bench."[7] John Brown, the senior United States senator from Kentucky, vigorously opposed his appointment.[8] But the new circuit judge had two more pertinent qualifications: he was a Federalist and he was a brother-in-law both of President Adams's influential advisor, Secretary of State and Chief Justice of the United States John Marshall, and of Kentucky's junior senator, Humphrey Marshall.[9]

McClung was born in Virginia in 1758, the son of a Scotswoman and an Irishman. According to the Marshall family's genealogist, the future circuit judge graduated from Washington College in 1785 and later studied law with Thomas Jefferson. After emigrating to Kentucky with his cousin Joseph McDowell (whose mother was a McClung), he was a member of the Kentucky Convention of 1787 and voted against separation from Virginia. He represented Kentucky in the Virginia legislature and joined the Danville Political Club. Around 1791 he settled near Bardstown. Two years later he married Susan Tarleton Marshall, the nineteen-year-old daughter of Colonel Thomas Marshall.[10] He represented Nelson County in the Kentucky Senate from 1796 to 1800 but his political career appears not to have been particularly distinguished before his appointment as circuit judge in 1801.

[5] Erwin C. Surrency, "Federal District Court Judges and the History of Their Courts," *Federal Rules Decisions*, XL (1966), 287.

[6] Harry Innes to Thomas Jefferson, Feb. 10, 1801, Thomas Jefferson Papers, Manuscript Division, Library of Congress (microfilm), roll 37.

[7] Thomas Todd to John Breckinridge, Feb. 17, 1802, Breckinridge Family Papers, Manuscript Division, Library of Congress, XXI, 3655.

[8] "Extract of a letter from a member of Congress, to a Gentleman in this place, dated Washington, Feb. 26, 1801," *Kentucky Gazette* (Lexington), Mar. 30, 1801. Evidently the custom of senatorial courtesy in appointing federal judges had not been developed.

[9] W[illiam] M[cClung] Paxton, *The Marshall Family* (Cincinnati, 1885), 72.

[10] *Ibid.*; The Political Club, Danville, Kentucky, Records, 1786-1790, Manuscript Dept., Filson Club, Louisville, Ky.

Contrary to tradition, McClung did sit on the Sixth Circuit bench during each of the three terms of its existence.[11] The Order Book of the court states that he was present almost every day. The court records do not reflect any major shift in philosophy or procedure during his tenure, although he was present during the peak of the internal revenue cases. One example may indicate something of the relationship between McClung and Innes. When the Sixth Circuit Court was established, it became customary for all the judges in attendance to sign each day's entries in the Order Book. On November 24, 1801, a new rule was announced that the "Proceedings shall be signed by the Judge presiding."[12] From that time on, the Order Books were signed only by Judge Innes, who was technically the subordinate.

When the Sixth Circuit Court and his judgeship were abolished by the Judiciary Act of 1802, McClung retired to pursue the life of a gentleman farmer. Some time after Christopher Greenup became governor in 1804, he appointed McClung to the Mason County Circuit Court. In 1811 he contracted a malignant fever while holding court at Augusta and died. The family genealogist reported that McClung "was distinguished for his high attainments as a lawyer, but most eminently for his unapproachable integrity as a judge."[13] The source for this assessment was Collins's *History of Kentucky*. It may be pertinent to note that Judge McClung's son, the Reverend John A. McClung, "contributed largely to Collins's first edition."[14]

The fourth judge to sit on the federal bench in Kentucky was the state's first United States Supreme Court justice, Thomas Todd. Born in 1765 in King and Queen County, Virginia, he was the son of Richard Todd and the former Elizabeth Richards, whose sister Catherine had married the Reverend Robert Innes. Todd's father died when he was eighteen months old, and his older first cousin Harry Innes took charge of his education. After two short enlistments in the Continental Army between 1779 and 1781, Todd lived with the Innes family until he began his career as a lawyer. He tutored the Innes children, read law

---

[11] Cf. Thomas Speed, *History of the United States Courts in Kentucky* (Louisville, 1896), 4.

[12] United States Court for the Sixth Circuit, in District Court Order Book C, 140. (Hereafter cited as DC OB.)

[13] Paxton, *Marshall Family*, 72.

[14] *Ibid.*, 171. John A. McClung wrote a major section in the original (1847) edition of Lewis Collins's *History of Kentucky*. It is reprinted as "Outline History" in Lewis Collins and Richard H. Collins, *History of Kentucky* (Louisville, Ky., 1924 [orig. publ. Louisville, 1874]), I, 247-328. The full description of Judge McClung states that he "was distinguished for his high attainments as a lawyer, but most eminently for his great unswerving and unapproachable integrity as a judge." *Ibid.*, II, 576.

with Innes, and studied surveying. When Innes emigrated to Kentucky, Todd remained with the family and accompanied them on their move a year or so later.[15]

Once in Kentucky, Todd began a minor career as recorder for almost every official gathering in the state. He was clerk for each of the ten Kentucky conventions 1784-1792, clerk of the federal district court 1789-1792, clerk of the Kentucky Court of Appeals 1792-1801, clerk of the Kentucky constitutional conventions in 1792 and 1799, sometime clerk of the Kentucky House of Representatives, and in 1793 and 1794, clerk of the Lexington Democratic Society.[16] He was also a disappointed candidate for governor in 1796. With uncharacteristic bitterness, he later wrote to his son that he lost the election because "numbers will prevail against talent and respectability and the electioneering intriguer supplant and undermine the independent and honest statesman."[17]

When a fourth seat was created for the Kentucky Court of Appeals in 1801, Todd moved up to judge. After the resignation of George Muter five years later, Todd became chief judge. In 1807 President Jefferson named him to the United States Supreme Court. Todd was to have the newly established seventh seat and to serve in the new Seventh Circuit Court.

The appointment of Todd was notable in two respects. The first is that since the new position on the Supreme Court was intended to give representation to the Ohio-Kentucky-Tennessee area, the president asked each member of Congress from those states to recommend two candidates. Todd is reported to have been on everyone's ballot, as either first or second choice.[18]

The second important aspect of the appointment is that its timing indicated an expression of confidence not only in the appointee but

[15] Standard biographical sources usually give the date of Todd's move to Kentucky as 1786, but it must have been earlier because he was clerk of the first Kentucky convention in 1784. William Elsey Connelley and E[llis] M[erton] Coulter, *History of Kentucky*, ed. Charles Kerr, I (Chicago, 1922), 227; Edward C. O'Rear, "Justice Thomas Todd," Kentucky Historical Society *Register*, XXXVIII (1940), 112-119.

[16] Connelley and Coulter, *History of Kentucky*, I, 321; Lowell H. Harrison, *John Breckinridge, Jeffersonian Republican* (Louisville, 1969), 54, 105; Harry Innes Papers, Manuscript Division, Library of Congress, XVIII, 2-166. Todd's assets included a notably legible handwriting, as can be seen in the federal court records.

[17] Thomas Todd to Charles S. Todd, Feb. 10, 1816, Todd Family Papers, MS Dept., Filson Club.

[18] Charles Warren, *The Supreme Court in United States History*, I (Boston, 1926), 301.

also in Judge Innes. The winter of 1807 was the critical point in Innes's career because it followed the Sebastian and Burr affairs in Kentucky. Henry Clay, recently elected United States senator, reported from Washington that despite the administration's assumption of Burr's guilt, no censure had fallen on Innes for his part in letting Burr escape.[19] And Buckner Thruston, the other senator from Kentucky, also wrote reassuringly: "Boyle . . . says the President is mostly inclined in favor of Colonel Todd, who will certainly meet our Support most cordially; The President knows the Connexion between Todd and yourself; this certainly argues that his Mind is not unfavorably impressed toward you, and ought to afford you some Consolation."[20]

There proved to be nothing improper about appointing Innes's cousin and protégé to share the new circuit bench. The circuit court never reviewed judgments of the district court. But the closeness of the relationship between the two men virtually guaranteed a continuation of the line of decision established by Innes and, apparently, approved by Jefferson. Innes, for example, had supported Kentucky's occupying claimant laws which protected the investment of small farmers from confiscation by larger and more powerful landholders. The president doubtless expected that Todd would continue to uphold Jeffersonian tenets in Kentucky, where the judicial branch was not dominated by Federalists.

The close connection between Todd and Innes was marked by mutual affection as well as a common agreement upon principles. Todd's first child was named Harry Innes Todd. Todd's letters to his sons as they grew up often suggested that they consult with their "Uncle Innes."[21] The family relationship was further reinforced the year after Innes's death, when the daughter of his second marriage, Maria Knox Innes, married Todd's third son, John Harris Todd.[22]

The community of ideas shared by the judge and the justice is shown, also, in Todd's letters to Innes reporting on the Burr trial at Richmond in September 1807.[23] Like his older cousin, Todd refused to

---

[19] Henry Clay to Thomas Todd, Jan. 24, 1807, James F. Hopkins and Mary W. M. Hargreaves, *The Papers of Henry Clay*, I (Lexington, Ky., 1959), 270.

[20] Buckner Thruston to Harry Innes, Feb. 18, 1807, Innes Papers, Library of Congress, xix, 165. Thruston had been Innes's recommendation for the Sixth Circuit Court appointment given to McClung in 1801. Innes to Jefferson, Feb. 10, 1801, Jefferson Papers, roll 37.

[21] Thomas Todd to Charles S. Todd, Aug. 23, 1808; Mar. 1, 1810; Feb. 17, 1811, Todd Family Papers, MS Dept., Filson Club.

[22] Innes Papers, Library of Congress, xviii, 2-166.

[23] Todd to Innes, Sept. 23, 1807, Innes Papers, Library of Congress, xviii, 2-92; Sept. 27, 1807, *ibid.*, 2-93.

be pressured into abandoning due process for political expediency, or into loosely defining treason.[24] The letters are particularly interesting because they describe Todd's own counterattack against Humphrey Marshall. Like Innes, Todd was in the process of suing the editor of the *Western World* for libel, and he gave Innes instructions for the trial. Todd was also trying to unearth evidence that Marshall was implicated in the Blount conspiracy, and that Marshall's son had been involved in Burr's "most diabolical" plans.[25]

Yet there were important differences between Todd and Innes. Despite his Jeffersonianism, Todd accepted Chief Justice Marshall's view of judicial authority and of national supremacy. While eulogies are notoriously unreliable, there was probably truth in the one written by Mr. Justice Story on Todd's death in 1826:

> He was not ambitious of innovations upon the settled principles of the law, but was content with the more unostentatious character of walking in the trodden paths of jurisprudence. . . . He steadfastly supported the constitutional doctrines which Mr. Chief Justice Marshall promulgated in the name of the Court . . . although bred in a different school from that of the Chief Justice.[26]

Todd was also less prosperous than Innes. He was unusual in that boom-or-bust period of Kentucky history because he was a successful lawyer with training as a surveyor who did not make a fortune out of land speculation. He never parlayed his surveyor's skills and his political connections into landholdings large enough to make himself wealthy.[27] One reason for his relative poverty may be that he lacked the initial investment capital: he is said to have begun his practice with thirty-seven-and-a-half cents, a horse, and a bridle.[28] He also seems to have found it more exciting to breed horses than to trade

[24] Todd testified, however, that he doubted the validity of Burr's title to the Bastrop lands on the Ouachita River, where Burr claimed that he intended to establish a settlement. Thomas Perkins Abernethy, *The Burr Conspiracy* (New York, 1954), 257. See Chapter Six.

[25] Todd to Innes, Sept. 23, 1807, Innes Papers, Library of Congress, xviii, 2-92; Sept. 27, 1807, *ibid.*, 2-93.

[26] Thomas Todd file, Manuscript Collection, United States Supreme Court Library, Washington, D.C.

[27] Willard Rouse Jillson, *The Kentucky Land Grants* (Louisville, 1925), reports that at one time Todd held five grants totaling 8,499 acres, not a large amount for the period. At least 1,000 acres derived from a grant made to veterans of the Virginia Continental Line. "Property Deed to John Fowler," Hopkins and Hargreaves, eds., *Clay Papers*, i, 379. Todd's letters to his son suggest that some of his land was lost to Henry Clay in a lawsuit. Thomas Todd to Charles S. Todd, Jan. 2, 1816; Jan. 10, 1816, Todd Family Papers, ms Dept., Filson Club.

[28] *Dictionary of American Biography*, s.v. "Todd, Thomas."

land.[29] Perhaps he was simply not greedy. In any case, as late as 1808, Todd was entirely dependent upon his salary. In admonishing his college-bound son to be frugal, he pointed out "how necessary it is to be prudent and economical and that upon an equal dividend of my Salary among a wife and five children, allowing $400 to each I shall have but a scanty sum to bear my expences in travelling to and attending the several Courts where official duty requires me."[30]

Todd and Innes did differ to some extent on matters affecting the federal court. As noted earlier, Todd apparently construed federal jurisdiction more narrowly: there were ninety causes dismissed "for want of jurisdiction" in the terms immediately following his appointment to the Seventh Circuit Court.[31] No longer did the federal court accept debt cases involving small sums that had been brought by British merchants.[32] There were also eight causes certified to the Supreme Court from 1807 until 1816, "the judges being opposed." The most significant of these was *Green* v. *Biddle*, raising the question of the validity of the Kentucky occupying claimant laws. Finally, the use of advisory juries in chancery suits died out after Todd joined Innes on the bench.[33] In the Seventh Circuit Court, fewer cases were heard each day and each term than formerly; fewer decisions were handed down. Apparently it took more time for two judges to confer than for one to decide alone. Perhaps Todd was not so hard a worker as Innes, who had often demonstrated an astonishing output. It had not been unusual for Innes to hear more than thirty cases or conduct a dozen jury trials on the same day.[34]

Yet except for the *Green* v. *Biddle* case, which came at the end of the period under discussion, the essential line of decision was unchanged after 1807 and the style of the Kentucky federal courts remained as it had been for nearly twenty years. Innes had spent almost two decades establishing the character of the courts and had acted upon 1,595 cases before Todd joined the federal bench. Only a judge with a very different view of jurisprudence could have greatly changed the courts' direction.

Consequently, the only judge in the Kentucky federal courts before

[29] Clay to Todd, Jan. 24, 1807, Hopkins and Hargreaves, eds., *Clay Papers*, I, 272; "Advertisement Concerning Buzzard," Feb. 17, 1807, quoted *ibid.*, 283; "Advertisement Concerning Buzzard," Mar. 7, 1808, quoted *ibid.*, 322-324.

[30] Thomas Todd to Charles S. Todd, Aug. 23, 1808, Todd Family Papers, MS Dept., Filson Club.

[31] See Chapter One and Appendix B.

[32] These cases are discussed in Chapter Seven.

[33] Occupying claimant laws and advisory juries are discussed in Chapter Eight.

[34] E.g., DC OB F, July 18, 1806, 486-500; *ibid.*, July 25, 1806, 509-519; DC OB G, July 31, 1806, 7-26.

61

1816 who was on the bench long enough and was in a position strong enough to challenge and change the character of the court was a man most unlikely to do so. Thomas Todd was distinguished by his personal loyalties. Furthermore, he had learned his law from Innes and shared his political philosophy. Like most lawyers with a judicial temperament, Todd believed that *stare decisis* (let the decision stand) was the spine of the law. He strengthened the traditions and reinforced the individual character of the federal courts in Kentucky, and thereby contributed to its stability and prestige.[35]

*   *   *

The Judiciary Act of 1789 provided, in addition to judges, three other officers for each federal court: marshals (who corresponded to sheriffs in English, colonial, and state courts), United States attorneys, and clerks. The clerks were more closely aligned with the judges than were the other officers of the court because they were appointed by the judges and served at their pleasure. In the Kentucky federal courts it is clear that personal and political allegiances were important in the selection process.

The first clerk of the district court was Thomas Todd, appointed by Innes on the opening day of the first session.[36] Todd resigned three years later to become clerk of the newly established Kentucky Court of Appeals, and for the next fifteen years his career developed in that court.

James G. Hunter, a Danville lawyer, succeeded Todd as clerk.[37] Within a few months of his appointment, Hunter became an active member of the Democratic Society and sponsored the public statements it issued.[38] Innes was well acquainted with Hunter through their

[35] Compare the amount of public protest registered over the three instances during this era when Kentucky state courts reversed themselves on important questions. The first occasion was when, in *Kenton* v. *McConnell* (1794), a majority of the Court of Appeals declared that the decisions of the Virginia Land Commission of 1779-1780 could be overturned. (The case was reargued in 1799 and reported in full for that year.) James Hughes, *A Report of the Causes Determined by the Late Supreme Court for the District of Kentucky and by the Court of Appeals in Which Titles to Land Were In Dispute*, 257-322. (1 *Kentucky Reports*.) The second came after Innes's death, when the occupying claimant laws were declared unconstitutional. The third was when state courts disallowed stay laws and replevin bonds and brought about the old court-new court battle of the 1820s.

[36] DC OB A, Dec. 15, 1789, 2.

[37] *Ibid.*, Dec. 18, 1792, 31; Maria T. Daviess, *History of Mercer and Boyle Counties* (Harrodsburg, Ky., 1924), 1-7.

[38] "The Democratic Societies of 1793 and 1794 in Kentucky, Pennsylvania, and Virginia," *William and Mary Quarterly*, 2d Ser., II (1922), 247.

common interest in the society, even though the judge was careful to keep his political sympathies out of the public eye. It is probable that his support of its purposes and members is reflected in Hunter's retaining the clerkship during the four most critical years of resistance to the internal revenue acts.

The third clerk was Thomas Tunstall, who followed Hunter on March 15, 1796. Tunstall was an old acquaintance of the judge. (Innes's papers include a promissory note indicating that he borrowed money from Tunstall in 1776.)[39] Tunstall, like Innes, shifted to the Sixth Circuit Court during its short life and returned to the district court when it was reestablished in 1802.[40] At the May 1807 session of the Seventh Circuit Court he was named clerk *pro tem* of that court as well as the district court. Both appointments were discontinued the following term.[41]

It is evident that the addition of Justice Todd to the circuit court influenced the choice of Tunstall's successor: this was John H. Hanna, the man who married Todd's daughter. Hanna was a Pennsylvania lawyer who came out to Kentucky to make his fortune, and was successful. He was described by a contemporary as "a fine clerk and a distinguished citizen . . . no man more trustworthy."[42] His honesty and industry brought him many rewards. At one time or another he owned the stagecoach line running from Louisville to Lexington, a large part of the land upon which Frankfort was built, and part interest in a number of cotton, woolen, and flour mills. Hanna was clerk of the Kentucky federal courts for forty-four years and did not resign until 1851. During his tenure he also became a leading citizen of Frankfort —president of the Farmers' Bank, supporter of the Widows' and Orphans' Home, donor of the sanctuary of the Episcopal church, and a member of the group who built the bridge over the Kentucky River.[43]

❋　　❋　　❋

The remaining officers of the court, the United States attorneys and the marshals, were presidential appointees. The former had indefinite tenure; the latter served for renewable four-year terms. Kentucky had only three marshals during the period 1789-1816. The first was Samuel

[39] Innes Papers, Filson Club.

[40] DC OB C, May 15, 1801, 51; Nov. 15, 1802, 316.

[41] United States Circuit Court for the District of Kentucky, Order Book A, May 4, 1807, 3; Order Book B, Dec. 9, 1807, 64. (Hereafter cited as CC OB.)

[42] Martin D. Hardin to Richard Rush, May 29, 1817, Misc. Letters, Dept. of State, M-179, roll 37.

[43] *Biographical Encyclopedia of Kentucky of the Dead and Living Men of the Nineteenth Century* (Cincinnati, 1878), 350.

McDowell, Jr., son of Judge McDowell of the old Kentucky District Court of Virginia. A member of a large Scots-Irish clan of vigorous Presbyterian and Federalist convictions, the younger McDowell pursued the duties of his office with the assistance of many of his brothers, brothers-in-law, and cousins, whom he appointed as his deputies. A cousin of William McClung and the Marshall family, McDowell was appointed to a third four-year term despite a lukewarm letter of recommendation by Humphrey Marshall.[44] There is little question that his tenure was dependent upon his political affiliations.[45]

The second marshal, Joseph Crockett, was recommended to President Jefferson as "a decided Republican."[46] Born in Virginia in 1742, Crockett served in the Revolutionary War and was discharged as a colonel. He came to Kentucky in 1784 to locate military warrants.[47] He surveyed lands and roads in Kentucky, sometimes in the employ of Colonel Thomas Marshall, but eventually lost most of his own claims. As a member of the Virginia legislature from the Kentucky District, Crockett opposed precipitate separation from Virginia. Nevertheless, he was elected to the first Kentucky General Assembly from Fayette County. His term as marshal coincided with effective enforcement of the internal revenue laws and brought him the highest fees in the nation. He received $452.33, in addition to his salary of $200.[48]

Seven years later, Secretary of the Treasury Albert Gallatin decided to wind up the business still remaining from the repealed revenue acts by transferring the duties of the supervisors of the internal revenue to the federal marshals.[49] Crockett was confused by his directives and

[44] Humphrey Marshall to John Adams, Nov. 20, 1799, Letters of Application and Recommendation During the Administration of John Adams, 1797-1801, M-406, roll 2, General Records of the Department of State, Record Group 59, National Archives; Paxton, *Marshall Family*, 58-62.

[45] Thomas Marshall Green, *Historic Families of Kentucky* (Baltimore, 1964 [orig. publ. Cincinnati, 1889]), 4; Otto A. Rothert, "Samuel McDowell's Letters to Andrew Reid," *Filson Club History Quarterly*, xvi (1942), 172-186.

[46] John Breckinridge to Thomas Jefferson, Feb. 16, 1801, Breckinridge Family Papers, xx, 3394. Breckinridge also recommended John Jouitt (Jouett) and Charles Wilkins, but with less enthusiasm. Breckinridge to Jefferson, Jan. 12, 1801, *ibid.*, 3377; Breckinridge to Jefferson, Mar. 2, 1801, *ibid.*, 3404.

[47] Samuel W. Price, *Biographical Sketch of Joseph Crockett* (Louisville, 1909), 9-23.

[48] Walter Lowrie and Walter S. Franklin, eds., *American State Papers, Miscellaneous: Documents, Legislative and Executive of the Congress of the United States*, i (Washington, 1834), 303.

[49] Albert Gallatin to Thomas Jefferson, Sept. 3, 1808, Internal Revenue Direct Tax, Correspondence 1807-1829, file 11713, General Records of the Department of the Treasury, Record Group 56, National Archives. (Hereafter cited as Internal Revenue Direct Tax Correspondence.)

charged the government for the salary due for taking on this responsibility while Supervisor Morrison was still handling it. Gallatin sternly replied, "The account is returned, that you may make another, in which that charge shall be omitted."[50] Crockett eventually made the correction, but it took him a long time to do so.

In 1811, Joseph Crockett was succeeded by his son Robert, and collections became more difficult. The younger Crockett was described as "a man of great energy and enterprise, but of an over sanguine temperament, and in consequence undertook more than he could accomplish."[51] He was continually getting involved in schemes that left him (and eventually his father) poorer than before. Except for a tour of duty in the War of 1812, Robert Crockett served as marshal until June 1817. In spite of whatever he may have accomplished in office, he failed to satisfy Treasury Department officials. As late as July 1816, they complained about partial accounts of five years' standing, "and these altogether deficient in the forms requisite for their settlement."[52]

A decade later, Joseph Crockett detailed his son's abortive ventures in a will that, upon his death in 1829, bequeathed to his daughters "whatever estate I may be in possession of . . . or monies due me from my son, Robert Crockett, for debts paid by me as his Security or otherwise."[53] A pension eventually arranged for Joseph Crockett may have permitted him to live out his remaining years in some dignity.[54] As for the Treasury Department, it finally ended its attempts to collect from Joseph Crockett in March 1823, with the notation that "he is dead and insolvent, ruined by his son."[55] He was not dead, but the money was uncollectable.

❀   ❀   ❀

The administrative problems of collection were minor in comparison with the difficulties of filling the remaining federal court position in

[50] Albert Gallatin to Joseph Crockett, May 22, 1810, *ibid.*

[51] Price, *Biographical Sketch*, 40.

[52] J. H. Smith to Robert Crockett, July 3, 1816, Internal Revenue Direct Tax Correspondence; J. H. Smith to Joseph Crockett, July 3, 1816, *ibid.* The problems encountered by the Treasury Department with the Crocketts were not at all unusual, according to records in the National Archives.

[53] Price, *Biographical Sketch*, 84.

[54] Henry Clay is said to have secured the pension by a private bill passed in Congress, but the published Clay papers contain no record of this. Cf. Price, *Biographical Sketch*, 11.

[55] George M. Bibb to Samuel Pleasanton, Mar. 9, 1823, Solicitor of the Treasury, Letters Received; United States Attorneys, Clerks of Courts, and Marshals, Kentucky 1804-1866, file 32092, Records of the Solicitor of the Treasury, Record Group 206, National Archives.

Kentucky, that of United States attorney. Eight appointments were offered in the first eleven years of the court and five were immediately declined. At first the difficulty may have been an illustration of President Washington's continuing problem of finding people willing to accept federal appointments.[56] Or it may have been a question of finding people with the proper qualifications, because the first appointee was overqualified, the second underqualified, and the third had the wrong political qualifications. But as time went on, it became increasingly evident that the most important reason the position was so hard to fill was that it carried with it duties no one wanted to perform.

The principal duty of a United States attorney was to bring suits against persons who were believed to be in violation of the statutes of the new nation. Until the Alien and Sedition Acts of 1798, the most controversial laws were the internal revenue measures. These statutes were exceedingly unpopular in Kentucky. They were so repugnant to most Kentuckians that enforcement proved to be impossible and, sometimes, even dangerous.

The records of the Kentucky federal court, Judge Innes's opinions, Treasury Department accounts, and private correspondence reveal that there was a whiskey rebellion in this state, once believed to have been generally (if reluctantly) in compliance with the internal revenue laws. Pennsylvania, where opposition to federal authority took the dramatic form of the Whiskey Rebellion, was not alone. Resistance was equally widespread in Kentucky, but much of the evidence was covered up at the time and has remained hidden ever since in government archives.[57] Many who knew better pretended that all was well there, while the population in fact engaged in massive civil disobedience and occasional violence.[58] Yet because it was inexpedient to acknowledge

[56] George Washington to Alexander Hamilton, Oct. 29, 1795, Harold C. Syrett et al., eds., The Papers of Alexander Hamilton, xix, 356-358.

[57] One of the most significant bodies of evidence is a collection of letters written by Colonel Thomas Marshall to Treasury officials describing the situation in Kentucky. These letters were discovered in 1954 among papers which had been removed from the Internal Revenue files at some unknown time in the past. The collection is correctly labeled "Whiskey Rebellion," and there are many references to affairs in Kentucky as well as in Pennsylvania. Whiskey Rebellion Papers, Record Group 58, Records of the Internal Revenue Service, National Archives. (Hereafter cited as Whiskey Rebellion Papers, National Archives.)

[58] Beginning in 1792, Hamilton was informed through the series of letters referred to in note 57, above, which were forwarded to him by Tench Coxe. E.g., Coxe to Hamilton, May 20, 1792, Syrett et al., eds., Hamilton Papers, xi, 405. Hamilton also knew, of course, that no whiskey tax money was forthcoming from Kentucky. Thomas Jefferson knew about the Kentucky situation because he was requested to forgive arrearages in order to obtain compliance, as described below.

the unpopularity of Hamilton's fiscal program, the Washington administration treated Pennsylvania as unique and singled it out for an experiment in the use of force to uphold federal authority.[59] Kentucky was protected from that experiment by its relative geographical isolation and by the administration's fear of snapping the bonds that held it in the Union. Even if an army could have been raised, transported, and supplied over the mountains (all of which are doubtful), it might well have thrown the West into the eager arms of France or Spain. As late as 1797, a Spanish agent reported:

There are only three motives that would impel them [the Kentuckians] to break the bonds uniting them to the other states, namely: 1. War with the French Republic; 2. Prohibition to navigate the Mississippi and settle in the territory of the King; 3. Inability to pay in silver the general taxes . . . or an attempt of the government to collect this sum by force. These are the main things that will determine their course of action.[60]

Kentucky has experienced many generations of antagonism toward revenue agents, but it is important to note that the resistance in the 1790s was not limited to a handful of mountain distillers. The population was nearly unanimous, and opposition to the whiskey tax included Kentucky's most respected leaders. Like the Pennsylvanians, they were "distillers through necessity, not choice, that [they] may comprehend

---

Edmund Randolph was told by George Nicholas, who was his brother-in-law, and by Senator John Brown, who gave him a copy of a letter from Kentucky which Randolph then passed on to Washington on Feb. 27, 1794, cited in note 78, below. The responses of the Washington administration are described in Chapters Two and Five.

[59] The administration took the official position that resistance to the internal revenue acts ended after Washington's Proclamation of Sept. 15, 1792, except in Pennsylvania. (This proclamation was published without comment in the *Ky. Gaz.* for six successive weeks, beginning Nov. 24, 1792.) Of even greater interest in Kentucky must have been Washington's State of the Union Message of Nov. 19, 1794 (published in the *Ky. Gaz.*, Jan. 3, 1795), which treated Pennsylvania as an isolated example. The pretense was continued by John Marshall in his biography of Washington, although Marshall knew from his own father the true situation in Kentucky. E.g., John Marshall, *The Life of George Washington, Commander in Chief of the American Forces During the War Which Established the Independence of His Country and First President of the United States*, II (New York, 1930 [orig. publ. Philadelphia, 1804]), 278-281, 402-415.

[60] Unidentified agent to Señor Don [*sic*] Manuel Gayoso de Lemos, Dec. 5, 1797. (Translated from the Spanish by the Military Intelligence Division of the War Department, March 13, 1934.) Letters Received by the Secretary of War, Unregistered Series 1789-1860, M-222, roll 1, Records of the Office of the Secretary of War, Record Group 107, National Archives.

the greatest value on the smallest size and weight."[61] They were probably unhappy about any form of taxation, although there is no evidence that they refused to pay the other excises of the era that were placed on such things as carriages and gold watches. But Kentuckians were angered when a distant government that seemed of little use to them placed a tax on their most exportable product. Only a few years earlier, many of them had rebelled against England in part because they believed that its legislature had unfairly taxed one part of the population without its consent. Time had not dulled their convictions. Nor had it brought much experience of gracefully accepting the will of the majority, or of sacrificing self-interest to national needs. The fragility of the new nation was clearly exposed when its statutes were ignored, and tax evasion was not only tolerated but also practiced by a large number of its citizens.

Because the government remained committed to collection of the excise despite petitions and protests, and force was out of the question, compliance could be achieved only through reliance on the peaceful processes of the legal system. It was the duty of United States attorneys to prosecute violators of federal laws. After passage of the internal revenue acts, it would have required someone with both courage and stature to undertake successfully such an assignment in Kentucky. And no one with those characteristics wanted the job.

George Nicholas, who was Washington's first choice for the post, was such a man. A member of the wealthy land-holding Carter family of Virginia, Nicholas ended his Revolutionary War service as a colonel and later achieved fame for his support of the 1784 struggle for religious freedom in Virginia and his eloquent defense of the federal Constitution in the 1788 state convention. He was a noted lawyer and legal scholar who held the first chair of law at Transylvania University.[62] Nicholas would have been an appropriate choice for judge of the federal court, but that position had been given to his friend Harry Innes, who often consulted him on matters of law and politics.[63] When Nicholas was offered the position as United States attorney in 1789 he

[61] The quotation is from a 1792 petition written by Albert Gallatin. Henry Adams, ed., *The Writings of Albert Gallatin*, I (New York, 1960 [orig. publ. Philadelphia, 1879]), 3.

[62] Matilda Nicholas Barrett, "George Nicholas, a Biographical Sketch" [1887], Bennett Young Collection, MS Dept., Filson Club.

[63] Among Innes's papers is a manuscript in Edmund Pendleton's handwriting describing Virginia land laws, especially the proper use of caveats. The manuscript has marginal notes in Nicholas's and Innes's handwritings. Innes Papers, Library of Congress, xxv, Pt. i, 5-254. Their joint decision not to report the 1797 Spanish offer was described in Chapter Two.

was probably not interested in this less prestigious appointment because he had extensive land claims and a large legal practice requiring his attention.[64]

James Brown, the twenty-four-year-old brother of Senator John Brown, was appointed in March 1790.[65] (The elder Brown probably arranged this appointment, as he had those of Innes and Nicholas.) James Brown had only recently moved to Lexington to practice law, after completing his education at William and Mary College. An able and ambitious young man who became secretary of state under Kentucky's first governor, Isaac Shelby, Brown later had a notable career in Louisiana as co-author of the Civil Code, secretary of the Territory, district attorney, and United States senator.[66] But in 1790 his career was just beginning, and he probably declined the opportunity to be United States attorney because he recognized his own inexperience, and because there was no salary and he could collect only the fees taxed by the court.[67]

The office was eventually filled by William Murray, a member of the Lexington bar, who presented his commission as attorney to the court when it convened in September 1791.[68] But six months before that, Congress had passed the first of the internal revenue acts, and Murray, who later helped organize the Democratic Society, clearly had no intention of trying to enforce them.[69] Colonel Thomas Marshall, the highest officer of the Internal Revenue Service in Kentucky, proceeded to

[64] George Nicholas to John Brown, Nov. 12, 1789, George Nicholas file, Kentucky Historical Society, Frankfort, Ky. Nicholas's notes on land cases tried in the Kentucky Court of Appeals were so complete that they were used by James Hughes and Thomas Todd when they prepared Vol. 1 of *Kentucky Reports*. 1 *Kentucky Reports*, vi.

[65] Thomas Jefferson to James Brown, Apr. 7, 1790, Domestic Letters of the Department of State, 1784-1906, M-40, roll 4, General Records of the Department of State, Record Group 59, National Archives. (Hereafter cited as Domestic Letters, Dept. of State, M-40.)

[66] Samuel M. Wilson, "The Early Bar of Fayette County," in *Addresses Delivered in Honor of John Marshall Day by Members of the Fayette County Bar* (Lexington, Ky., 1901), 50. Brown married wealthy Ann (Nancy) Hart, sister of Henry Clay's wife, and in the 1820s was United States minister to France. Hopkins and Hargreaves, eds., *Clay Papers*, 1, 150n.

[67] 1 Stat. 73, sec. 35. The official appointment of William Murray, dated Feb. 27, 1791, notes the resignation (not refusal) of Brown, but there is no evidence in the district court records that he ever took the oath of office or performed any official duties, although he was admitted to practice in April 1790. Misc. Letters, Dept. of State, M-179, roll 5; DC OB A, Apr. 1, 1790, 1.

[68] DC OB A, Sept. 20, 1791, 10. There is no explanation for Murray's absence from the June term.

[69] "The Democratic Societies," *WMQ*, 2d Ser., II (1922), 239; Wilson, "Early Bar of Fayette County," 51.

organize the district and appointed collectors, but he got no cooperation from the United States attorney in prosecuting violators of the
law. Except for taking the oath of office and collecting allowances for
attending court, Murray seemed to have no public duties.[70] He never
asked for indictments from the grand juries and never prosecuted any
suits, either civil or criminal, in the name of the United States. In December 1792 he resigned to become attorney general of Kentucky, and
once again the office of United States attorney was vacant.[71]

In February 1793 the president turned again to George Nicholas.
By this time, Commissioner of Internal Revenue Tench Coxe had offered a compromise to distillers in order to achieve compliance with
the law. Taxes were to be excused for the first year, from July 1, 1791
until July 1, 1792. This was not enough for Nicholas, who refused his
second appointment. He defended his position in a letter to Colonel
Marshall:

> I have encouraged no man to oppose the law; I have recommended
> it to all who have applied to me for that Purpose, to comply with it;
> I have refused to give instructions how the distillers might evade
> the law; I have declined giving any general opinion on the Practica-
> bility of enforcing the law; but after suits have been brought, I have
> upon being employed in them, given an opinion as to the decision
> that would Probably take place in those Particular cases. In all fu-
> ture applications, except where the defendants shall have been
> guilty of a clear breach of the Peace, I shall hold myself at liberty
> to appear for them, and to endeavor to show that their cases do not
> come within the law, or ought not to be punished under it.[72]

Nicholas did cooperate enough to recommend Thomas T. Davis for
the office, but Marshall thought him a poor suggestion. "His character
as a man of genious and information I have never heard mentioned
but in very moderate terms. I have no great hopes from this Gentle-
mans assistance. He can be no match for Colo Nicholas at the bar."[73]

Meanwhile, the president had made a different selection in Novem-

[70] DC OB A, Sept. 20, 1791, 13; Jan. 12, 1792, 18; Mar. 20, 1792, 26.
[71] William Murray to Jefferson, Dec. 7, 1792, Misc. Letters, Dept. of State,
M-179, roll 8.
[72] Nicholas to Marshall, Aug. 25, 1793, Whiskey Rebellion Papers, National
Archives.
[73] Marshall to Edward Carrington (supervisor of the revenue in Virginia),
Mar. 20, 1794, *ibid*. Davis, a Jeffersonian and friend of Innes, was not appointed.
Davis later served in Congress and as a judge of the Indiana territorial court.
An application by him for a writ of *habeas corpus*, denied by Innes, is described
in Chapter Seven.

ber. This time he chose John Breckinridge, a Virginia lawyer who had moved to Kentucky earlier in the year.[74] The new nominee, however, had already accepted appointment as attorney general of Kentucky. In January he declined the federal post without explanation.[75] Colonel Marshall believed that he knew the reason:

> No Federal Atto. as yet undertakes to act in this Country, it is no more than I have for some time foreseen, I suspect it to be a part of the plan of those who wish to defeat the law; men of Character and known abilities are recommended, but whose principles and Connections are known to be adverse to the Law, from which it necessarily follows that they will refuse the appointment.[76]

The colonel may have been mistaken in suspecting conspiracy but he was correct in his assessment of the "principles and connections" of Breckinridge, Nicholas, Brown, and Murray. At the very time that he was appointed, Breckinridge was chairman of the Democratic Society and was writing "A Remonstrance of the Citizens West of the Mountains to the President and Congress of the United States." The document vigorously criticized the government for its failure to secure the free navigation of the Mississippi River and candidly stated that the people of the interior were not willing to share the burdens of government while they did not share its benefits. Breckinridge was a most unlikely person to wish to serve as attorney. He was a Jeffersonian who would gain fame for introducing Jefferson's resolutions against the Alien and Sedition Acts to the 1798 Kentucky legislature. He later became a senator, and was appointed attorney general of the United States just before his death in 1806. Few positions could have been less tempting in 1794 than the assignment of prosecuting Kentuckians under an unpopular federal law that was leading to violence in Kentucky as in Pennsylvania.

Colonel Marshall had already experienced many problems in trying to retain collectors, because they were so often intimidated by the population. In February 1794 there was a particularly brazen nighttime attack upon a collector whose money, saddlebags, and records were stolen. The money and saddlebags were later found, but the records were not. Marshall, despairing of a federal prosecution, sug-

[74] Harrison, *John Breckinridge*, 40.
[75] Breckinridge to the secretary of state [Edmund Randolph], Jan. 13, 1794, Misc. Letters, Dept. of State, M-179, roll 11.
[76] Marshall to Carrington, Mar. 20, 1794, Whiskey Rebellion Papers, National Archives. Marshall also complained to Tench Coxe, commissioner of internal revenue, on the same date. *Ibid.*

gested that the suspected assailants be charged in "Bourbon [state circuit] Court, where my son Alexander is States atto[rney] who I know will do his duty."[77]

The suggestion that members of the Marshall family might cooperate where others had not may have been passed on to President Washington. In any event, the next appointment went to Marshall's son-in-law, William McClung, in June. But Federalist McClung was no more interested in the position than the Republicans had been. Edmund Randolph wrote to the president: "William McClung has refused to accept his Commission, as Attorney for the district of Kentucky. I suspect, that we must see some turn in the minds of the people there, before anybody will venture upon an office, which will be chiefly conversant in the excise penalties."[78]

With no federal attorney in Kentucky, Hamilton advised Commissioner of Revenue Tench Coxe to hire private counsel to prosecute suits there. The instructions went out to Marshall, who replied to Coxe, "You tell me that I may call in the assistance of any other attorney. This you may depend sir is not attainable."[79] Nevertheless, the colonel again asked George Nicholas and promised him "liberal fees."[80] But Nicholas still refused.[81] It was not until 1796 that Marshall could at last write that William Clarke, who had recently come to Kentucky from Maryland, would accept the office of attorney if it were offered to him. Commissioner Coxe was advised that "it will perhaps be neces-

[77] Marshall to Carrington, Mar. 20, 1794, *ibid.*

[78] Randolph to Washington, Oct. 22, 1794, Domestic Letters, Dept. of State, M-40, roll 7. (The same letter is in Misc. Letters, Dept. of State, M-179, roll 12.) John Brown had sent Randolph a letter stating that "no lawyer who has a reputation to loose will accept that Office. Perhaps H[umphrey] Marshall or [William] McClung—but what would be the consequence? They are fully as odious to the People as the Excise, and would probably be mobb'd if the[y] attempted to discharge the functions of that Office." Randolph passed this on to Washington, Feb. 27, 1794, *ibid.*, roll 11. It is an interesting commentary on the appointment policies of President John Adams that McClung's refusal of this obligation in 1794 was no bar to his acceptability as a midnight appointment for circuit judge in 1801.

[79] Marshall to Coxe, May 29, 1794, Whiskey Rebellion Papers, National Archives.

[80] Marshall to Nicholas, Oct. 8, 1794, *ibid.*

[81] Humphrey Marshall later contended that Nicholas had agreed in 1796 to accept appointment as district attorney for a limited time, a fact that Nicholas vigorously disputed. Oliver Wolcott's recollection was like Marshall's, but Wolcott could not produce the evidentiary letter which Marshall wanted in order to embarrass Nicholas. Humphrey Marshall to Oliver Wolcott, Jr., Sept. 24, 1798, Oliver Wolcott, Jr., Papers, Connecticut Historical Society, Hartford, x, 41; Wolcott to Marshall, Oct. 20, 1798, *ibid.*, xxxv, 75.

sary to furnish him with a Copy of the Acts of Congress which I believe cannot be had here."[82]

Armed with a copy of the statutes and an interim appointment, William Clarke presented his commission to the court at its December 1796 term.[83] Little is known about him before that date, but over the next four years he was to make a noticeable impression in Kentucky.[84] No longer were the internal revenue laws ignored: Clarke brought 55 criminal charges and 176 civil suits in his determined effort to get compliance. But an outsider had little chance against the equally determined population. And Clarke was evidently not as skillful as his adversaries. It was hard to get indictments, harder still to get convictions, and even the civil suits ran afoul of legal technicalities upheld by Judge Innes.[85] In the end, not one of Clarke's defendants paid the full penalties or debts provided by the laws.

Fortunately for Clarke, his tenure coincided with an era of peace with the Indians and the promise of free navigation of the Mississippi by the Spanish, or he might have precipitated the secession of Kentucky or violence to himself.[86] His bumbling efforts earned the contempt of the judge, censure from the Treasury Department, and, eventually, the embarrassment of his earlier supporters. By 1800 such an impasse had been reached that the Marshalls arranged to have Clarke kicked upstairs to become chief judge of the newly created court of Indiana Territory.[87] He left Kentucky a year before his successor took office and went to Vincennes, where he opened a general store, held court, and died of pleurisy in 1802.[88]

[82] Marshall to Coxe, Aug. 14, 1796, Whiskey Rebellion Papers, National Archives.

[83] DC OB A, Dec. 20, 1796, 136. The Sept. 24 appointment was confirmed Dec. 22, 1796. John C. Fitzpatrick, ed., *The Writings of George Washington from the Original Manuscript Sources, 1745-1799*, xxxv, 241n.

[84] Clarke was evidently suggested by Attorney General Charles Lee, among others. Washington to the secretary of state [Timothy Pickering], Oct. 10, 1796, Fitzpatrick, ed., *Writings of Washington*, xxxv, 241. Apparently members of the Marshall family were also involved in the appointment. Marshall to Coxe, Aug. 14, 1796, Whiskey Rebellion Papers, National Archives. On Clarke, see "Hopewell Rogers Index," n.p., n.d. (typescript), Filson Club.

[85] These cases are described in Chapter Five.

[86] The Treaty of Greenville with the Indians was concluded in August 1795; the Treaty of San Lorenzo with Spain was signed in October 1795.

[87] The secretary of state [John Marshall] to the president [John Adams], Aug. 26, 1800, Clarence Edwin Carter, ed., *The Territorial Papers of the United States*, vii, *The Territory of Indiana 1800-1810* (Washington, D.C., 1939), 18. See, also, Clarence E. Carter, "William Clarke, First Chief Justice of Indiana Territory," *Indiana Magazine of History*, xxxiv (1938), 1-13.

[88] Judge [Henry] Vanderburgh to the secretary of state [James Madison], Nov. 15, 1802, Carter, ed., *Territorial Papers*, vii, *Indiana*, 78.

It was Joseph Hamilton Daveiss who finally ended the resistance of Kentuckians to the revenue laws—on the eve of their repeal. Daveiss was a fervent Federalist who had adopted his middle name in honor of Alexander Hamilton, whom he extravagantly admired. He was also a protégé of the Marshalls and would soon become, by marriage, a member of the family.[89] Daveiss's Scots-Irish parents brought him to Kentucky from Virginia in 1779, when he was five years old. At eighteen he served under Major John Adair guarding the transportation of provisions to forts north of the Ohio River.[90] He later studied law under George Nicholas and began to practice in 1795. When Humphrey Marshall arranged the appointment as United States attorney, Daveiss was serving as a representative from Mercer County in the Kentucky General Assembly.[91]

Although Daveiss's commission was dated December 1800, he did not present it to the court until its November 1801 term. During that year he won a major case in the United States Supreme Court, which brought him huge landholdings in the Green River country.[92] He may also have worked out some kind of arrangement between the new administration of Thomas Jefferson and the Jeffersonians in Kentucky, because it is obvious from the Kentucky federal court records that a new day had dawned. Daveiss was a vigorous and competent prosecutor, and the docket was immediately flooded with cases. In cooperation with James Morrison, who had succeeded Colonel Marshall as inspector of the revenue in 1797, Daveiss brought 317 civil suits for Debt (owed by distillers who had failed to pay taxes), 161 of these in his first term in office.[93] After repeal of the internal revenue laws in 1802, Daveiss tenaciously pursued delinquent collectors, customs authorities, postmasters, and army contractors. In all of these actions, he enjoyed a notable degree of success. Daveiss also prosecuted twenty-eight other criminal actions. Here, however, his conviction rate was much lower for a variety of reasons, many of which related to Judge Innes's strict adherence to due process.[94]

Throughout Daveiss's tenure, he and the judge were continually on the verge of political warfare outside the courtroom. Daveiss was close-

[89] Daveiss married Nancy Marshall in 1803.

[90] Daveiss, *History of Mercer and Boyle Counties*, 52. In the Burr affair in 1806, Daveiss subpoenaed Adair in order to forestall the dismissal of the second grand jury. The case is described in Chapter Six.

[91] Humphrey Marshall to Joseph Hamilton Daveiss, Nov. 24, 1800, Joseph Hamilton Daveiss and Samuel Daveiss Papers, MS Dept., Filson Club.

[92] *Wilson* v. *Mason*, 1 Cranch 45 (1801), is described in Chapter Eight.

[93] See Chapter Five.   [94] See Chapter Six.

ly associated with Humphrey Marshall, and the two arranged financing for a newspaper, the *Western World*, in order to give public expression to their Federalist convictions. It was this paper that revived the charges of a Spanish conspiracy against Judge Sebastian and Judge Innes and their associates in 1806.

The climax of Daveiss's career came in November of that year, when he tried to get an indictment against Aaron Burr. Innes, who probably doubted Daveiss's intentions more than Burr's innocence, believed that there was no legal way to bring Burr to trial within the traditions of due process. After a year of sending warnings to President Jefferson about Burr's activities in Kentucky and preparing the case, Daveiss was bitterly and publicly critical both of the president and of the judge. The attorney's intemperance led to his dismissal in March 1807.[95] He returned to his law practice and wrote memoirs detailing his grievances. In 1811, he obtained a commission as major under William Henry Harrison when hostilities against the Indians were resumed. Whatever antagonisms the former attorney may have generated by his energetic prosecutions, they were apparently forgiven by his death at the Battle of Tippecanoe. Grateful Kentuckians named Daviess County in his honor four years later.[96]

The next attorney for the United States was George M. Bibb. Born in Virginia, he attended Hampden-Sidney and William and Mary Colleges and moved to Kentucky in 1798.[97] Bibb was a member of the Kentucky House of Representatives when he was appointed attorney. He held this position only a year before resigning in March 1808 to become a judge of the Kentucky Court of Appeals. He later had a successful career as United States senator, chief judge of the Court of Appeals, chancellor of the Louisville Chancery Court, and secretary of the Treasury under President Tyler. He also published four volumes of *Kentucky Reports*.

The United States attorney with the longest tenure in the period covered by this study was Robert M. Wickliffe, who served from 1808 until 1819. Wickliffe was born in Pennsylvania in 1775, while his parents were traveling from Virginia to Kentucky.[98] He was another of George Nicholas's law students, and was practicing in Lexington at the time of his appointment. After his resignation, he was a member of the Kentucky House of Representatives, and from 1825 until 1833,

95 See Chapter Six.
96 Wilson, "Early Bar of Fayette County," 49. Note the reversal of the letters "ie" in the spelling of Daviess County.
97 *Ibid.*, 53.
98 *Biographical Encyclopedia of Kentucky*, 66.

of the Kentucky Senate. Wickliffe had a long and important political career as a member of the "Bardstown faction" before his death in 1859. He was also said to have "probably accumulated a larger fortune than any of his contemporaries," a notable distinction in that era of land speculation and legal maneuvering.[99]

By 1816, twenty-one men had been appointed to the federal court in Kentucky. Probably they, like other Americans, were proud that they lived under a government of laws. But none of the veterans of that generation would have contended that laws operated automatically. It seems peculiarly fitting that it was a former attorney of the court, George Bibb, who wrote, "The Constitution is on paper, and men are the agents by whom its action on the people is to be given and regulated."[100] He might as accurately have stated that statutes are on paper, and men are the agents by whom they are enforced. Certainly anyone who had witnessed the earlier difficulties of filling his office appreciated the importance of the human element in the functioning of law. And many Kentuckians must have recognized that the character of their federal court was determined in large measure by the stature and convictions of those who served it—and, during one critical period, of those who refused to serve, as well.

[99] *Ibid.*

[100] George M. Bibb, *Reports of Cases at Common Law and In Chancery Argued and Decided in the Court of Appeals of the Commonwealth of Kentucky, Fall Term 1808, to Spring and Fall Terms 1809* (3d ed., Louisville, 1904), 4. (IV *Kentucky Reports.*)

CHAPTER FOUR

The Procedures of the Courts

As the structure and jurisdiction of the federal courts in Kentucky were defined in federal statutes, and the reputation and professionalism of their officers may be deduced from biographical information, so the style and character of those courts may be seen by examining the procedures followed throughout their first generation. The most distinctive aspect of these procedures was their rigorous adherence to the antiquated technicalities of English law. The writs, the forms of action, the pleadings, and the judgments were all consistent with traditional English practice. It is clear from their records that the Kentucky federal courts were very conservative. They made no apparent compromise with tradition, no progress toward the flexibility of modern legal practice. Their caseload reflected their era, but their procedures reflected the past.

What went on in the Kentucky federal courts was, therefore, markedly different from what usually has been thought typical of the period. For many years American legal history has been dominated by the assumption that American law and legal practice in the postrevolutionary era was intensely and consciously Anglophobic. For example, it has been said that "political conditions after independence had brought about a general distrust of English law, which was prolonged by the rise of Jeffersonian democracy at the beginning of the nineteenth century."[1] Yet there is no evidence of this distrust in the Kentucky federal courts between 1789 and 1816. Nor do the records bear out the statement by another observer that "the Revolution engendered widespread hostility toward everything English, especially the common law."[2] Similarly, it has been thought that until the second decade of the nineteenth century "ignorance of the English equity system was the rule."[3] But a large number of the private suits in the court of Harry

[1] Roscoe Pound, "A Hundred Years of American Law," in *Law: A Century of Progress, 1835-1935* (New York, 1937), I, 14.

[2] Richard E. Ellis, *The Jeffersonian Crisis: Courts and Politics in the Young Republic* (New York, 1971), 112. See also Max Radin, "The Rivalry of Common Law and Civil Law Ideas in the American Colonies," in *Law: A Century of Progress*, II, 428; Morton J. Horwitz, "The Emergence of an Instrumental Conception of American Law, 1780-1820," in Donald Fleming and Bernard Bailyn, eds., *Law in American History*, Perspectives in American History, V (Cambridge, Mass., 1971), 292.

[3] William F. Walsh, "The Growing Function of Equity in the Development of the Law," in *Law: A Century of Progress*, I, 153. James Kent and Joseph Story are

77

Innes were equity cases and they were managed with careful attention to the forms and practices of English equity courts.

Evidence compiled by historians who have worked in court records and lawyers' papers challenges these assertions of unenlightened legal Anglophobia, but has received less public attention. Yet this increasing body of data points to an opposite conclusion: that the animosity felt toward the English political and imperial connection was not extended to the English legal system. From the established settlements of Massachusetts, New York, and Virginia, to the frontiers of the Indiana and Michigan Territories, it was English law and legal forms that defined American jurisprudence.[4] There may well have been widespread impatience with the technicalities that often made justice expensive and inaccessible, and certainly there were scattered incidents of local resistance to the courts.[5] But the fathers and sons of the American Revolution concentrated on trying to make the old system more responsive, instead of destroying it or creating a more rational system to supersede it, as their counterparts in Napoleonic France did during these years.[6]

---

generally believed to have been the progenitors of equity in the United States. But see Stanley N. Katz, "The Politics of Law in Colonial America: Controversies over Chancery Courts and Equity Law in the Eighteenth Century," in Fleming and Bailyn, eds., *Law in American History*, 257-285.

[4] William Wirt Blume, "Civil Procedure on the American Frontier: A Study of the Records of a Court of Common Pleas of the Northwest and Indiana Territories (1796-1805)," *Michigan Law Review*, LVI (1957), 161-224; William Wirt Blume, ed., *Transactions of the Supreme Court of the Territory of Michigan 1805-1814* (Ann Arbor, Mich., 1935); Elizabeth Gaspar Brown, *British Statutes in American Law 1776-1836* (Ann Arbor, Mich., 1964); Elizabeth Gaspar Brown, "Frontier Justice: Wayne County 1796-1836," *American Journal of Legal History*, XVI (1972), 126-153; Francis S. Philbrick, "Law, Courts, and Litigation of Indiana Territory, 1800-1809," *Illinois Law Review*, XXIV (1929), 1-19, 193-219; L. Kinvin Wroth and Hiller B. Zobel, *The Legal Papers of John Adams* (Cambridge, Mass., 1965); Julius Goebel, Jr., *et al.*, eds., *The Law Practice of Alexander Hamilton* (New York, 1964-69); Julius Goebel, Jr., *Antecedents and Beginnings to 1800*, in Paul A. Freund, ed., *The Oliver Wendell Holmes Devise History of the Supreme Court*, I (New York, 1971); Herbert A. Johnson *et al.*, eds., *The Papers of John Marshall*, I (Chapel Hill, N.C., 1974); William E. Nelson, *Americanization of the Common Law; The Impact of Legal Change on Massachusetts Society, 1760-1830* (Cambridge, Mass., 1975).

[5] Nelson, *Americanization of the Common Law*, 5, 67-72.

[6] Common law was, of course, superseded by English, colonial, state, and federal statutes, all of which had the effect of "amending" English law. But passage of such statutes was more indicative of the general acceptance of the binding quality of English judicial decisions than of legal Anglophobia. However, anti-British attitudes probably were responsible for passage of a widely cited Kentucky statute of 1808 that purported to nullify post-1776 English statutes and decisions. The impact of this Kentucky action on state law is analyzed in Brown, *British Statutes*, 130-135. Lewis N. Dembitz stated that it was ignored in the Kentucky federal

Modern historians often share the impatience with technicalities because the formal rhetoric and classical pleadings of English law tended to prolong the proceedings, obscure the results, and lend an air of incomprehensible unreality to actual cases and controversies. Yet because American law is derivative, it is necessary to understand traditional English legal practice at least in general terms.

At the time the American Constitution was written and the Kentucky courts established, English civil law was divided into fairly separate systems: law and equity, each practiced in different courts. The older, common law, was relatively inflexible, but its procedures had to be followed first if they applied to the circumstances at hand. In the (common) law courts, an aggrieved person, on advice of counsel, chose one of a number of specific forms of action by which he might gain redress of his grievance. For example, if the aggrieved was owed a fixed sum of money, he could choose an action of debt; if he was injured by a broken contract under seal, he could choose an action of covenant; if his injury was the indirect consequence of another's action, he could choose case (formally titled trespass on the case). Each form of action had its distinguishing writs, formal pleadings, admissible evidence, and potential judgment.

After choosing the form of action, the aggrieved then applied to a chancellor or one of his subordinates for the appropriate writ (there were approximately three hundred available) and made a declaration of his grievance according to a prescribed formula. In England, a writ was a written order issued on behalf of the crown. Writs were directed to a sheriff and instructed him to perform some particular duty, such as to inform the defendant of the nature of the charge against him, to require the defendant to satisfy the grievant, or to bring him into court to explain if he did not satisfy the aggrieved. Writs did not act directly upon the accused. But the issuance of an initial writ marked the beginning of a series of highly developed traditional procedures by which wrongs could be redressed under the jurisdiction of the appropriate law court.

These courts then received pleadings from the lawyers. The classical pleadings were intricate verbal formulae repeated letter-perfect, each in proper order, and exchanged between parties until a crucial point of factual dispute had been isolated. The "issue" was then "joined," and the matter came to trial. At the trial, the judge determined the law

---

courts. Lewis N. Dembitz, *Kentucky Jurisprudence* (Louisville, Ky., 1890), 7. See also Lawrence M. Friedman, *A History of American Law* (New York, 1973), 95-100.

(proper procedures, admissibility of evidence, relevant precedents, and applicable statutes), disinterested witnesses gave oral testimony, and a jury tried the facts. In suits at common law, "twelve good men and true, sworn well and truly to try the issue joined," decided whether the plaintiff or the defendant was correct on the factual issue in question. After they had reached their decision, the judge then announced how the law applied to it; in other words, the judge pronounced the judgment of the court.

If a plaintiff or his counsel had chosen the wrong form of action to achieve the redress he wanted (i.e., applied for the wrong writ), or departed from the established rhetoric in his pleadings, or if there existed no writ to cover his particular circumstance, his case was at least temporarily lost. He might pursue it through another form of action or different writs, if these existed to meet his needs. But if there were none that applied, the aggrieved had no remedy at law, although he might in equity. The common law courts acknowledged no deviation from tradition: the phrase "no writ, no right" expresses their rigidity and the limitations on their jurisdiction.

Courts of chancery developed in England under the chancellor, who was the keeper of the king's conscience. The purpose of these courts was to provide equity (fairness) in situations that were not covered by law, or that could not be decided fairly under law. After exhausting the possibilities of remedy at law, the petitioner (now called the complainant) could apply to the equity (chancery) courts for relief. Over the centuries chancery courts also developed an established set of procedures and decisions, but they remained distinguishable from the law courts in several ways. Chancery courts required evidence in writing instead of oral testimony, and they acted directly upon the individuals concerned. Juries were not used to find the facts, and equity judges (chancellors) could tailor decisions to fit the peculiar circumstances of an individual case. Awards could be made to both litigants, in differing amounts; such a balancing of interests was not possible in law. Chancery courts were more flexible, although by the end of the eighteenth century, not necessarily speedier than the law courts.

The most obvious difference between the American and the English court systems was a structural one: in the United States, each federal court heard both law and equity cases, instead of one or the other as in England. For although they acknowledged the distinction between law and equity, the Founding Fathers did not establish separate federal courts to exercise the different jurisdictions. Article III, section 2, simply stated that "the [federal] judicial Power shall extend to all

Cases, in Law and Equity. . . ." Congress might have set up separate inferior courts of law and of equity in the Judiciary Act of 1789, but did not. Two years later, the Seventh Amendment was ratified. Its guarantee of the right of jury trial in law cases involving more than twenty dollars required some separation of the caseload in federal courts, but their unitary structure was retained. Originally, this unusual but not unique combining of law and equity within each federal court probably reflected both frugality and the expectation that the lower federal courts would have a small caseload.[7] Edmund Pendleton, at least, believed that Congress had created "a blended jurisdiction" because "it no doubt was Oeconomical as otherwise a Chancellor for each state must have been appointed, with perhaps little to do."[8] Pendleton preferred separate courts and expected that future Congresses might establish them. This has never been done, although well into the twentieth century, federal courts had a "law side" and an "equity side."

From their inception, therefore, all federal courts entertained cases brought under two different kinds of law. It is probable that (as in Kentucky) different procedures were adopted for each kind. Except for the early years when there was little business in his court, Judge Innes arranged the docket to separate the law cases from the equity cases, and they were often heard on different days. As required by section 16 of the Judiciary Act of 1789 (and by English tradition), no suit in equity could be sustained if a remedy lay at law, and actions at law had to be completed before any related equity matters could be ex-

---

[7] Some state courts heard both law cases and equity suits. In Virginia, at least, problems resulted from this circumstance. E.g., Edmund Pendleton to Harry Innes, Nov. 9, 1791, David John Mays, ed., *The Letters and Papers of Edmund Pendleton*, II (Charlottesville, Va., 1967), 581. The rather surprising departure from tradition in establishing a blended jurisdiction in the federal courts seems never to have been questioned, although other aspects of the intentions of the Framers and the Ellsworth committee have been scrupulously examined. See, for example, Charles Warren, "New Light on the History of the Federal Judiciary Act of 1789," *Harvard Law Review*, XXXVII (1923), 49-132; Goebel, *Antecedents and Beginnings*, 457-508. The mistrust of equity these authors describe derived from two related factors: the absence of the right of trial by jury in chancery courts, and the power that English chancellors had because their authority was limited neither by precedent nor by juries. However, it seems likely that, as in earlier times, it was not equity itself that aroused suspicion but chancery courts (and particularly their administration). See Katz, "The Politics of Law," in Fleming and Bailyn, eds., *Law in American History*, 261, 265. In any case, the blending of jurisdictions in the federal courts, whether intended as an economy or as a check upon the supposed prerogative of chancellors, marked an important step toward modern practice.

[8] Pendleton to Innes, Nov. 9, 1971, Mays, ed., *Pendleton Papers*, II, 581.

plored by bringing a suit in chancery. For the most part Innes retained the historically different language of the separate jurisdictions: the initiator of a law suit was a plaintiff, of an equity suit a complainant; the phrase, "It is considered by the court that . . ." prefaced judgments at law, while the phrase "It is ordered by the Court" preceded interlocutory and final decrees in chancery. However, in Kentucky the person against whom a chancery suit was directed was called the defendant, as in law, and not the respondent, as was more common in equity.

The First Congress not only blended the jurisdictions of law and equity, it also blurred the traditional differences between the kinds of evidence acceptable to law courts and equity courts. In England, law courts required that evidence be given by oral testimony, while chancery courts required that evidence be given in written form. But sections 15 and 30 of the Judiciary Act of 1789 made both kinds of evidence admissible in both kinds of cases. The former section specified that "all the said courts of the United States, shall have power in the trial of actions at law . . . to require the parties to produce books or writings . . . which contain evidence . . . under circumstances where they might be compelled to produce the same by the ordinary rules of proceeding in chancery." The latter section stated "[t]hat the mode of proof by oral testimony and examination of witnesses in open court shall be the same . . . in the trial of causes in equity . . . as of actions at common law." Yet it permitted depositions (written testimony), under certain circumstances, "in any civil cause."[9]

Innes evidently believed that section 30 superseded state practice (which permitted depositions in equity) unless the exceptional circumstances were clearly applicable. But requiring oral testimony in chancery suits was, he wrote, tedious and troublesome both to the court and to litigants.[10] Waiting for witnesses caused innumerable continuances in "7 causes out of 10 on the Equity side of the Docket," and he complained that the inconveniences of the requirement were

[9] 1 Stat. 73. Section 15 was apparently intended to extend discovery procedures available in chancery to law. Goebel, *Antecedents and Beginnings*, 483-501. Section 30 permitted depositions from persons who (1) lived more than 100 miles from the court, or (2) were bound on a voyage to sea, or (3) were about to leave the United States or the district, or (4) were "ancient or very infirm." Examples of law cases in which depositions were permitted are: *Adair* v. *DeGraffenreidt*, District Court Order Book A, Mar. 18, 1794, 56; *Berry* v. *Starns*, *ibid.*, June 17, 1795, 99; *Coleman* v. *Wilkins*, *ibid.*, June 21, 1796, 117; *Gibbs* v. *Christy*, *ibid.*, July 11, 1798, 207; *Horner* v. *Singleton*, District Court Order Book B, Mar. 11, 1799, 34. (Hereafter cited as DC OB.)

[10] Innes to John Brown, Mar. 18, 1798 (typescript), Innes Papers, Manuscript Division, Library of Congress, xxviii, 9-212.

"so apparent that Gentlemen of the barr are defeating the law by con-
senting in many instances to take depositions."[11] Innes thoroughly dis-
approved of such avoidance of the intent of the statute and repeatedly
urged that it be amended. His petitions were finally granted in 1802,
when the Jeffersonians' judiciary act permitted federal courts to accept
depositions wherever they were allowed in state practice.[12]

Departures from tradition were difficult for a traditionalist like Innes
and he made as few as possible.[13] Yet for some unknown reason he permitted common law cases to be brought under only eight of the dozens
of available forms of action: case, covenant, debt, detinue, ejectment,
trespass, writ of dower, and writ of right.[14] What is even more surprising is that there were no cases in trover or assumpsit, as were common
in other courts during the period. The Order Books did not repeat the
early stages of procedures in law, that is, the filing of the declaration
or the application for a writ.[15] But after the initial issuance of process
the court's respect for custom is evident in its careful observation of the
proprieties that had become enshrined in centuries of English jurisprudence. Declarations were answered by demurrers or an appropriate
formal plea; replications by rejoinders, surrejoinders by rebutters, followed by surrebutters, until the issue was joined. All of these were
carried on in the antique language of the formal pleadings and spread
across the Order Books.[16]

[11] Innes to John Breckinridge, Dec. 27, 1801, Breckinridge Family Papers,
Manuscript Division, Library of Congress, xxi, 3559.

[12] ii Stat. 166, sec. 25. Jefferson described himself as having been "once a great
advocate for introducing viva voce testimony," but changed his mind after learning
that in Kentucky and Virginia "it worked inconveniently." Thomas Jefferson to
Breckinridge, Jan. 29, 1800, Breckinridge Family Papers, xviii, 3164.

[13] Like an English chancellor, he adopted the somewhat uncommon practice of
using advisory juries (in equity cases dealing with land), for reasons suggested in
Chapter Eight.

[14] These terms (and others) are defined in the glossary (Appendix E). Case,
covenant, debt, detinue, and trespass are discussed in Chapter Seven; ejectment,
writ of dower, and writ of right in Chapter Eight. Actions at law employed to
enforce the revenue acts are discussed in Chapter Five; criminal charges unrelated
to the revenue acts in Chapter Six.

[15] Some of these papers, although not all of them, are included in the Complete
Record of the Seventh Circuit Court, after May 1807. The Complete Record is
not, however, a record of all of the cases heard in the circuit court. For example,
the Complete Record for the November term 1807 includes papers for 32 cases,
but the court at that term heard 64 new cases, 191 old cases, and handed down
56 judgments. Similar discrepancies are found for all of the terms, and the grounds
for inclusion or exclusion of cases in the Complete Record are not known.

[16] For a description of these pleadings, see Nelson, *Americanization of the
Common Law*, 72-77. The modernization of pleading observed in Massachusetts as
early as 1776 is not evident in the Kentucky federal courts during Innes's tenure.

This devotion to the rituals of the common law meant that the Kentucky federal courts retained the ancient pleadings of ejectment cases, with lengthy fictitious exchanges between mythical legal contestants, long after that practice had been abandoned in the state courts. A Kentucky statute of December 18, 1800, provided that "[i]n actions of Ejectment, it shall be lawful for the Plaintiff to declare in his proper name . . . against the Defendant in his proper name . . . and instead of the fictitious suggestions of lease, entry and ouster to state that he is legally entitled to the premises."[17] Even though the federal court followed state laws (as required by section 34 of the Judiciary Act of 1789) in much more sensitive matters like the occupying claimant acts, it preferred the older way here, as cumbersome and confusing as it was. So John Doe, Richard Roe, John Den, Richard Fen, and many other characters with ingenious alliterative names continued to sue one another throughout this period.

The court was also strict about maintaining the limitations on joinder. Because of the narrowly defined areas of common law actions, a plaintiff often had to file several suits to achieve his remedy. If he had suffered a financial loss from a broken contract, he might be required to file two suits: one action in covenant, and another action in debt. If a dual partnership defaulted, the plaintiff had to sue one member, pursue that case through judgment, and then sue the second member. A creditor hoping to recover money borrowed by one individual at five different times had to file five different suits and wait for each to reach judgment separately.[18]

Attorneys were reminded that this was a court that expected them to discharge their duties properly. If a lawyer was not present when his client's case was called, the cause was dismissed and the counsel's absence noted in the records. When they signed complaints, they attached "p.q." (*pro querente*: for the plaintiff) to their names. They were required to observe the litany of the pleadings. Judge Innes once admonished counsel: "The Latitude contended for by Mr. Attorney goes at once to destroy that System of Good pleading which has stood the test for Ages past and which I hope will continue to be strictly attended to by Judges."[19]

[17] C. S. Morehead and Mason Brown, *A Digest of the Statute Laws of Kentucky,* I (Frankfort, Ky., 1834), 583.
[18] A federal statute passed in 1813 (III Stat. 21) made it possible to combine more than one action in a single suit. But because it was passed so near 1816, it had little effect upon the caseload of the court in our period.
[19] *Morrison* v. *Jewell*, in [Harry Innes], "Cases in the Court of the United States for the District of Kentucky, from its first Organization to the year 1806 Inclusive," United States Court for the Western District of Kentucky, Louisville, 83-91.

Yet for the modern reader, this continuing repetition of form and language is almost totally unenlightening. Except for the litigants' true names, there is little to distinguish one covenant case from another covenant case, or one debt case from another debt case. The chancery suits present a striking contrast. Equity evidence fills page after page, because all of the paper processes associated with equity (wills, depositions, warrants, patents, surveys, accounts, and orders) were copied along with the proceedings of each day's docket. Every chancery suit seemed to involve a different set of variables, although almost all were long, complicated, and continued on the records for many years.

The hard-pressed clerk was permitted only standardized abbreviations, such as "ha fa" for the writ *habere facias possessionem,* "sci fa" for the writ *scire facias,* "Chy" for chancery, and "exon" for execution. Few allowances were made for the problems of hand copying records after busy terms, and no free thinking was permitted. In March 1800, a term during which 243 cases were heard in fourteen days, Judge Innes announced new rules requiring the minutes to be written up before the next sitting, or a fine of five dollars would be levied. The clerk was also ordered not to take any step on the Rules Docket without instructions in writing signed by the litigant or his counsel, or a fine of fifty cents would be charged. Furthermore, he was to report to the judge, under penalty of ten dollars, any processes not returned by the marshal by noon on the Saturday preceding the next term.[20] (Evidently Thomas Tunstall had been lax in performing his duties.)

Much of the time of the court, especially in its early years, was taken up by Innes's supervision of the details of judicial administration: granting continuances to plaintiffs, complainants, and defendants; ordering their appearances at upcoming terms; permitting the amendment of declarations and answers; naming commissioners to take depositions at a time and place convenient to the counsel of both parties; designating persons to evaluate improvements and waste under the Kentucky occupying claimants laws; charging arbitrators to resolve disputes; and ordering surveyors to "go upon the lands in controversy on the [blank] day of [blank] if fair, if not then on the next fair day and then and there lay off and survey the same." Defendants were often slow in appearing, commissioners late in reporting, and surveyors careless about following the instructions of the court, so that such orders might be repeated term after term.

It is not surprising that it took years for most cases to reach completion, both in law and in equity. In addition to other problems, many of

[20] DC OB B, Mar. 27, 1800, 342.

the private cases rested upon diversity jurisdiction and defendants were not within an area that could be served conveniently by the marshal. In many cases, the Order Books stated: "It appearing to the Court that the Defendant is not an inhabitant of this District, it is ordered that he enter his appearance on the first day of next Court," three or six months later. A copy of the appearance order was placed in newspapers in the county where the land in dispute lay or the event in dispute had occurred, and in the county where the court was held, for twelve weeks preceding the next session. Such orders were often repeated for several terms until the defendant obtained counsel to appear for him in Kentucky.

While cases were continued time and time again, the Order Books occasionally note: "This cause is continued until next Court, on condition that the parties then be prepared for trial." Sometimes the court itself was unexpectedly adjourned by bad weather, illness, or Indian trouble. But if it was held, the parties were expected to be there on the day appointed. A tardy plaintiff might discover his cases dismissed for failure to prosecute, a late defendant adjudged in default, regardless of how long their suits had been before the court.

The monotony of entries in the Order Books rarely lifts to reveal whatever flexibility may have existed in the management of the docket. But an occasional entry suggests that the court was not as rigid as the forms through which it carried on its business. For example, in an 1814 writ of right case, the unsuccessful tenants (defendants) moved for a new trial, basing their motion on four points of law. At the conclusion they pleaded that "if the counsel for Tenants is mistaken in all these points of law, then the Tenants move for a new trial because of the mistake of the counsel in preparing and managing their defense."[21] The argument prevailed, and a new trial was awarded at which judgment went for the tenants.[22]

In 1803 a successful plaintiff swore out an execution six weeks after judgment, despite a court order staying execution for three months. The defendant protested at the next term of court, and the judge admitted that while the proper action would have been a writ of error *coram nobis*, "inasmuch as the Plaintiff [would be] thereby delayed and put to costs, the court is willing to proceed in this summary way: the [previous] execution is hereby quashed, and the Plaintiff is given leave to sue out another."[23] This is an example of how Innes occasion-

[21] *Green* v. *Watkins*, Circuit Court Order Book C, May 23, 1814, 446. (Hereafter cited as CC OB.)

[22] *Green* v. *Watkins*, CC OB D, Nov. 25, 1815, 303.

[23] *Davidson and Goddard* v. *Wilson and Eastin*, DC OB D, Mar. 24, 1803, 158.

ally demonstrated a flexibility that reinforced the substance of the court's power.

A plaintiff with five ejectment cases on the docket once showed up nine days after he had been found in default for failure to appear and his cases had been nonsuited. He asked the court to set aside the nonsuits and to reinstate his cases because he said he had been detained on the Ohio River by high winds. Furthermore he had thought that the suits would not be tried that term because he heard that one of the judges was ill. (Justice Todd was absent from this term.) Despite objections by the defendants, Judge Innes sustained the plaintiff's motion, and his cases were returned to the docket.[24]

Such reinstatements were not infrequent, but they were seldom explained. In fact, the reappearance of apparently terminated cases occurred so often that it is one factor that rendered the statistical totals of the work of the court out of balance. Another major factor was the number of interlocutory (provisional) decrees in equity suits not identified by that term. The number of cases pending was not the remainder when judgments were subtracted from cases previously docketed. Sometimes previous judgments were set aside without explanation. At other times a case reappeared because of action taken by the winner to enforce the judgment of the court, or by the loser to postpone it. An application for an injunction or a *supersedeas*, or for writs of *fieri facias, capias ad satisfaciendum*, or *venditione exponas*, all brought cases that had seemed completed back on the Order Books as active causes.

A large number of pending suits also ceased to be active without any explanation. There are probably a number of reasons why cases remained open in the records when they were actually finished. There must have been a great amount of untidy clerical housekeeping, including unnoted self-executing writs, unmarked office dismissions, and other actions in the clerk's office that were not recorded in the Order Books. Many litigants simply disappeared. Others dropped their cases or reached agreement without informing the court. By 1816, one-third of the private causes docketed were technically still pending, although many of these had been inactive for years.

But despite inevitable irregularities in their holographic records and occasional evidence of leniency, the style of the Kentucky federal courts was typically manifested by their insistence upon tradition, form, and authority. This, of course, extended to management of the one area of lay participation—the role of juries. Judge Innes, espe-

---

[24] *Blight* v. *Carr, Blight* v. *Shacklett, Blight* v. *Woolfolk, Blight* v. *Richard Stith, Blight* v. *William Stith*, CC OB C, May 4, 1814; *ibid.*, May 13, 1814.

cially, always retained a firm hand over their activities in civil cases. While the facts were the jurors' business, as the law was his, it is clear that he did not encourage their independence. It made no difference whether defendants denied the charges against them by pleading the general issue or by special pleading: juries had little latitude in civil suits.[25] In private cases unrelated to the internal revenue acts, for example, jurors almost invariably found for the plaintiffs. This result, and the fact that sometimes more than a dozen jury trials were held in a single day, indicate that directed verdicts must have been common although the phrase was never recorded.[26] The judge also did not hesitate to set aside facts found by juries.[27] On one occasion, refusing a motion made by counsel to instruct the jury "that they were at liberty to think for themselves," Judge Innes instead admonished the jurors that they were "absolutely bound by the opinion of the Court."[28] Counsel formalized his disagreement by filing a bill of exceptions, but the judge's instructions prevailed.[29]

It was uncommon for the Order Books to report that a jury failed to reach a verdict, although juries were often discharged without making a finding. The technique usually employed for dismissing a jury was to withdraw a juror, "whereupon the jury was discharged." Sometimes juries were excused after reporting, "if the law be for the Defendant, then we find for him; if the law be for the Plaintiff, then we find for him." The judges generally "took time" on these cases and announced judgment a term or two later.

[25] A special plea was a denial of some specific fact in the plaintiff's declaration; pleading the general issue constituted a denial of all the allegations. William E. Nelson has written that the former gave more authority to the court (because only the judge could know the legal consequences of the jury's finding) and the latter gave more authority to the jury (because they then had some discretion in applying the law to the facts). The growing use of pleading the general issue that Nelson has observed in Massachusetts between 1760 and 1830, and which he believes had the effect of broadening the base of decision making, is not evident in the Kentucky federal courts during the period 1789-1816. Nelson, *Americanization of the Common Law*, 21-35.

[26] It is also likely that the high proportion of acquittals in the government's criminal cases against distillers was due to Innes's instructions to juries. This is described in Chapter Five. Appendix B gives judgments on private suits; Appendix C, judgments on the government's cases.

[27] E.g., *Watts v. Massie*, DC OB F, July 25, 1805, 176.

[28] *Buck and Brander v. Casey*, CC OB B, Nov. 9, 1810, 400. This case was unusual because it had been appealed from the Kentucky General Court to the Court of Appeals and then removed to the federal court.

[29] Bills of exceptions were formal objections to the judge's rulings, which were written in the Order Books at the time judgment was rendered and signed by the judge. They were signified by a hand-drawn seal which resembled a four-leaf clover without the stem.

Judge Innes may have been authoritarian in his management of juries, but he appears not to have been capricious. In criminal cases unrelated to the revenue acts he was particularly careful to respect the judgment of jurors, even when he disagreed with them.[30] He did not rush them to judgment but continued trials longer than was then customary in England. However, his handling of the few criminal trials stands in marked contrast to his management of the hundreds of civil suits, where jury deliberations seem often to have been *pro forma*. But even when he opposed a jury finding in civil suits, he conscientiously tried to balance English traditions with the requirements of the American Constitution.

For example, a jury in 1805 found for a defendant, a former collector of revenue, who owed the government $1,419 in taxes collected but not paid over to the government. The case had begun back in 1802, and had been continued, for many reasons, for nine terms. (According to the custom of the time, the collector was charged with arrears of $4,000, the amount of his bond; the exact amount owed was learned from the final judgment, which did not come until May 1810.) Judge Innes did not agree with the jury's finding but felt constrained by the provision of the Seventh Amendment which states that "no fact tried by a jury, shall be otherwise reexamined in any Court of the United States, than according to the rules of the common law." When he granted the government a new trial he explained his reasons in one of the few written opinions recorded in the Order Books:

> In a case with strong evidence on *both* sides, like this one, the Court ought not to grant a new trial. The *Jury* is the proper judge of which scale of evidence preponderates. [Many precedents cited from English reports.] On the other hand, there are cases where new trials have been granted. [Other English precedents cited.] The principle which actuated the Courts in the last recited cases was, for the attainment of Justice Courts ought tenaciously to adhere to decisions which establish the rights to property. Yet in points of practice they ought to vary as experience shall evince their convenience or inconvenience.
>
> The great object of Courts is to preserve the rights of the people and to do Justice in the case of contests. . . . The verdict in this case did not meet my approbation and as the practice of granting a new trial when there is evidence on both sides has been established by

[30] See Chapter Six, especially Innes's joining in a petition for a pardon for the defendant Berry, found guilty of mail robbery.

Judges of the first eminence, I feel myself supported in granting the present motion.[31]

This opinion by Judge Innes is typical of his frequent reliance upon English precedents. In this instance, his use of authorities on both sides of the question reflected the state of English law, which had not then "attained any systematic clarity" on the matter of control over civil juries.[32] Granting a new trial, despite a jury finding for the defendant, was one of several permissible means of control by judges that was current in England in this period.

Another illustration of the degree to which the Kentucky federal judges controlled their court was the frequency with which they terminated cases. Since judicial termination of a cause had the effect of favoring the defendant, these actions tended to redress the balance which was otherwise heavily weighted in favor of the plaintiffs; when cases went to trial, juries almost always found for them. Despite the directed verdicts that must have lain behind those juries' decisions, it is clear that the judges were also concerned with the rights of defendants, because in 24 percent of the civil cases docketed they forbade the continuation of the legal action in their court. Sometimes this reflected the limitations on federal jurisdiction, a consideration of which Justice Todd was much more sensitive than was Judge Innes. But more often they both exercised the latitude permissible in contemporary English practice by using a variety of terminating options. Of a total of 320 cases that were formally terminated by the judges, they quashed and dismissed 289 cases for various reasons, including want of jurisdiction, and declared 31 plaintiffs nonsuited. The courts even used compulsory nonsuits (when the plaintiff failed to sustain his case with sufficient evidence), suggesting that the judges were consciously following English custom.[33]

Another reason for ending cases, and the one that best reflects the combination of lengthy, cautious litigation and limited life expectancy,

[31] *U.S.* v. *Moore*, DC OB F, Mar. 26, 1805, 39.

[32] Edith Guild Henderson, "The Background of the Seventh Amendment," *Harvard Law Review*, LXXX (1966), 299. The jury's unlimited right to acquit in a criminal case, except in criminal libel cases, was well established by this time. *Ibid.*, 290.

[33] See Appendix B. Nonsuits were ruled out in Virginia in 1794. Henderson, "Background of the Seventh Amendment," 301. No nonsuits were found in reported Kentucky state court cases during this period. It is possible that there were some in unreported Court of Appeals cases, but the case papers were destroyed by fire. Achilles Sneed, *Decisions of the Court of Appeals of the State of Kentucky from March 1, 1801 to January 18, 1805 Inclusive*, ed. Harvey Myers (Cincinnati, 1869), v. (II *Kentucky Reports.*)

was the notation that "the Plaintiff [or Defendant] having departed this life, this cause abated." These must have been cases in which there were no known heirs and the litigant had died intestate, because section 31 of the Judiciary Act of 1789 expressly provided that pending law cases could be continued to judgment by executors or administrators. Chancery cases, however, were frequently reinstituted through bills of revivor. Many land cases were continued on the docket in this way, while others, involving great quantities of land, were not. If there were heirs, they evidently decided not to pursue this litigation, which was often an expensive and risky gamble in Kentucky.

The Kentucky federal court also followed the English custom of taxing costs and awarding them to the winner. (Costs were distinct from damages, which were assessed by juries and awarded to the successful plaintiff.) At this time, costs in Kentucky, as in England, included attorneys' remuneration as well as court fees.[34] All of these expenses were standardized and noted in the rules. The total amount of money involved could be considerable, especially for a cause continuing over many terms requiring writs, depositions, service of process, witnesses, juries, and lawyers. Yet many plaintiffs and complainants evidently achieved their purposes by the mere filing of their suits. The large number of unterminated causes suggests that many defendants did not contest the action or answer the court. They probably just disappeared, and it was generally expensive, uncertain, or even unnecessary to pursue them.

There were several provisions regarding costs that tended to protect the innocent to a greater degree than he is protected today. For example, the initial internal revenue act provided that a defendant might recover his costs if the case resulted in a verdict for him, or in a nonsuit.[35] The following year the statute was amended to deny this reimbursement in cases where the informer or plaintiff was an officer of the government "specially authorized to commence such prosecution," if the court certified that there was reasonable ground for bringing the charges.[36] Yet in the internal revenue cases arising at the end of the decade in Kentucky, the court regularly allowed costs to the innocent defendant to be collected from the informer even when he was a revenue officer or the attorney for the district. This policy went further than a statute passed in 1799, providing that the United States was

---

[34] The Process Act of Sept. 28, 1789 provided that the fees charged in federal courts should be the same as those of the supreme court of the state. 1 Stat. 93, sec. 2.

[35] 1 Stat. 209, sec. 42.   [36] 1 Stat. 278, sec. 5.

responsible for the fees of the court when a cause brought under the penal statutes was discontinued, nonsuited, or judgment went for the defendant.[37] There is abundant other evidence that the court was unsympathetic with criminal prosecutions under the revenue acts; apparently it wished to protect the defendants even in civil cases. Although Judge Innes may have exceeded the intentions of the statutes, no protest is recorded in the records.

Those who did lose their cases were not without redress: chancery suits could be appealed to the United States Supreme Court, and law cases could be carried there on writs of error. (A writ of error petitioned the high court to reexamine matters of law in the record, but not matters of fact.) When counsel disagreed with the decisions of the court, objections were stated in bills of exceptions and noted in the Order Books. Although there were dozens of bills of exceptions in the records, only forty-four private cases were carried to the Supreme Court.[38] It is likely that the expense deterred all but the most determined and wealthy litigants—those who had much to gain but who could also afford defeat.

The records of the federal courts in Kentucky show that in addition to hearing cases, they also performed naturalization proceedings for new citizens. Section 8 of Article 1 of the Constitution provided that "Congress shall have power . . . to establish an uniform Rule of Naturalization," and Congress implemented this in 1795.[39] Although it has been suggested that the statute was implemented only by state courts until 1906, this was not the case in Kentucky.[40] Whether Kentucky state courts exercised the concurrent authority authorized by the statute cannot be known until or unless those court records can be found. But the federal court did accept statements of intent and affidavits that residence requirements had been met from eighteen persons during this period. The judges then administered an oath by which the applicant swore to support the Constitution and "that he doth absolutely and entirely renounce and abjure all allegiance and fidelity to any foreign prince, potentate, state, or sovereignty whatever, particularly to [that of his native land]."[41]

[37] 1 Stat. 626.

[38] Thirty-nine cases dealt with land and are described in Chapter Eight. The others were: two related detinue cases, two debt cases, and one case in covenant. (Five other suits were prepared by the U.S. attorneys.)

[39] 1 Stat. 414.

[40] Leonard D. White, *The Federalists: A Study in Administrative History* (New York, 1948), 395.

[41] Statement of William Kelley, DC OB A, July 9, 1798; George Hamilton, *ibid.*; David Bell, *ibid.*; Henry Clarke, *ibid.*; George Clarke, *ibid.*; John Mullanphy,

Overlooking a federal court's performance of naturalization cere-monies is an illustration of the imperfect conclusions previous scholars have been able to draw when they have not studied court records themselves. The naturalization procedures are probably not important. But more serious is a misjudgment of the character of courts, which seems to have occurred because scholars have used scattered memoirs or statutes to generalize about what actually went on in the hundreds of courtrooms of the new nation. The Order Books, written opinions, and related papers of the federal courts in Kentucky from 1789 until 1816 demonstrate that the procedures in these courts, at least, were very different from the style usually attributed to lower courts in that period.

It is possible that these courts were unique. Judge Innes once wrote that "where a Court is composed of a single Judge, he can adopt Rules regulating the proceedings in suits."[42] Judge Innes's choice of tradi-tional procedures, his insistence on maintaining the separation between law and equity, his rigorous demand for strict pleading, his narrow definitions of the common law actions, and his dominance over juries may all have been unusual for a judge in his generation. Yet it seems more likely that he was a typical, if not universal, figure. Where else would lawyers and judges who had been educated in the traditions of English law look for precedents and procedures but in English sources?

It has long been recognized that the War for Independence was a limited revolution for political autonomy, not one that drastically or immediately changed the existing social or economic order. Why should it be assumed that resistance to the legal authority of Parlia-ment required resistance to the familiar legal system of Englishmen? It may be that scholars have been mesmerized by Anglophobia, se-duced by frontier theory, and misled by egalitarianism to construct a version of legal history that does not always coincide with fact.

Even in Kentucky, Judge Innes's ideas about how to manage a court need not have endured for twenty-seven years if they were incom-patible with the expectations of the population. It is conceivable that Judges McClung and McNairy could have altered the direction of the

---

DC OB D, July 9, 1803; Adam Caldwell, *ibid.*; James Mitchell, *ibid.*; James Hughes, *ibid.*; Thomas Greavor, DC OB E, April 14, 1804; George Greer, *ibid.*, Nov. 26, 1804; Johannes Goodman, DC OB F, July 13, 1805; Stephen Louis Hus Deforges, CC OB A, May 12, 1807; Henry Newberry, *ibid.*, May 13, 1807; Nich-olas Clarke, CC OB B, July 15, 1808; John Venice, *ibid.*, Nov. 20, 1810; Owen Riley, CC OB C, May 9, 1812; John Adam Markley, *ibid.*, June 2, 1813.

[42] Draft opinion, *Thompson* v. *Davis*, Innes Papers, Library of Congress, XXI, Pt. ii, 1-185.

court, if only briefly, in 1801-1802, had they wanted to. Judge Innes might easily have been impeached if he had not had popular support in 1806-1808. Certainly Justice Todd could have changed the procedures after the Seventh Circuit Court was established in 1807. But none of these things came to pass, and the courts remained essentially the same throughout the period. It should be noted that of all the criticisms that were made of the judges and of the laws they were called on to enforce, there were no charges that this was a Tory court, or that its formalities prevented the attainment of equal justice under law. On the contrary, the caseload indicates that it was a highly respected and popular institution.

The evidence contained in the records of the Kentucky federal court suggests that a reassessment of American legal history is needed. The judges, clerks, marshals, attorneys, and the prominent lawyers who practiced before its bar, were born and educated in the colonies. Like most Kentuckians, they were vigorous supporters of the political revolution against England. Yet clearly all were loyal to the English legal system and comfortable with its precedents. The court was indeed affected by the environment: the substance of its caseload reflected the newness of the nation and the unsettled conditions of the frontier. But the procedures, practices, and principles of the court were nonetheless as consistent with the English judicial tradition as that first generation of Americans knew how to make them.

CHAPTER FIVE

The Internal Revenue Laws and
Their Enforcement

THE United States was by far the most frequent single plaintiff in the federal courts in Kentucky from 1789 to 1816. During those years, the government brought 775 suits: 100 criminal charges and 675 civil actions. Ninety-five percent of these cases resulted from the internal revenue laws passed in the new nation's first decade. The unpopularity of these laws constituted a serious challenge to the power of the national government and to the authority of its courts in Kentucky. How the courts met this challenge is revealed in a variety of long-forgotten contemporary sources.

Certain federal statutes may be enforced both by criminal and by civil procedures, and both methods were used in Kentucky. Criminal charges could be brought in one of three ways. If one or more members of a grand jury believed from their own knowledge that a federal statute had been violated, the grand jury could issue a presentment. If a competent public officer (such as a revenue inspector) in the course of his duties suspected such a violation, he could file an information with the court. If the United States attorney for the district had reason to suspect a violation, he could submit an indictment to the grand jury requiring their concurrence in the form of "a true bill." Civil procedures to enforce the internal revenue acts were simpler and were based upon the assumption that if a distiller had failed to pay his taxes he owed a debt to the government. If that appeared to be the case, the internal revenue supervisor could file an action in debt "on behalf of himself and for the benefit of the United States." Whether the charges were true was a fact to be determined by petit juries in all criminal cases, and in civil cases where more than twenty dollars was involved.

The United States Court for the District of Kentucky was slow in getting underway: the first five terms were taken up by the promulgation of rules of procedure, the appointment of court officials, and the admission of attorneys. It was not until June 1791 that Judge Innes issued an order that "the marshal . . . shall constantly summon a Grand Jury of twenty-four freeholders" at least fifteen days before the convening of the court, to attend the first day of each term.[1]

1 District Court Order Book A, June 21, 1791. (Hereafter cited as DC OB.)

Issuance and service of this order did not, however, insure the attendance of the grand jurors. The first group was discharged because only fourteen of the twenty-four appeared. Among those missing was James Speed, a prominent citizen of Mercer County who had administered the oath of office and the oath upholding the Constitution to Judge Innes when the federal court first opened.[2] But the judge did not tolerate the absence of any grand juror, even Speed. All of the delinquents were summoned to attend the next court. Those who did not then appear, including Speed, were served with attachments.[3] When Speed did appear in March, his earlier absence was excused, and he was foreman of the grand jury for that term.[4]

The names of the members of the panels do not indicate that the marshal sought out leading citizens for grand juries. While prominent men were included on the lists (Speed, Peter Casey, John Haggin, William Kennedy, for examples), the remainder seem to have been otherwise undistinguished citizens. All were treated equally: upon failure to appear, summonses were issued. If the absentee appeared at the following term, his absence was invariably excused. If he did not, the summons was followed by an attachment, then by an alias attachment, and finally by a forty-shilling fine. Those who did appear were rewarded. They were paid fifty cents for one day's attendance, and from fifty cents to two dollars for travel expenses. In addition, they served as petit jurors in as many as five trials, for each of which fifty cents was paid.

The difficulty of assembling a large enough panel was temporarily resolved by the adoption of a new rule in the September 1792 term of the court, ordering that any sixteen of the grand jurors summoned should be a sufficient number to constitute a grand jury.[5] Even this rule did not secure an adequate number the following March. In any case, these early grand juries were largely inactive, probably in part because of the limitations imposed by the instructions of the judge. For Judge Innes, who had eloquently described "the first Grand Inquest which hath been assembled in this District under the General Governance of the United States" as the "*Guard*" and "*Protector* of the Citizen" against the "*Arbitrary* arm of the Executive," nevertheless listed only eleven offenses as coming within the grand jury's jurisdic-

[2] Thomas Speed, *Records and Memorials of the Speed Family* (Louisville, 1892), 57; DC OB A, Dec. 15, 1789, 1.

[3] DC OB A, Sept. 20, 1791, 10; Jan. 12, 1792, 14.

[4] *Ibid.*, Mar. 20, 1792, 21.   [5] *Ibid.*, Sept. 18, 1792, 30.

tion.[6] These were: treason; misprision of treason; forgery of any public security of the United States; passing any such forged public security; stealing, falsifying, or avoiding any record, process, or other proceeding of any of the courts of the United States; perjury in any oath taken pursuant to any of the laws of the United States; subornation of perjury; bribery; obstructing the execution of process of the United States; the rescue of persons convicted or awaiting trial on capital offenses under the laws of the Union; and offenses committed within the Indian territory.

The list given to this federal grand jury is striking in its restraint, especially when it is compared with other instructions that Innes had given to state grand juries when he was a judge of the Kentucky District Court of Virginia. Those earlier jurors had been exhorted to report a wide variety of offenses, including "Blasphemy, Profane cursing and swearing, Adultery, Fornication, Breaking of the Sabbath and Drunkenness."[7] It is clear that Innes believed that many offenses came under the common law jurisdiction of the state that were not cognizable in a federal court. The list is striking, also, because the judge did not instruct the federal grand jurors that the federal internal revenue laws were matters for their attention. Since he knew that "all the penal laws of the state" were within the cognizance of a state panel, he must have known that the penal laws of the United States were within the cognizance of a federal panel.[8] Furthermore, Judge Innes must have been aware that the internal revenue laws were being violated throughout Kentucky.

The first of the internal revenue acts, a long and complicated statute with sixty-two sections, had been passed on March 3, 1791. It was followed over the next eight years by a half-dozen other major acts, all designed to make the collection of the tax on domestic distilled spirits more efficient, effective, and acceptable.[9] But acceptance was

6 Draft address, undated but prepared for the grand jury which convened Jan. 12, 1792. Harry Innes Papers, Manuscript Division, Library of Congress, xviii, 2-123.

7 Draft copy of an "Address to the Grand Jury" [1784?], ibid., 2-120.

8 Ibid., 2-123. Both the Judiciary Act of 1789 and the Internal Revenue Act of 1791 referred explicitly to the authority of federal courts over cases arising from federal statutes. 1 Stat. 73, secs. 9, 11; 1 Stat. 199, sec. 42. State courts were given concurrent jurisdiction over internal revenue cases arising more than 50 miles from a federal district court in 1794. 1 Stat. 378, sec. 9.

9 1 Stat. 199, 1 Stat. 267, 1 Stat. 275, 1 Stat. 378, 1 Stat. 512, 1 Stat. 626. Additional laws passed during this period amended and supplemented the principal statutes and specified procedures.

rare in Kentucky, where the population generally was opposed both to the excise and to the purpose for which it was raised.

The whiskey tax was designed by Secretary of the Treasury Alexander Hamilton to defray the cost to the federal government of its recent assumption of the debts of the states. Most Kentuckians thought that they had already done their part in absorbing state debts by accepting depreciated currency and by purchasing Virginia treasury warrants for Kentucky lands, which were proving to be worth little more than the paper they were written on. They strongly objected to paying taxes to a government that seemed uninterested in solving either of their most pressing problems: protecting them from the Indians or securing the free navigation of the Mississippi from the Spanish. Moreover, a tax on domestic distilled spirits appeared to them to be discriminatory because it did not fall equally on all citizens in all parts of the country.[10] It seemed unfair because whiskey was often the only common medium of exchange in the West, where specie was rare. And it seemed oppressive because it taxed their most valuable export. Whiskey had the greatest worth per unit of weight or volume, an important consideration when transportation was exceedingly difficult.[11]

Resistance to the internal revenue laws seems to have begun as early in Kentucky as in Pennsylvania, where it has received more attention because there a federal army was ultimately required to put down rebellion.[12] By March 1792, Colonel Thomas Marshall who, as inspector of the Seventh Survey of the Eleventh District (Virginia), was the highest revenue officer in Kentucky, was already complaining to his superior about "the many violent enemies the law had."[13] Although inspections had evidently been attempted, Marshall had been forced to postpone collections because his collectors' official commis-

[10] "Papers Relating to What is Known as the Whiskey Insurrection in Western Pennsylvania, 1794," *Pennsylvania Archives*, 2d Ser., iv (Harrisburg, 1890), 5.

[11] At this time production averaged 1½ to 2 gallons per bushel. Henry G. Crowgey, *Kentucky Bourbon* (Lexington, 1971), 61. The only export of comparable value was tobacco, which was much bulkier.

[12] Richard H. Kohn, "The Washington Administration's Decision to Crush the Whiskey Rebellion," *Journal of American History*, lix (1972), 567-584. The similarity of events in Pennsylvania can be seen in Jacob E. Cooke, "The Whiskey Insurrection: A Re-evaluation," *Pennsylvania History*, xxx (1963), 316-346; William Miller, "Democratic Societies and the Whiskey Insurrection," *Pennsylvania Magazine of History and Biography*, lxii (1938), 324-350; Leland D. Baldwin, *Whiskey Rebels* (Pittsburgh, 1939).

[13] Thomas Marshall to Edward Carrington, Mar. 8, 1792, Whiskey Rebellion Papers, Record Group 58, Records of the Internal Revenue Service, National Archives. (Hereafter cited as Whiskey Rebellion Papers, National Archives.) In 1794 Marshall's district was reorganized and renamed the District of Ohio. i Stat. 270.

sions had not yet arrived and "had we made the least slip advantage would have been taken of it."[14]

Marshall's problems were compounded by confusing, complicated, and sometimes unworkable statutes. Distillers were expected to register their stills and to keep complete records—but they did neither. The law distinguished between distilleries in cities, towns, and villages on one hand (which were taxable according to the quantity and proof of the distilled product), and country stills on the other (which were taxable according to the capacity of the still). Rating the tax of the former was impossible because of the absence of records. Computing the tax of the latter was equally inexpedient: Colonel Marshall quickly complained about "the impracticability of measuring the stills on account of their being all at work."[15] Other statutory distinctions between distilleries and private stills were inapplicable in Kentucky, where almost every farmer was a distiller. And the provision that the penalties of the law were not to apply to persons who owned only one still not exceeding fifty gallons encouraged many to ignore the law altogether.[16]

Congress was as inexperienced in drafting excise laws as it was unfamiliar with conditions on the frontier, and for once Alexander Hamilton's expertise was unequal to the task.[17] The very flexibility of the procedures created confusion. And Kentuckians who were opposed to the excise in principle took advantage of all the loopholes, leaving the burden of proof on the harassed agents.[18]

These collectors were to receive a percentage of the duties collected, or half the penalties and forfeitures recovered in suits when distillers

[14] Marshall to Carrington, Mar. 8, 1792, Whiskey Rebellion Papers, National Archives.

[15] Ibid.

[16] 1 Stat. 199, secs. 15, 21, 36, 43; 1 Stat. 267, sec. 1. Section 15 of the latter statute, passed in May 1792, lowered duties but contained a bribe (or threat) to those on the frontier: any deficiency in the expected excise was to be made up from money raised for the protection of the frontiers.

[17] Hamilton's key role in suggesting legislation and drafting procedures for implementing it is thoroughly documented in Harold C. Syrett, et al., eds., The Papers of Alexander Hamilton, VII-XVIII.

[18] Because country stills and those under 400-gallon capacity in cities, towns, and villages were rated according to capacity, owners who produced high proof whiskey held a great competitive advantage over owners of larger stills and distilleries, whose products were taxed according to proof. When this was pointed out by Edward Carrington, Marshall's superior in Virginia, he was instructed to avoid discussing the matter and exposing the defect in the law. Tench Coxe to Carrington, June 30, 1792, Letters Sent by the Commissioner of the Revenue and the Revenue Office, 1792-1807, M-414, roll 1, Records of the Internal Revenue Service, Record Group 58, National Archives. (Hereafter cited as Letters Sent, Revenue Office, M-414.)

were found guilty of refusing to pay the tax.[19] But there were no suits because the attorney for the district refused to bring charges, and grand juries did not return presentments. The act also offered revenue officers the option of distress (or distraint) and sale, a summary procedure by which the supervisor could issue a warrant to the marshal, who was then authorized to sell as many of the goods and chattels of a delinquent as were needed to realize the amount of money due to the government. If insufficient funds were realized from the sale, the offender could be imprisoned. Regardless of the statutory provisions, Judge Innes believed that distraint (seizure) required some overt act of defiance, and evidently the marshal shared the judge's views. In any case, the procedure could not have been expected to make the law any more popular. Colonel Marshall acknowledged that "distraining I fear will not at present answer our purposes."[20]

Pecuniary incentives were not enough, even after the colonel offered to contribute his one percent to get better enforcement in Nelson, Madison, and Mason Counties.[21] Inspection trips were so hazardous that he was obliged to accept the resignation of several collectors, and retained others only by shifting their assignments to other counties where the opposition was not yet organized. He refused one resignation because "no [other] person worthy of trust living in Nelson [County] could be got to accept" the job—a comment, incidentally, which indicates that opposition to the law transcended political loyalties, because Nelson County was a center of Federalist sentiment.[22]

In October 1792, Commissioner of Revenue Tench Coxe tried to be helpful by reporting that in Maryland, "aid to the Government has been derived from information being given by the trade. No persons are so much concerned to prevent infractions of the laws as the fair complying distiller."[23] But in Kentucky, as the court records show, no mem-

---

[19] The total costs of collection were not to exceed 7%. The collectors originally were allocated 4% for collections in cities, towns, and villages, and 5% for country stills. The percentage was continually raised and the distinction between cities and countryside eliminated. Colonel Marshall received a salary and a percentage of collections. (In 1794 his salary was $600.) Syrett *et al.*, eds., *Hamilton Papers*, VIII, 191; XII, 96; XVIII, 167.

[20] Marshall to Carrington, Mar. 8, 1792, Whiskey Rebellion Papers, National Archives.

[21] *Ibid.* Commissioner of the Revenue Tench Coxe was impressed by Marshall's "spirit and liberality" in contributing his percentage to the collectors and planned "to make it known in the proper places." Coxe to Carrington, Oct. 23, 1792, Letters Sent, Revenue Office, M-414, roll 1.

[22] Marshall to Carrington, Mar. 8, 1792, Whiskey Rebellion Papers, National Archives.

[23] Coxe to Marshall, Oct. 31, 1792, Letters Sent, Revenue Office, M-414, roll 1.

ber of the general public was willing to act as an informer even for half the penalties and forfeitures. And the collectors had enough problems without filing informations against distillers.

Soon Marshall and the collectors stood alone. In December 1792, the United States attorney for the district resigned his office, and for four years there was no one to prosecute violators of the law.[24] The revenue officers could only threaten and cajole, and neither method was effective.[25] In the spring of 1793, Collector Brooks was assaulted in Nelson County.[26] Later, in the summer, Collector Hubble bought some whiskey for the army only to have it "rescued" from him.[27] The following winter Hubble spent the night with a distiller, and while they slept the house was attacked and Hubble's money, saddlebags, and records for Mason and Bourbon Counties were stolen.[28] Some time later, the collector of Fayette County was pulled from his horse, tarred, and rolled in leaves.[29]

What was equally remarkable was the role of the federal court. During all this period, grand juries were convened who proffered no presentments. No informations were filed with them and, of course, no indictments were handed down in the absence of a federal attorney. Marshall and his superior in Virginia, Edward Carrington, were forced to resort to civil procedures. In December 1793, Carrington brought two suits in case, apparently to recover the value of the stolen whiskey.[30] The suits were continued at the March 1794 term and dismissed

[24] William Murray preferred to become attorney general for Kentucky, and a state statute prohibited state officials from holding federal positions. Murray to the secretary of state [Thomas Jefferson], Dec. 7, 1792, Miscellaneous Letters of the Department of State, 1789-1906, M-179, roll 8, General Records of the Department of State, Record Group 59, National Archives. (Hereafter cited as Misc. Letters, Dept. of State, M-179).

[25] Both are reflected in advertisements in the *Kentucky Gazette* (Lexington). See, for examples, *Ky. Gaz.*, June 18, 1791; Mar. 24, 1792; Apr. 21, 1792; Apr. 28, 1792; Nov. 24, 1792; Jan. 12, 1793; July 27, 1793; Aug. 31, 1793; Nov. 23, 1793; Feb. 22, 1794.

[26] Coxe to Carrington, Mar. 27, 1793, Letters Sent, Revenue Office, M-414, roll 1.

[27] George Nicholas to Marshall, Aug. 25, 1793, Whiskey Rebellion Papers, National Archives.

[28] Marshall to Carrington, Mar. 20, 1794, *ibid.*; *Ky. Gaz.*, Feb. 22, 1794. Part of the money and saddlebags were later recovered, but the records were never found.

[29] Coxe to William Clarke, May 11, 1797, Tench Coxe Section, Coxe Papers, Manuscript Collection, Historical Society of Pennsylvania, Philadelphia.

[30] Case was a form of action used to recover damages which were the indirect consequence of the defendant's act. *Carrington* v. *Saunders, Carrington* v. *Trotter*, DC OB A, Dec. 17, 1793, 44.

in July. To add insult to injury, Carrington was ordered to pay the defendants' costs.[31]

Meanwhile, Alexander Hamilton thought of an ingenious way to secure compliance. Since the Treasury Department was already in the business of purchasing supplies for the army, it occurred to Hamilton that distillers might be persuaded to pay their taxes in whiskey.[32] When he was in western Pennsylvania with the troops during the Whiskey Rebellion, he wrote to Coxe: "It has been much insisted upon, that this part of the Country could not without oppression pay the duty in cash. The supply of the Western Army enables us to ac- comodate [sic] in this particular, an option may therefore be either to pay in cash or in Whiskey."[33]

But most Kentuckians would not be humored into compliance. Ap- parently the only distillers who took advantage of Hamilton's offer were those who sold whiskey to the army. Interestingly enough, these sales were arranged by middlemen like Thomas Marshall and Thomas Carneal—who, because they were also revenue officers, were able to require payment as a condition of purchase.[34] The whiskey credited to duties in this way went to the army. But no money was forwarded from Kentucky, and evasion of the excise continued.[35]

Eventually an earlier concession was repeated. In 1793, Secretary of State Thomas Jefferson had agreed to forgive arrearages for the first year upon the promise of distillers that they would pay the tax

[31] Ibid., Mar. 18, 1794, 54; July 22, 1794, 61. Nicholas had strongly recom- mended to Marshall that the suits be dropped. Nicholas to Marshall, Aug. 25, 1793, Whiskey Rebellion Papers, National Archives.

[32] The Treasury Department had taken over this function from the War De- partment after St. Clair's defeat had been attributed in part to the inefficiency of earlier supply arrangements. Legislation authorizing the transfer was passed in February 1792 (1 Stat. 279). John C. Miller, The Federalist Era 1789-1801 (New York, 1960), 147; Leonard D. White, The Federalists: A Study in Administrative History (New York, 1948), 121.

[33] Hamilton to Coxe, Nov. 17, 1794, Whiskey Rebellion Papers, National Ar- chives. A copy of this letter, addressed to Henry Miller (acting quartermaster gen- eral of the militia army), is in Syrett et al., eds., Hamilton Papers, xvii, 376.

[34] Marshall to Coxe, Mar. 20, 1794, ibid. For their dual roles and purchase ad- vertisements, see Ky. Gaz., Nov. 24, 1792; Mar. 29, 1794; Jan. 17, 1795.

[35] Walter Lowrie and Walter S. Franklin, eds., American State Papers, Finance. Documents, Legislative and Executive of the Congress of the United States, 1 (Washington, 1834), 390, 391, 562, 593, 618; Coxe to John Brown, Mar. 30, 1797, Coxe Papers; Coxe to Marshall, Jan. 2, 1796, Letters of Tench Coxe, Com- missioner of the Revenue, Relating to the Procurement of Military, Naval, and Indian Supplies, 1794-1796, M-74, Records of the Bureau of Indian Affairs, Record Group 75, National Archives; Treasury Department [Oliver Wolcott] to Thomas Carneal, Oct. 21, 1797, Oliver Wolcott Papers, Manuscript Collection, Connecticut Historical Society, Hartford, xxxiii, 44.

in the future.[36] An extension of the grace period had been refused in 1793, but by 1795 the administration was willing to try again.[37] When James Innes returned from his placating mission to Kentucky to inform residents there about the reopened negotiations for navigation of the Mississippi, he evidently convinced the central government that there was no possibility of securing compliance unless arrearages accruing before 1794 were forgiven.[38] The Treasury Department apparently believed that a bargain had been struck, but both Hamilton and his successor, Oliver Wolcott, underestimated the determination of Kentuckians. Five years later Wolcott complained bitterly: "Influential Gentlemen of the State of Kentucky gave assurance in 1795, that by forebearing to demand the duties and penalties which had accrued prior to July 1794, a general compliance with the Law, would be thenceforward assured. A compromise was authorized on the principles suggested, but without securing the desired effect."[39]

By 1796 the Treasury Department was becoming desperate. Military action was inadvisable if not impossible, and the carrots of payment in whiskey and forgiveness of arrearages and penalties had been rejected. The stick of legal action was all that remained. But Wolcott had become suspicious about the absence of activity in the federal court, and he wrote Coxe to instruct Colonel Marshall to consider bringing suit. Equal application of the law was clearly not what Wolcott had in mind, as an early draft of his letter reveals:

The first demand ought to be made of those delinquents, whose examples in opposition to the Law has been most influential. If they shall manifest a disposition to submit to the Law . . . the Supervisor ought to settle with them. . . . If however, opposition is made to a compromise on these Principles, suits ought to be commenced against this class of Men generally. With respect to persons of inferior consideration and influence, suits may be suspended until further instructions shall be received. In making the experiment care

[36] Thomas Jefferson to George Nicholas, July 15, 1793, Domestic Letters of the Department of State, 1784-1906, M-40, roll 5, General Records of the Department of State, Record Group 59, National Archives. (Hereafter cited as Domestic Records, Dept. of State, M-40.) It was Jefferson's refusal to extend the grace period that prompted Nicholas to decline, for a second time, the appointment as United States attorney for the Kentucky District. Nicholas to Marshall, Aug. 25, 1793, Whiskey Rebellion Papers, National Archives.
[37] Hamilton to Coxe, Nov. 17, 1794; Jan. 27, 1795, Whiskey Rebellion Papers, National Archives.
[38] See the account of James Innes's mission in Chapter Two.
[39] Wolcott to Thomas T. Davis, Feb. 25, 1800, Innes Papers, Library of Congress, XXI, Pt. i, 1-89.

~~should be taken to render it so general as that the issue may com-~~
~~pletely demonstrate, the efficacy of judicial concern~~ [crossed out in
original]. If for any reason it shall appear adviseable [*sic*] to the
Supervisor to institute some of the suits in the State Courts no objections will be made at the Treasury.[40]

This strategy was, for the time being, as unsuccessful as its predecessors.[41] Marshall could find no attorneys to assist him, and except
for the suits in case brought earlier by Carrington in the federal court,
its records indicate that term after term passed with no hint that
federal statutes were being avoided or evaded. Grand juries were regularly empaneled, but until March 1795 they did nothing but approve
the First Census.[42] Their only presentment during this period was
against Andrew Holmes, charged with retailing wine at his tavern in
violation of an act that laid duties on foreign wines and foreign distilled spirits.[43] That presentment was quashed at the next term for
"uncertainty and informality," and no grand juries were empaneled
at any of the succeeding six terms.[44] The marshal was evidently violating the rule adopted in June 1791 that required a grand jury at
each term. But there is no indication in the records that he was cen-
sured by the judge, although Innes did not hesitate to reprimand the
marshal (and the clerk) for inattention to their duties on other occasions.

There was still no United States attorney for the Kentucky District

[40] Wolcott to Coxe, June 27, 1796, Wolcott Papers, xxxi, 49. The final draft
omitted the words crossed out. Wolcott to Coxe, June 27, 1796, Whiskey Rebellion Papers, National Archives. Coxe transmitted the final draft verbatim to Marshall. Coxe to Marshall, June 30, 1796, Letters Sent, Revenue Office, M-414, roll
2.

[41] The strategies apparently did not work in Pennsylvania, either, according to
a letter written by Coxe's successor to Marshall's successor. William Miller, Jr. to
James Morrison, June 2, 1798, Whiskey Rebellion Papers, National Archives.
Furthermore, Oliver Wolcott doubted that even the military action there had been
successful in securing compliance. In 1799 he wrote President Adams that "though
the insurrection has been suppressed the spirit which occasioned it still exists, and
the friends of government and its officers have lost much of the influence which
they once possessed." Wolcott to Adams, Nov. 18, 1799, Wolcott Papers, xl, 68.

[42] DC OB A, Jan. 12, 1792, 18. The failure of grand juries to act is further
evidence of the nonpartisan nature of the resistance to the whiskey tax. Under
Kentucky statute, grand jurors were summoned by the marshal, and this practice
was followed in the federal court. Harry Innes to John Breckinridge, Dec. 27,
1801, Breckinridge Family Papers, Manuscript Division, Library of Congress, xxi,
3559. The federal marshal during this period was Samuel McDowell, Jr., a cousin
of the Marshalls and a strong Federalist.

[43] i Stat. 376; DC OB A, Mar. 17, 1795, 82.

[44] DC OB A, June 17, 1795, 97. "Informality" meant lack of legal form.

104

to take the initiative in prosecuting suits. Even Colonel Marshall's son-in-law, William McClung, had declined the office. The colonel suspected some kind of conspiracy and he expressed his frustration repeatedly in letters, including one to his son John, upon his appointment as United States attorney general:

> Now I hope we may be informed why we have no Attorney in this State for the United States. I have complained of this in every letter I have written on the subject of revenue. I cannot possibly have the revenue collected, as no one will comply with the laws without compulsion, and the government has not put it into my power to compel compliance. This I have tried, but without success. . . . there might be political reasons assigned for the neglect. But if that be the case, why am I repeatedly written to by the Commissioner of Revenue, as if it was expected that I could go on with the business in the same manner as if there were no impediment.[45]

Matters seemed about to change in December 1796, when William Clarke accepted appointment as attorney for the district, and the four-year vacancy in that office finally ended. On the day after he presented his commission of office to the court, the grand jury brought presentments against James Smith and Peter Utman for having forcibly obstructed a revenue collector.[46] Responding to the new situation, Judge Innes promulgated new rules "to regulate penal laws when fines and imprisonment are instituted, or fines only."[47] The rules provided for issuance of subpoenas, conditions for default judgments, acceptable pleadings, and other details which were to be completed "in the same manner as in Common Law." The only unexpected requirement was that the attorney for the district was to file an information on every presentment, stating the charge and the informer's name and residence.[48]

---

[45] Thomas Marshall to John Marshall, Nov. 6, 1795, quoted in W[illiam] M[cClung] Paxton, *The Marshall Family* (Cincinnati, 1885), 22. Colonel Marshall apparently did not realize that his son had declined the appointment, just as he had earlier refused to serve as United States attorney for the District of Virginia, possibly for the same reasons that others had refused the office in Kentucky. George Washington to Alexander Hamilton, Oct. 29, 1795, Syrett *et al.*, eds., *Hamilton Papers*, xix, 357.

[46] DC OB A, Dec. 21, 1796, 142.

[47] *Ibid.*, Dec. 23, 1796, 143-145.

[48] *Ibid.* Theoretically a presentment resulted from an allegation made by a member of a grand jury, but the result of this rule was that subsequent presentments carried the names of informers who were revenue agents and not grand jurors.

The movement toward criminal litigation continued at the March term, when two related charges were brought. One was a presentment against Peter Smelzer for keeping an unregistered still (on an information filed by a collector); the second was an indictment against Joseph Steele for assault and battery against another revenue agent. Of equal significance was Clarke's response to the instructions given by Commissioner Coxe to Colonel Marshall the preceding June: he filed informations against men whose opposition to the law he believed had been influential. And the attorney chose to make examples of two who were unquestionably prominent: Thomas Jones, justice of the peace for Bourbon County and an elector of the state senate, and United States Senator John Brown, Judge Innes's closest friend.[49]

Colonel Marshall, confident that at last the forces of law and order had triumphed over neglect of duty, resigned his inspectorship. He wrote to President Adams:

> It may possibly be asked why, after holding the office during the most critical of troublesome times, I should now resign it, when I am no longer insulted, and abused. . . . In truth, this very change . . . furnishes a reason. . . . For having once engaged in the business of revenue I presently found myself of sufficient importance with the enemies of the Government here to be made an object of their particular malevolence—and while this was the case, I was determined not to be driven from my post.[50]

But Marshall's confidence was premature. No grand juries were empaneled at the next two terms of the court (in June and November 1797) nor did the new attorney file any more informations. Marshall and Carrington, it seemed, could depend only on each other. In November, Carrington filed four suits in debt, and Marshall filed one. Both men sued in their own names "and for the benefit of the United States" against four different defendants.[51] Despite Coxe's instructions, however, none of these defendants appears to have been particularly prominent. One was the man whom Carrington had sued in case in

[49] DC OB A, Mar. 22, 1797, 151; William Clarke to Tench Coxe, May 11, 1797, Coxe Papers; W. T. Smith, *A Complete Index to the Names of Persons, Places and Subjects Mentioned in Littell's Laws of Kentucky* (Lexington, Ky., 1931), 97.

[50] Marshall to Adams, Apr. 28, 1797, Misc. Letters, Dept. of State, M-179, roll 15.

[51] Marshall's and Carrington's cautiousness in observing the proprieties (suing in their own names and for the benefit of the United States) is in marked contrast to the carelessness of Clarke, noted below.

1793; another was sued by both Carrington and Marshall, so that there were only four defendants although there were five suits.[52]

This second use of civil actions proved little more productive than the first. Carrington discontinued the cases against three of the defendants and paid the costs. The fourth defendant, sued by both Carrington and Marshall, confessed judgment for $165.72 in 1798 but was able in 1802 to get a *supersedeas* staying proceedings on collection.[53]

A similar examination of the disposition of the earlier cases indicates that the first four criminal charges (those against Smith, Utman, Smelzer, and Steele) were also proving futile. The charge against Utman was abated by his death. The charge against Smith was continued at every term until July 1798, when he was able to prove to the satisfaction of the court that process had been served on the wrong James Smith. He then recovered his costs from Clarke. A new information was filed and new process issued against James Smith, merchant. This case, like many others, remained open throughout the remainder of the period under examination.[54] The charges against Smelzer and Steele, brought in March 1797, were continued the following June. In November Steele's charge was quashed for informality. Smelzer's case was continued until March 1798, when it was discontinued on the motion of Clarke, with the defendant paying costs.[55]

Still the attorney persevered. He filed an information against Dudley Mitcham for using an unregistered still and got a presentment from the grand jury in March 1798.[56] But then no grand jury was empaneled in July, and Clarke could only file informations against two more distillers, John Shawhan and James Caldwell.[57] It was uphill work. Finally, in November 1798, Judge Innes announced a new rule:

No person shall on whom any process shall be served returnable to this Court, or has a Suit depending herein, or who may be sum-

[52] *Carrington* v. *Saunders, Carrington* v. *Ravenscraft, Carrington* v. *Helm,* DC OB A, Nov. 20, 1797, 169; *Carrington* v. *Horine, Marshall* v. *Horine, ibid.,* Nov. 21, 1797, 174.

[53] The action may have been used because of Marshall's death in 1802. No further proceedings were recorded that might have revived the debt case in the name of his heirs or in the name of the United States. *Marshall* v. *Horine,* DC OB A, July 9, 1798, 196, 197; *Horine* v. *Marshall,* DC OB C, Nov. 20, 1802, 368; Dec. 1, 1802, 418.

[54] DC OB A, Mar. 21, 1797, 147; June 20, 1797, 162; Nov. 20, 1797, 170; July 12, 1798, 211; DC OB B, Nov. 19, 1798, 4.

[55] DC OB A, Mar. 21, 1797, 146, 147; June 20, 1797, 162; June 21, 1797, 165; Nov. 20, 1797, 168, 170; Nov. 21, 1797, 171; Mar. 12, 1798, 180.

[56] *Ibid.,* Mar. 12, 1798, 178.   [57] *Ibid.,* July 12, 1798, 211.

moned as a witness in any suit or question depending in the Court, *or who is a distiller of Spirits within this district* [italics added], shall be summoned as a Grand Juror; and the Marshall before he summons a Grand Juror is directed to make the necessary inquiry agreeably to this Regulation.[58]

The new rule had an immediate impact: the November grand jury issued presentments against five persons for operating unregistered stills.[59] For the first time in the seven years since passage of the internal revenue act, grand jurors brought charges based on their own knowledge of violations of the law. And once begun, the trend continued: in March 1799, thirteen distillers were presented; in July, another; in November, five more; in March 1800, an additional six. The charges were substantially the same in every case.[60] And, meanwhile, Clarke continued to file informations. He brought five in November 1798, two in March 1799, and one each in March and November 1800.[61]

However, these presentments and informations were not followed by convictions. When the cases came to trial, it became evident that petit jurors refused to convict their neighbors of criminal charges when their only crime was violating the revenue acts. As Judge Innes had pointed out in his address to the first federal grand jury:

> Trials by Jury have from time immemorial been considered as the basis of Liberty . . . They are the great bulwark which intervenes between the Magistrate and the Citizen. . . . In Criminal cases . . . no Offender can be arraigned at the Bar, until his Offence hath been inquired into by the Grand Inquest . . . and found to be true by

[58] DC OB B, Nov. 26, 1798, 27. The rule was evidently put into effect before it was recorded in the Order Book.

[59] *U.S.* v. *Trimble, U.S.* v. *Bush, U.S.* v. *Hardwick, U.S.* v. *Lewis, U.S.* v. *McKenney,* DC OB B, Nov. 19, 1798, 1. Because of the limitations on joinder, two presentments were made for two of these men (Trimble and Bush) for failure to enter on two different dates. The total number of presentments was, therefore, seven.

[60] *U.S.* v. *Trimble, U.S.* v. *Hockaday, U.S.* v. *Singleton, U.S.* v. *Bayer, U.S.* v. *Galbraith, U.S.* v. *Dodson, U.S.* v. *Ellis, U.S.* v. *Stewart, U.S.* v. *Bogio, U.S.* v. *Gouge, U.S.* v. *Wills, U.S.* v. *Peeples, U.S.* v. *Logan,* DC OB B, Mar. 12, 1799, 44-48. *U.S.* v. *Farrow, ibid.,* July 8, 1799, 87; *U.S.* v. *Jackman, U.S.* v. *Teter, U.S.* v. *Adams, U.S.* v. *Shackleford, U.S.* v. *Price, ibid.,* Nov. 18, 1799, 130, 131; *U.S.* v. *Randolph, U.S.* v. *Allen, U.S.* v. *Dawson, U.S.* v. *Spaulding, U.S.* v. *Keith, U.S.* v. *Barbee, ibid.,* Mar. 11, 1800, 238, 239.

[61] *U.S.* v. *Beauchamp, U.S.* v. *Payton* (two charges), *U.S.* v. *Lee* (two charges), DC OB B, Nov. 11, 1798, 16; *U.S.* v. *Trimble, U.S.* v. *Bush, ibid.,* Mar. 11, 1799, 34, 36; *U.S.* v. *Heath, ibid.,* Mar. 10, 1800, 229; *U.S.* v. *Robinson, ibid.,* Nov. 18, 1800, 479. The list of names indicates that the Scots-Irish did not dominate the distilling industry, as is commonly supposed.

the voice of twelve of them at least, his trial then comes on before a Petit Jury where a unanimous voice is necessary to find him guilty.[62]

Petit jurors in Kentucky apparently saw themselves as such a "great bulwark" between the government and its citizens, and Judge Innes assisted them by rigidly maintaining procedural safeguards. The cases of Brown, Jones, Trimble, and Bush illustrate how the judge and the jurymen prevented enforcement of the unpopular revenue laws through criminal charges.

John Brown's case was the simplest of these, but even it required five terms (twenty months) to come to judgment. Clarke filed the information in March 1797, and secured a writ of *venire facias ad respondendum* (summoning a defendant against whom a misdemeanor has been charged). When Brown did not appear in June, a *capias ad respondendum* (ordering the marshal to take the defendant and keep him for trial) was issued. This was followed by an *alias capias ad respondendum* in November. There is no mention at all of the case at the March 1798 term, possibly because Brown was then attending Congress.[63] Brown pleaded not guilty in July and "putteth himself upon the country," the traditional request for a jury trial.

At the trial in November it turned out that Brown was being prosecuted not for any misconduct on his part but because a former owner of his still had failed to enter it or pay duties on it. The court disagreed with the government's contention that the proceedings were *in rem* (against the still) and disallowed evidence relating to the alleged transgressions of the former owner. This left the jury free to acquit Brown. Lack of proof and poor pleading appear to have accounted for Clarke's failure to prosecute successfully one of Kentucky's most prominent Jeffersonians.[64]

The charge against Thomas Jones (the Bourbon County justice of the peace) was more complicated, continued longer, and gave Innes an opportunity to expose Clarke's supposed incompetence. The initial information filed in March 1797 was quashed for informality, and Clarke had to file a second one charging Jones with using two un-

---

[62] Draft address, Innes Papers, Library of Congress, xviii, 2-123.

[63] Innes had written to him in Philadelphia, on other matters, in January. Innes to Brown, Jan. 28, 1798, Brown Family Papers, Special Collections Department, Margaret I. King Library, University of Kentucky, Lexington. Brown's membership in the Senate may explain his earlier absences as well.

[64] *U.S. v. Brown*, DC OB A, Mar. 22, 1797, 151; June 21, 1797, 166; Nov. 20, 1797, 170; July 9, 1798, 196; DC OB B, Nov. 22, 1798, 17.

registered stills. The defendant "craved oyer" (heard the charges) in June and pleaded not guilty in November. The following March, the case finally went to trial. It had been seven years since the first revenue act had been passed, and this was the first time a charge of failure to enter and pay duties had gone to a petit jury.

But after hearing the evidence, Innes instructed the jury to find a special verdict "as the case was new and might create some difficulty," and the jury did as it was told.[65] This meant that the jury found facts (that the stills were in a condition to be used, that indeed they had been used, and that they had not been entered according to law), but did not determine the guilt or innocence of the defendant. Their finding concluded, "If the law be for the Plaintiff, we find for the Plaintiff; if the law be for the Defendant, then we find for him." Clarke then moved for a *venire facias de novo* (a writ summoning another jury for a new trial) because he said that the special verdict was "imperfect" and insufficient for the court to base a judgment upon. Proceedings were continued until the next term, when the arguments were repeated.

Clarke was determined to get another trial and find a jury that would convict, and he bolstered his motion with citations from Blackstone, *Bacon's Abridgment, Coke's English King's Bench Reports*, and *Viner's Abridgment*. He insisted that the prosecution "related to property in which the government had acquired a right (i.e., the stills) and did not affect the liberty of the citizen," and concluded that it was therefore a civil prosecution.[66] The judge was "not sufficiently advised of and concerning the premises" and continued the case another term.[67] Four days after Brown's acquittal in November, Innes denied the motion for a new trial against Jones. Clarke then filed errors to arrest the judgment, and the case was continued again.[68] Finally, on the last day of the term in July 1799, Judge Innes read a long, carefully prepared opinion to the court.[69]

The judge began mildly enough by recapitulating the facts and

[65] *U.S. v. Jones*, DC OB A, Mar. 22, 1797, 151; June 20, 1797, 162; Nov. 21, 1797, 173; Mar. 12, 1798, 179-182.

[66] *U.S. v. Jones*, Draft opinion, Innes Papers, Library of Congress, xxvii, Pt. i, 8-71.

[67] *U.S. v. Jones*, DC OB A, July 10, 1798, 222.

[68] *U.S. v. Jones*, DC OB B, Nov. 26, 1798, 28; Mar. 13, 1799, 51.

[69] *U.S. v. Jones*, DC OB B, July 12, 1799, 110; July 15, 1799, 128. The final opinion is in [Harry Innes], "Cases in the Court of the United States for the District of Kentucky, from its first Organization to the year 1806 Inclusive," United States Court for the Western District of Kentucky, Louisville, 19. (Hereafter cited as Innes Opinions.)

defining the issues: whether this was a civil or a criminal proceeding, and if it was a criminal one, whether a *venire facias de novo* could be awarded for imperfection in the verdict. He then launched into a ten-page exposition apparently designed to squelch what he considered were the pretensions of the United States attorney. The court believed that the case was one of criminal and not civil law. The judge defined the term "information," distinguished between prosecutions *in rem* and *in personam*, and described the difference between summary and regular proceedings. He also expounded on public wrongs, the English antecedents of American jurisprudence, the history of excise laws, what is meant when a verdict is "full," and the proper use of a writ *venire facias de novo*. In refuting Clarke's arguments, Innes cited Blackstone, *Hawkins' Pleas of the Crown*, *Raymond's English King's Bench Reports*, *Morgan's Essays*, Strange, Coke, and other sources.[70] The court admitted that the statutes did not answer the question of further prosecution, so that "resort must be had to the common law." But he lectured the attorney on the hazards of reciting cases found in compilations extracted from reports "which, when examined, are not always correct." Finally, the judge said that it would be inconsistent with general practice to grant new trials in criminal cases for imperfections in the verdict. He was compelled, he added, to decide against the motion, discharge the defendant, and order the entire proceedings quashed.

The opinion leaves the distinct impression that Judge Innes was not simply explaining his decision but was exploiting an opportunity to overwhelm Clarke with a tour de force of legal erudition. It was apparent that the court would not tolerate any blurring of the distinctions between civil and criminal prosecutions and would insist upon strict adherence to traditional due process. As it turned out, the judge's intransigence in criminal proceedings was shared by petit jurors. Of the fifty criminal charges brought from December 1796 through November 1800 (the period of Clarke's tenure), not one of the accused paid the full fines, penalties, or forfeitures provided by the laws. It made no difference whether the charge was distilling without a license or obstructing revenue agents: criminal charges simply were not acceptable. Seven cases went to petit juries, and in every instance the jurors found for the defendants. Judge Innes then ordered their accusers to pay the costs of the suits. Failure to appear and plead resulted in eight default judgments, but two of these were later set aside.

[70] Many of these are unidentifiable because the manuscript abbreviations are illegible, but it is clear that Innes was generous with English legal citations.

Two other defendants acknowledged their failure to enter and pay duties; they were assessed only those duties and the costs of the suits, minus the district attorney's fees. The remaining thirty-three cases were abated by the death of the defendants, or quashed, dismissed, or discontinued.

Among the defendants were two men who were evidently being harassed by Clarke and the grand jurors, but Innes and the petit jurors refused to cooperate. Nothing in the records explains why William Trimble and Ambrose Bush inspired such attention, but the number and variety of charges against them indicated that they were marked men. Bush was unique among the defendants because he made peach brandy as well as whiskey; Trimble was the father of two sons who became even more prominent than he was—the older, Robert, succeeded Innes as judge of the district court, and later succeeded Todd as justice of the Supreme Court; the younger, John, was appointed to the "new" Court of Appeals by Governor Desha in 1825, and was offered the district court post by President John Quincy Adams.[71]

William Trimble first appeared in the Order Books in November 1798, when he was presented by a grand jury on two counts of using stills which had not been entered and on which duties had not been paid. Bush was also presented twice at that term on the same charges, and their cases seem to be related because the two defendants acted as surety for each other in the actions brought against them.[72] The following March another grand jury again presented Trimble on the same charges, specifying different dates.[73] While the grand jury was deliberating, Supervisor of Revenue James Morrison filed civil suits for debt against Bush and Trimble, and, in addition, Clarke filed informations against them.[74]

The first of all the charges against Trimble to come to trial was a debt case, in July 1799. He pleaded that he "doth not owe the debt in the declaration demanded," and a petit jury agreed.[75] The finding was important because this was the first civil suit brought under the revenue acts that had reached a jury. The result was not, however, surprising:

[71] Interview with Edna Talbott Whitley (Mrs. Wade Hampton Whitley), Paris, Kentucky, Nov. 6, 1970.
[72] DC OB B, Nov. 19, 1798, 2.
[73] Ibid., Mar. 12, 1799, 47.
[74] Ibid., Mar. 11, 1799, 34, 35.
[75] Ibid., July 8, 1799, 85. As discussed below, the declaration apparently specified the duties that had accrued before the stills were entered, and not the penalty for failure to enter. The judge's opinion is in Innes Opinions, 103.

five members of the jury had similar causes pending before the court.[76]

The marshal's choice of petit jurors, and the court's acceptance of them, seem clearly to have been in violation of the spirit of the rule regarding grand jurors announced in November 1798, which had resulted in the first grand jury charges not based on informations. The officials of the court were evidently unsympathetic with Clarke's methods. What is perhaps more surprising is that Clarke apparently did not challenge the selection process. But it might not have made any difference if he had. Although all nine civil and criminal charges against Trimble and Bush eventually went to petit juries, in every instance the jurors found for the defendants or acquitted them.

This July 1799 term was a personal disaster for Clarke. He was subjected to a scathing lecture on legal history in the Jones case and he lost the civil suit against Trimble. To add to Clarke's embarrassment, Morrison brought an action of debt against *him* for failure to pay internal revenue duties. (A juror was withdrawn at his trial to avert a verdict, probably because agreement was reached.)[77] Finally, completing Clarke's humiliation, Commissioner of Revenue Miller strongly criticized the handling of the Trimble case in a letter to Morrison:

> The interests of the United States have been committed by this defeat, in a way that is mortifying. . . . It is an important concern to avoid the introduction of suits, unless in cases of urgency. . . . In such cases and none others, in my opinion, ought there [be] resort to proceedings which must become expensive, tedious, and . . . uncertain in their decision.[78]

The Revenue Office wanted Clarke and Morrison to use the statutory provision for distraint (seizure) and sale, a method earlier rejected even by the determined Colonel Marshall.[79] Clarke unwisely complied with Miller's request, and the result was the wounding of the marshal and his deputy when they tried to serve a writ of *fieri facias*.[80] Ob-

[76] Dudley Mitcham, DC OB A, Mar. 12, 1799, 178; Robert Peeples, DC OB B, Mar. 12, 1799, 47; William Ellis, *ibid.*, 46; John Galbraith, *ibid.*, 45; and Ambrose Bush, whose cases were cited above.

[77] *Morrison* v. *Clarke*, DC OB B, July 13, 1799, 113.

[78] Miller to Morrison, Oct. 23, 1799, Letters Sent, Revenue Office, M-414, roll 2.

[79] See Chapter Three. Distraint and sale was first specified as a method of enforcement in the act of Mar. 3, 1791, i Stat. 199, sec. 23; and later in i Stat. 597, sec. 15; iii Stat. 22, sec. 28; and iii Stat. 366, sec. 2.

[80] The incident occurred Apr. 13, 1800. *U.S.* v. *Caldwell*, *U.S.* v. *Matthew Hemphill*, *U.S.* v. *John Hemphill*, *U.S.* v. *Andrew Hemphill*, DC OB B, Nov. 17,

viously distraint and sale were unlikely to gain the cooperative support of the marshal, and given the attitude of Kentuckians toward the revenue acts, such procedures also were unlikely to be any more productive than criminal charges.

Criminal charges had failed; distraint and sale had misfired. But there remained a third way to achieve compliance with the revenue acts: to bring civil suits for debt (for the amount of duties accrued) against noncomplying distillers. In November 1798, Supervisor James Morrison decided to experiment with this new procedure and chose his defendants carefully. He brought six suits against Stith and Thomas Daniel of Jefferson County. The Daniel brothers were major distillers —and Stith Daniel had been appointed a revenue collector by Colonel Marshall.[81] When their cases were continued in March 1799, Morrison continued the experiment by filing seven more debt cases. In July, the government won its first victory of any kind in the eight years since passage of the internal revenue acts: a petit jury assessed the Daniel brothers $259.12½; $928.38¾, and $231.25.[82] It was an instructive lesson for the defendants, who thereafter acknowledged their debts.[83] It was also instructive for Morrison, who vigorously pursued the new policy. He filed twenty-three more debt suits in July, sixty-three in November, forty-eight in March 1800, twelve in June, and twelve in November. Even more notable was that the government won fourteen more judgments in July 1799, nineteen in November, eighty-one in March 1800, twenty in June, and seven in November.

But the victory proved to be a limited one. During these same months, twenty-six judgments went for the defendants, and twenty-seven judgments that had earlier gone for the government were set aside. The judge and the attorney for the district were on a collision course: Innes was absolutely rigid about legal technicalities and Clarke was notoriously casual about form. Some defendants were able to get judgments arrested because suits had been brought in the name of the United States, instead of in the name of Supervisor Morrison "for the

---

1800, 468. Caldwell confessed and was sentenced to one hour in jail, a fine of $40, and costs; the Hemphills found it convenient to move out of the district and their cases never came to trial. DC OB C, Nov. 18, 1802, 323.

[81] *U.S. v. Stith and Thomas Daniel*, DC OB B, Nov. 21, 1798, 10; *Ky. Gaz.*, Nov. 24, 1792; Nov. 15, 1794.

[82] Fractions of cents were not uncommon in the judgments of the court but they were usually expressed in mills. *U.S. v. Daniel* (three cases), DC OB B, July 12, 1799, 104, 105.

[83] DC OB B, Nov. 21, 1799, 185.

use of the United States."[84] Other defendants pleaded successfully that no demand for payment could be proved, whereupon their cases were dismissed. A third group pleaded that revenue agents (who were often the only witnesses) were inadmissible as witnesses because of their interest in the judgment. (During this period, no one could testify in a proceeding if he had a pecuniary interest in its result.) Since the collectors received six percent of their collections and fifty percent of all penalties and forfeitures, Innes refused their evidence and judgments went for the defendants.

The pleading which brought the most serious disagreement between Innes and Clarke was that offered by Trimble and upheld by Innes in a July 1799 debt case. Trimble claimed that no duty could be collected on stills that had not been entered. Innes agreed that a distiller could be charged the penalty for not having entered his still, but not the duties which might have accrued during the period of nonentry. Clarke had apparently failed to specify the penalty in his declaration, and sued only for the duties. He was so vehement in his opposition to the judge's ruling that Innes suspected that complaints about him were being made to the Treasury Department. He wrote to Thomas T. Davis, a member of the House of Representatives, to find out what Clarke might be reporting. After two inquiries from Davis, Secretary of the Treasury Oliver Wolcott acknowledged that there had been some correspondence concerning Innes's ruling in the Trimble case.[85]

Wolcott assured Davis that Clarke's "representations" had "ever been temperate and respectful," and that "the decision of the Judge must be conclusive, in case it shall not be controuled by a Superior Judicial Tribunal."[86] What apparently frustrated Secretary Wolcott (and perhaps Clarke, as well) was that most of the Kentucky distillers had

---

[84] While it is not now possible to prove that this oversight was Clarke's, and not Morrison's, other evidence makes it seem likely. Innes reported in March 1800 that Morrison was "well convinced of Clarke's incompetency and wishes to get rid of him." Innes to Brown, Mar. 5, 1800, Innes Papers, Library of Congress, xxviii, 9-217. In any event, it was Clarke's responsibility to see that the government's suits were prepared properly. His successor found it necessary to amend the identification of the plaintiff in at least 21 of the government's cases during his first term in office. See DC OB C, Nov. 16, 1801, 52-54.

[85] Davis to Innes, Feb. 28, 1800, Innes Papers, Library of Congress, xxvii, Pt. i, 8-2; Wolcott to Davis, Feb. 25, 1800, ibid., xxi, Pt. i, 1-89.

[86] Wolcott was apparently hoping that one of Clarke's cases would be carried to the United States Supreme Court. Innes was not opposed to this because he thought it would give him an opportunity to expose Clarke's incompetence. Wolcott to Davis, Feb. 25, 1800, Wolcott Papers, xxxvii, 146; Innes to Brown, Mar. 18, 1798, Innes Papers, Library of Congress, xxviii, 9-210.

never lived up to the 1795 agreement (that arrearages would be forgiven and compliance assured). While the Treasury Department duly noted the amount of excise in its reports, the figures were always identified as "accrued" and never as "paid." By the spring of 1800, the administration had lost the earlier optimism occasioned by Clarke's appointment. He had failed to secure the cooperation of the people, and he was clearly no match for the distillers, their lawyers, or the federal judge.

Meanwhile, Innes was having his own doubts about the Trimble case. The legal principle he had asserted was consistent with his insistence on technical distinctions and traditional procedures. Yet he thought it necessary to write to Edmund Pendleton, the old and respected Virginia jurist and friend of the Innes family, describing the legal problem and asking his opinion. Pendleton's reply reinforced Innes's judgment:

> When a duty is laid on an Article, the collection of which is predicated on a step to be taken previously . . . and a penalty imposed on him for neglecting to take that step, the penalty and not the duty is recoverable; penalties being generally a substitute for what they are intended to inforce and are estimated so as to be more than adequate. The legislature may make it additional to the duty by express words . . . which gives force to the Opinion that the penalty is the rule where the law is silent, as in the present case.[87]

The man whom Innes once referred to as "the luminous Pendleton" closed his letter with reassurance: "But why a clamor about your jedgment? do they expect you'l pursue their Opinions or your own? if they think you erred, let them carry it before the Superior Court and have the error corrected. And why are you made uneasy by the Clamor, who are alone accountable to God and yr conscience for the rectitude of your Judgmt."

Clarke's failure to win support in the community and Innes's lack of respect for him eventually took their toll of the attorney. When the March 1800 grand jury made six presentments, Clarke immediately moved to quash them, presumably because he would not or could not effectively prosecute the cases.[88] Even the number of new actions in debt brought by Morrison dwindled in the June term: Innes said that

[87] Pendleton to Innes, Nov. 3, 1799, Innes Papers, Library of Congress, XXI, Pt. i, 1-87. The adequacy of the penalty may be seen in the Trimble opinion. The duty was 54¢ per gallon per year; the penalty was $250 and forfeiture of the still.
[88] DC OB B, Mar. 11, 1800, 238, 241.

he, too, had become convinced of Clarke's incompetence.[89] By then it was apparent to all that Clarke's effectiveness had ended. Finally, the Marshalls in Kentucky used their connections in the Adams administration to remove Clarke from a situation that must have become for them, as it certainly was for him, "exceedingly difficult and embarrassing."[90] Fortunately for them, Governor William Henry Harrison was eager to get judges appointed to the new court for the Indiana Territory, and the chief justiceship there offered a convenient berth. President Adams was in no hurry to make the appointment but the combined pressure from Governor Harrison, Secretary of State John Marshall, and Secretary of the Treasury Wolcott brought him around.[91] Clarke was given a recess appointment in October 1800 which was confirmed by the Senate in December, and in January he took the oath of his new office.[92]

Meanwhile, there was a strange interregnum in Kentucky while the Marshalls were arranging to have a political ally (and future brother-in-law) appointed in Clarke's place.[93] Clarke did nothing after he learned of his new appointment, and although his successor's commission was dated December 1800, it did not arrive in Kentucky until spring and was not presented to the court until November.[94] During these months someone prepared a statement of the caseload of the Kentucky federal court which, when it was published in December 1801, contained serious errors. By understating both the number of cases docketed and the number of cases decided, "it implies to *some* (say Fed[eralists]) that injustice has been done to the interest of the U.S.," complained Judge Innes.[95] It may not have been Clarke's parting shot, but Innes thought that it was, and wrote indignant letters to

[89] Innes to Brown, Mar. 5, 1800, Innes Papers, Library of Congress, xxviii, 9-217.

[90] Wolcott to Clarke, Aug. 5, 1800, Wolcott Papers, xxxviii, 38.

[91] John Marshall to Adams, Aug. 26, 1800, Miscellaneous Permanent Commissions, Appointment Office Files, B (1789-1802), Department of State, quoted in Clarence E. Carter, "William Clarke, First Chief Justice of Indiana Territory," *Indiana Magazine of History*, xxxiv (1938), 1-13; Carter, ed., *The Territorial Papers of the United States*, vii, *The Territory of Indiana 1800-1810* (Washington, 1939), 20.

[92] Carter, *Territory of Indiana*, vii, 16-19.

[93] Humphrey Marshall to Joseph Hamilton Daveiss, Nov. 24, 1800, Joseph Hamilton Daveiss and Samuel Daveiss Papers, Manuscript Dept., Filson Club, Louisville, Ky.

[94] Daveiss to Breckinridge, Jan. 2, 1802, Breckinridge Family Papers, xxi, 3573; DC OB C, Nov. 16, 1801, 125.

[95] Innes to Breckinridge, Jan. 14, 1802, Breckinridge Family Papers, xxi, 3611.

Senator Breckinridge and Secretary Madison to get the matter straightened out.[96]

In November 1801, Joseph Hamilton Daveiss became attorney for the district. From the day he presented his commission to the court it was obvious that a new regime had begun. Daveiss was energetic and competent, and those qualities proved to be more important than his Federalism, his membership (by marriage) in the Marshall family, and his alliance with Humphrey Marshall. Innes and Morrison could work effectively even with a political enemy if he was capable, and the Kentucky distillers soon learned that their ten-year escape from internal revenue taxes had ended. Ironically, their compliance was achieved only after Jefferson had been elected, and the taxes were being repealed.

Daveiss began his first day in court by getting two indictments from the grand jury, amending earlier cases brought by Clarke, and with Morrison docketing 121 civil cases in debt against distillers. One of the indictments charged a distiller with obstructing the service of a process for distraint and sale, a procedure that had not grown more popular with time. The other eventually resulted in the only petit jury conviction on a grand jury indictment against a distiller during the entire period under examination. Daveiss had chosen his case carefully, and the finding was undoubtedly influenced by evidence that the defendant had used two pistols to prevent service of a warrant charging that

[96] *Ibid.*; Innes to Madison, Jan. 14, 1802, Misc. Letters, Dept. of State, M-179, roll 19. The clerk of the Kentucky court vehemently denied that the errors had been committed in his office. Thomas Tunstall to Daveiss, Jan. 14, 1802, Daveiss Papers. Julius Goebel, Jr., believed that such errors were perpetrated by the administration to show that there was little business in the lower federal courts and thereby justify repeal of the Federalists' Judiciary Act of 1801, 11 Stat. 89. If so, the strategy failed to take into account its effect on Innes, one of the few Republican federal judges. Julius Goebel, Jr., *Antecedents and Beginnings to 1801*, in Paul A. Freund, ed., *The Oliver Wendell Holmes Devise History of the Supreme Court of the United States*, 1 (New York, 1971), 569-573. The original statistics were: private suits commenced, 670; decided, 445; depending, 225; government suits instituted, 196; decided, 21; depending, 175. The corrected statistics were: private suits commenced, 870; decided, 624; depending, 246; government suits instituted, 294; decided, 249; depending, 45. Neither the original statistics nor the corrected ones (confirmed by Tunstall in an accompanying statement, breaking down the number of cases by terms of the court) correspond with those compiled for the present work. Those of Innes and Tunstall are greater, and Tunstall's statement included terms when the court did not meet, according to the Order Books. The discrepancies remain inexplicable unless actions were recorded in the clerk's records that do not appear on the Order Books. If this is true, the Kentucky federal courts were even busier than the present study indicates. Cf. Innes to Madison, Jan. 14, 1802, Misc. Letters, Dept. of State, M-179, roll 19; *American State Papers, Miscellaneous*, 1, 320, 325; Appendices A, B, and C below.

he had hidden spirits to evade payment of the excise. Obviously, even in Kentucky the use of firearms was considered excessive.[97]

Daveiss even secured a jury conviction on an information filed against a distiller.[98] But criminal prosecutions were relatively unprofitable, and the outcomes of other informations were similar to the results during Clarke's tenure: three were dismissed, one discontinued, three defendants acknowledged their debts and paid costs, one judgment went for the defendant, and two judgments went for the government. Forfeitures and fines resulting from these were later remitted by Secretary of the Treasury Albert Gallatin who was, of course, unsympathetic with the revenue laws.[99]

The massive docketing of debt cases during Daveiss's first term indicated his awareness that compliance with the internal revenue acts could most successfully be achieved through civil action. He was careful not to risk failure through sloppiness in procedure: all of the 161 suits filed in November 1801, and the 51 filed in May 1802, were brought in the name of the revenue officer (usually Morrison) "for the use of the United States." (As noted earlier, Daveiss amended earlier declarations to comply with this technicality.) After his first term, Daveiss seldom used criminal charges to enforce the revenue acts. The Jeffersonians repealed the internal revenue taxes in April 1802, but a few cases continued to trickle in until the five-year statute of limitations took effect. Altogether, Daveiss filed 315 debt cases during the six years he was attorney.[100] The message must have been clear to Kentucky distillers: few of Daveiss's cases ever went to juries, as most defendants acknowledged their debts and paid the duties. And al-

[97] The defendant was released on $300 bail provided by Thomas Marshall, Jr., and the judgment was later arrested because of errors in the warrant. Innes's opinion stressed not only the heinous nature of the crime but also the danger of general warrants and quoted the Fourth Amendment as well as English decisions. The proceedings may be traced in *U.S.* v. *Mannen*, United States Court for the Sixth Circuit, DC OB C, Nov. 17, 1801, 106; *ibid.*, May 17, 1802, 191; United States Court for the District of Kentucky, DC OB C, Nov. 17, 1802, 345; *ibid.*, Nov. 18, 1802, 349; *ibid.*, Nov. 29, 1802, 413; *ibid.*, Dec. 2, 1802, 434, 437; DC OB D, Dec. 3, 1802, 15; *ibid.*, Dec. 6, 1802, 31.

[98] *U.S.* v. *Pleu*, DC OB C, Nov. 30, 1801, 179; May 17, 1802, 193; Nov. 24, 1802, 387; DC OB D, Mar. 17, 1803, 107; *ibid.*, July 5, 1803, 195; *ibid.*, Nov. 7, 1803, 304.

[99] Gallatin's own political career originated in Pennsylvania, where he acted as a moderate during the Whiskey Insurrection. His understanding of the problems of the distillers is indicated by his 1792 petition quoted in Chapter Three at n. 61. Authority to remit forfeitures and penalties was granted in the first internal revenue act, 1 Stat. 199, sec. 43.

[100] He also filed 79 other charges, some of which are described in Chapter Six, making a total of 394 prosecutions.

though Kentuckians grumbled until the excise was repealed, they belatedly registered their stills and paid their taxes.[101]

One of the most conspicuous aspects of this large number of debt cases was the policy of the court regarding sureties. The defendants in these suits were always accompanied in court by someone who "undertook" for them.[102] With the docketing of the government's cases, it became clear that the financial responsibility required of sureties was minimal, or that it was waived. Most defendants in the debt cases in November 1801, for example, undertook for each other. While some prominent persons were included in these lists, it is likely that many others were simple farmers with few liquid assets, except perhaps their whiskey. Not all the sureties could possibly have been substantial persons either in terms of community standing or financial resources.

The court's acceptance of other defendants as sureties may have marked an important departure from traditional surety practice. English courts permitted only persons of considerable position (originally, only the nobility) to be sureties; in modern American practice, financial responsibilty is required. The acceptance of sureties who were defendants in similar debt cases may have been a practical response, prompted by numbers and necessity, to a problem of legal policy. It is doubtful whether there was within reach of the Kentucky federal court a large enough group of substantial citizens to undertake for hundreds of defendant distillers. It is also doubtful whether the capital of persons who did have money and property could have provided surety for so large a number of litigants. On the other hand, failure to require any surety at all would have been a greater violation of tradition, and might have been interpreted as license to avoid the necessary commitment to the court.

[101] G. Thompson to Breckinridge, Feb. 6, 1802, Breckinridge Family Papers, XXI, 3641; Joseph Crockett to Breckinridge, Feb. 9, 1802, *ibid.*, 3647. These are among the letters that were misconstrued by Charles Warren. They, like others, express resentment of the whiskey tax and the Federalist judiciary act, but not of the federal court in Kentucky. Warren's misunderstanding is discussed in Chapter One, n. 27.

[102] The pleading was, for example, "John Hambleton, Jr. came into court and undertook for John Hambleton, Sr., that if he shall be cast in the action aforesaid he shall satisfy and pay the condemnation of the Court or render his body to prison in discharge of the same or on failure thereof that he will do it for him." *LeClair* v. *Hambleton*, DC OB A, Dec. 16, 1794, 77. This pleading was repeated in the Order Books for every defended debt case, private and public—some 800 times. Julius Goebel, Jr., describes this as "bail"; the term in the Kentucky federal court records was "security." Both refer to what today would be called "surety"—the guarantee of payment by a person other than the defendant in a civil case, in the event of his failure to pay a judgment; cf. Goebel, *Antecedents and Beginnings*, 522-534.

Theoretically, any defendant unable to provide a surety might be bound over to the marshal for custody, but frontier Kentucky certainly did not possess custodial facilities for hundreds of its citizens. Nor would it have served the public interest to incarcerate so large a proportion of the working male population. In the absence of studies of procedure in other federal courts it cannot now be known whether the experience in Kentucky's federal courts was part of a pattern, or whether it was unique. Judge Innes's flexibility regarding sureties may have been a creative method of maintaining the forms of the past under unprecedented pressures. There is no evidence in the court records that any surety for a distiller-debtor was ever pursued further by the court, although sureties for persons who held bonded official positions were often called to account when the officials were delinquent.

These cases account for the remainder of Daveiss's civil prosecutions. As the number of new cases involving distillers declined, the number of cases involving collectors of revenue rose. It was soon apparent that the government had almost as much difficulty collecting from revenue agents as those agents had earlier experienced trying to collect from distillers. Daveiss charged fifteen former collectors with delinquency. With the exception of one collector who died, every one of these cases went to juries, and in every instance the jurors found for the United States. When the collectors failed to pay their judgments, Daveiss proceeded against their sureties, which resulted in another group of suits.

The list of delinquent collectors included almost every prominent agent in Kentucky, with the conspicuous absence of Thomas Marshall and James Morrison.[103] (Marshall was once slow in rendering his accounts, however.)[104] But the others owed amounts that on the face of the record were astonishing, because those with unsettled accounts were liable to the United States for the total amount of their bonds, which—depending on rank—ranged from $2,000 to $20,000. (The most common amount was $6,000.) The actual arrearages computed from the final judgments were far lower—generally less than $400 (from $64.23 to $5,202.71), but even small amounts were hard to collect.

Because Daveiss's prosecutions against the collectors were initiated

[103] *American State Papers, Miscellaneous,* I, 285, lists 17 collectors for the Kentucky District. The list is not entirely accurate, because it omits some names that appeared frequently in the Order Books, and includes others who, if they served, were inactive or did not give evidence in prosecutions against the distillers.
[104] Miller to Morrison, June 28, 1798, Letters Sent, Revenue Office, M-414, roll 2.

during Jefferson's administration, it might seem that the administration ordered these charges filed for purely political reasons.[105] Most of the collectors had been appointed during the Washington and Adams administrations, usually upon the recommendation of Thomas Marshall, and most of them were probably Federalists. But a variety of evidence makes it doubtful that these Kentucky cases can be explained only on a partisan basis. First, it is unlikely that Daveiss would have cooperated so vigorously in prosecuting members of his own party, unless that was quid pro quo for enforcement against the distillers. Second, Kentucky jurors had a well-established history of resisting government pressures, and it is almost inconceivable that they would have found so many guilty verdicts if the evidence had not sustained the charges, even against the former collectors. But finally, there are masses of records among Treasury Department, Internal Revenue Service, and Post Office Department papers indicating that delinquency on the part of second-, third-, and fourth-level government appointees was very common during this period. Honest men who rendered their accounts promptly and completely were the exceptions; most were notoriously casual about handling public funds and government contracts.[106]

The suits against collectors and other officials and their sureties, like private cases, dragged on for years. Government cases ceased to be controversial, perhaps because any latent emotionalism was drowned in a sea of legal minutiae. The identity of the prosecutors became irrelevant as Daveiss was succeeded by Bibb, and he by Wickliffe. In

[105] Carl E. Prince, "The Passing of the Aristocracy: Jefferson's Removal of the Federalists, 1801-1805," *Journal of American History*, LVII (1970), 565-575.

[106] Similar conclusions about the prevalence of delinquency were reached by Leonard D. White in *The Jeffersonians* (New York, 1951), 163-182; and by Malcolm J. Rohrbough in *The Land Office Business* (New York, 1968), 271-302. For records in the National Archives reflecting widespread delinquency, see: Letters Sent by the Postmaster General, 1789-1836, M-601, rolls 1-11, Records of the Post Office Department, Record Group 28; Internal Revenue, Letters Sent, 1803-1819, General Records of the Department of the Treasury, Record Group 56; Internal Revenue Assessors, Duties on Household Goods, 1815-1816, *ibid.*; Internal Revenue Direct Tax, Correspondence, 1807-1829, file 11713, *ibid.*; Letters Sent by the Commissioner of the Revenue and the Revenue Office, 1792-1807, M-414, rolls 1-3, Records of the Internal Revenue Service, Record Group 58; Solicitor of the Treasury, Letters Sent, 1820-1830, file 12229, Records of the Solicitor of the Treasury, Record Group 206; Register of Suits Directed to be Instituted Against Sundry Persons [by the] Solicitor of the Treasury, 1791-1821, file 18182, I, *ibid.*; Return of Executions Which Have Been Received by the Marshal, Statement of Executions Issued on Judgments Rendered in Suits on Treasury Transcripts, 1821-1830, file 26889, *ibid.*; Solicitor of the Treasury, Attorneys' Returns, 1821-1830, II, List of Suits Decided and Pending in the Circuit Court of the United States for the District of Kentucky, file 34508, *ibid.*

1807, the suits against former officials (except, for some as yet unknown reason, postmasters) were, like the rest of the docket of the district court, transferred to the new Seventh Circuit Court where some action was noted at almost every term. But years passed before they reached judgment. For examples: *U.S. v. Evans* (a collector appointed in 1797) began in March 1800, and judgment for the plaintiff came in November 1811; *U.S. v. Jennings* began in July 1804, and reached judgment in November 1814; *U.S. v. Arthur* began in July 1803, and was still pending in November 1815. Other suits were still unfinished in the third decade of the nineteenth century. Unfortunately, there was no procedure for clearing the Treasury Department books of hopeless accounts, so they remained on the books while successive administrations persisted in trying to collect by going to executors or administrators of decedents' estates when necessary.[107]

While these government suits moved slowly through the circuit court, the private caseload of that court grew enormously and greatly overshadowed them in number. The district court, left with only the postmasters' cases, seemed moribund and often did not meet. In December 1814 the district court suddenly flickered into life again, and once more a rapidly increasing number of suits appeared on its docket. Its Order Books make it apparent that the passage of a dozen years had not changed the convictions of some Kentuckians about paying taxes on whiskey. When the War of 1812 required new amounts of money, old sources of revenue were revived, and once again it became necessary in Kentucky for the United States attorney to file informations against the errant to secure compliance with internal revenue laws.[108] While these criminal charges moved toward jury trials, the attorney for the district filed sixty-two civil suits for debt. These debt cases were brought to judgment much more quickly than those from the first series of tax laws, suggesting that the court had learned from

[107] White, *Jeffersonians*, 166.

[108] The applicable statutes were: an act requiring licenses for stills, July 24, 1813 (III Stat. 42); an act laying duties on distilled spirits, Dec. 21, 1814 (III Stat. 153); an act requiring licenses for retailers of wine and spiritous liquors, Aug. 2, 1813 (III Stat. 72). To judge from the records in the National Archives, it is likely that there were also evasions of the direct taxes imposed on land and improvements, dwelling houses, and slaves, July 22, 1813 (III Stat. 22); on refined sugar, July 24, 1813 (III Stat. 35); on carriages, July 24, 1813 (III Stat. 40); on gold and silver watches, Jan. 18, 1815 (III Stat. 186); and stamp duties on notes and bonds, Aug. 2, 1813 (III Stat. 77). The Kentucky District Court Order Books do not clearly indicate which taxes were not being paid. The final section of this Order Book contains the only seriously damaged pages of the 5,000 examined for this study, and parts of many of them are illegible. DC OB G, 358-416.

experience even if the population had not. When defendants did not appear at the next term, the attorney moved for default judgments, and juries immediately assessed the damages and costs.[109] Toward the end of the second term in which this strategy was used, defendants began to acknowledge their debts and thereby save themselves some of the costs.[110] Even with this more expeditious way of handling the government's suits, however, many of these cases were incomplete at the end of 1816.

To some extent, this examination of the disposition of internal revenue cases in Kentucky's federal courts distorts the picture of their work. They would have been busy courts if they had handled only private suits. In only four of the twenty-seven years studied were more government causes docketed than private ones. Yet it may have been the internal revenue cases that justified the existence of the lower federal courts in Kentucky. Their private caseload, which came under a jurisdiction concurrent with the states, might have heavily burdened the state courts. But because the federal judges carefully followed the decisions of the state courts (as required by section 34 of the Judiciary Act of 1789), the results would probably have been the same in either set of courts in Kentucky. Similar judgments also would probably have been reached had the criminal docket been in the state, rather than the federal courts, because petit jurors in state courts would have been equally opposed to convicting their neighbors of criminal charges for violating the internal revenue laws.

The ultimate enforcement of the revenue acts through civil procedures may have been the one part of the federal courts' caseload that made the federal courts in Kentucky essential. By the mid-1790s the Kentucky state court system was the object of considerable dispute. Among other things, the Court of Appeals decision in *Kenton* v. *McConnell* (1794), which stated that the findings of the Virginia Land Commission of 1779-1780 were reversible, cast doubt upon thousands of land titles in the state and brought severe criticism from many people who were part of the landholding and political establishment. It is doubtful whether the state courts before 1801 had sufficient prestige to have enforced the internal revenue laws effectively even in civil actions. (Thomas Todd joined the Court of Appeals bench in 1801, and it seems to have been more highly regarded after that.)

While the federal court had not lost prestige before 1795, it had not gained much influence, either. It is true that its inactivity until after

[109] DC OB G, May term, 1815, 373-387.
[110] *Ibid.*, Dec. 7, 1815, 413, 414.

the Treaties of San Lorenzo (with Spain) and Greenville (with Indians in the Northwest Territory) may have prevented overt rebellion against the federal government during a period when it seemed of little use to many Kentuckians. But ignoring the challenge posed by the internal revenue acts made the court an uncertain and unpredictable institution in the minds of the people. It had to resolve the problem of compliance if it was to have any weight in the community.

The arrival of William Clarke forced Innes to find acceptable ways of enforcing the public statutes. Not until 1799 did the outline clearly emerge. The most important element was the use of civil rather than criminal procedures: suing for the amount of the debt, rather than charging distillers with criminal acts for failing to enter their stills and pay taxes. Next, the court began requiring compliance by revenue officers and other government officials who had evaded or avoided the law. Morrison's charge in July 1799 that Clarke had failed to pay his taxes, and the jurors' finding at the same term that the Daniels brothers owed hundreds of dollars, marked the adoption of this policy. Paired with this strategy was the rejection of the selective enforcement policy against prominent Republicans that had been recommended by the Treasury Department. When jurors found for the defendant John Brown in November 1798, and for the defendant Trimble the following July—against the government in both instances—they were showing their repudiation of the Federalists' instructions. Finally, the people needed assurance that the protections of traditional due process would be available to them. When, also in July 1799, Innes ruled that duties were not collectable on stills that had not been entered, and accompanied his decision with an opinion full of references to English legal precedents, he furnished the security that had been needed.

That term marked the turning point. Effective mass enforcement would await the arrival of Joseph Hamilton Daveiss and the promise of repeal. But the court's assumption of responsibility dated from July 1799. The second Kentucky constitutional convention, which convened a week after the opening of the July court term, enhanced Innes's prestige when it accorded him positions of authority. And soon the entire caseload of his court showed a marked increase. Until that year the court had almost as little private as public business, as if Kentuckians withheld their personal litigation until they knew what the federal court would do about the public statutes. It is surely more than coincidence that the expansion of the private caseload accompanied the growth of the government's cases in 1799. Apparently this was the time the community and its leaders gained confidence in their federal

125

court, however repugnant they found some of the laws it was called upon to enforce. And from then on, it assumed an increasingly important role in Kentucky.

Inferior federal courts in other states may have been superfluous during the early years of the republic. But the federal courts in Kentucky justified their existence by their handling of the internal revenue cases. Judge Innes's carefully timed enforcement of the laws; his devotion to due process despite pressure from the government; his insistence upon equal justice; and his supervision of hundreds of cases against distillers made his courts a necessary part of the judicial system. While it took ten years to achieve compliance with the internal revenue laws in the federal courts, this probably never would have been accomplished in the state courts. And because the court successfully met the challenge of enforcing unpopular statutes, it became an institution that was both trusted and respected.

CHAPTER SIX

Criminal Charges in the Courts

J UDGE Innes's political judgment and judicial skill enabled the federal court to survive the challenges of the internal revenue acts with a notable degree of prestige and authority. He was equally competent in handling a wide variety of criminal charges that soon followed. In these cases, Innes, and later Todd, construed criminal statutes narrowly and the rights of defendants broadly, and paid the same scrupulous attention to traditional English standards of due process as they did in the rest of the docket. The criminal caseload was not large because neither judge believed that federal jurisdiction extended to common law crimes, but their management of the twenty-two other criminal charges brought in their court gives further evidence to support the court's general reputation for fairness.

The first criminal charges unrelated to the revenue or licensing acts were brought by Joseph Hamilton Daveiss. Two days after he took office he filed informations alleging violations of the 1797 stamp act, which had been designed to raise money to protect the nation from the threat of France.[1] The Adams stamp act was no more popular among Jeffersonians than the parliamentary stamp act had earlier been among the colonists.[2] It also encountered a remarkable amount of administrative bungling: failure to complete and distribute the dies for the stamps in time meant that the effective date of the law had to be postponed.[3] In Kentucky, the effort to enforce it reflected Daveiss's partisanship. He chose defendants by their political affiliation and brought charges against John Robinson and against Nathaniel Hart, brother of Henry Clay's father-in-law.[4]

[1] 1 Stat. 536.
[2] James Morton Smith, *Freedom's Fetters: The Alien and Sedition Laws and American Civil Liberties* (Ithaca, 1956), 260.
[3] Oliver Wolcott to Tench Coxe, July 13, 1798, Whiskey Rebellion Papers, Record Group 58, Records of the Internal Revenue Service, National Archives. (Hereafter cited as Whiskey Rebellion Papers, National Archives.)
[4] *U.S.* v. *Robinson*, District Court Order Book C, Nov. 18, 1801, 116. (Hereafter cited as DC OB.) *U.S.* v. *Hart*, *ibid.*, 117. Robinson may have been the "John Robison" described in an 1806 letter as an "acquaintance" of Henry Clay's. John Wood to Henry Clay, Oct. 9, 1806, James F. Hopkins and Mary W. M. Hargreaves, eds., *The Papers of Henry Clay*, I (Lexington, Ky., 1959), 244. Robinson was accused of having made a promissory note on unstamped paper in August 1798. Hart was charged with having antedated a note of July 1798 so that it purported to have been made before the statute went into effect.

This proved to be an ill-considered tactic by Daveiss, and might well have jeopardized the public support he needed to prosecute successfully the civil cases against distillers. For Hart—who had Henry Clay as his defense attorney—was indignant, and angrily threatened to bring suit for malicious prosecution.[5] At the trial next May, Innes instructed the jury that the evidence was insufficient to support the issue, and the government was nonsuited. The judge then ordered the informer, Walker Baylor, to pay Hart's costs.[6] Robinson's case went to trial in November, and after his jury found him innocent, he, too, recovered costs from his informer.[7]

These two cases were the only ones brought in Kentucky under the controversial legislation of the Adams administration. William Clarke had not dared to try to enforce the sedition act, but had he done so, it is highly unlikely that Innes and the other Republicans would have tolerated charges against fellow Jeffersonians. (The act had expired by the time Daveiss took office.) In contrast to others, this was one federal court whose judge did not harangue grand juries to search out critics of the government. On the contrary, Innes reminded them that they were to be "a strong barrier between the supreme power of the government and the citizen," and that their duty was to shield the people from "unjust persecutions."[8] Kentucky grand juries were neither apathetic nor apolitical; and given their choice, they preferred to use Federalist statutes against Federalists.

In 1802, a criminal case with more serious implications came to the attention of the court, involving the alleged murder of three Indians by three white men. Although relations between the settlers and the Indians had improved after the Treaty of Greenville in 1795, there were still occasional acts of aggression. The Indians had given up a large section of the southeastern part of the Northwest Territory in exchange for permanent possession of the rest, but the attitude of frontiersmen had not been changed by this cession any more than by earlier ones. Indians were still considered expendable by Anglo-Americans, particularly when they thought they would go unpunished.

[5] Nathaniel Hart to John Breckinridge, Nov. 19, 1801, Breckinridge Family Papers, Manuscript Division, Library of Congress, xx, 3513. Hart had recently won a suit against Walker Baylor, the informer, in the Kentucky Court of Appeals.
[6] DC OB C, May 17, 1802, 194.   [7] Ibid., Nov. 24, 1802, 385.
[8] Kentucky Gazette (Lexington), Dec. 1, 1800. Compare Richard D. Younger, The People's Panel: The Grand Jury in the United States, 1634-1941 (Providence, R.I., 1963), 50-54. The assumption that "it was the uniform practice of federal judges" to encourage prosecutions under the Sedition Act of 1798 is doubtless linked to the assumption that they were all Federalists, but Innes was not. Smith, Freedom's Fetters, 183.

In 1797, in what three years later became Indiana Territory, three white men had gained the confidence of three Delaware Indians by inviting them to go hunting. The white men were two brothers named Martin and John Williams and their friend John Crutchlow; the Indians were James and George Gillaway and the wife of one of them. The Williams party got the Indian men drunk enough to lure them into the woods one at a time and kill them. Then the woman was murdered with a tomahawk and her body thrown into the Ohio River with a stone around the neck.

The alleged murderers boasted freely of their deed to settlers in the area, who resented such provocation of peaceful Indians. These settlers reported that the dead Indians' property had been displayed by the Williams party and volunteered to testify against them. John Williams was awaiting trial, when, in 1802, he escaped from the Knox County jail in the Indiana Territory and fled to Kentucky with his brother and Crutchlow.[9]

The governor of the territory, William Henry Harrison, applied to Kentucky Governor James Garrard to deliver them up, but before the warrants were issued for their arrest, Martin Williams voluntarily surrendered to Judge Innes in Frankfort.[10] The judge granted Williams $2,000 bail for appearance at the November court and immediately informed Garrard. It is surprising that Innes granted bail to a murder suspect, but this was a quid pro quo for Williams's promise to surrender his brother.[11] Ten days later, the judge wrote to Harrison for a statement about the case and the names and addresses of witnesses, in order to serve subpoenas upon them.[12]

Judge Innes's assumption of jurisdiction, another peculiarity of this case, was based upon Martin Williams's surrender, which had been conditional upon the promise of trial in Kentucky.[13] Innes's initiative in the matter was not disputed by Harrison, at least partly because of the difficulty of getting witnesses to come to Vincennes. Still, Harrison wished the trial might be held there, "where it would have been easy

9 Clarence Edwin Carter, ed., *The Territorial Papers of the United States*, VII, *The Territory of Indiana 1800-1810* (Washington, D.C., 1939), 55n.

10 The surrender was evidently arranged through an attorney named Gilmore. Harry Innes to the secretary of war [Henry Dearborn], Oct. 14, 1802, Harry Innes Papers, Manuscript Division, Library of Congress, XXI, Pt. ii, 1-145.

11 *Ibid.*; Innes to the governor of Kentucky [James Garrard], July 12, 1802, *ibid.*, Pt. i, 1-137.

12 Innes to William Henry Harrison, July 22, 1802, *ibid.*, 1-138.

13 Innes to the secretary of war, Oct. 14, 1802, *ibid.*, Pt. ii, 1-145. Federal jurisdiction extended to murder committed within any place under the sole and exclusive jurisdiction of the United States. 1 Stat. 112.

for a number of the chiefs to attend to witness the fairness of the transaction."[14] As it was, he hoped to persuade one or two of the chiefs to go to Frankfort as observers.

Harrison was concerned about the chiefs because he was then under pressure from President Jefferson to get them to relinquish land along the Wabash River, even though the request for this cession was in direct violation of the Treaty of Greenville. Jefferson was convinced that the expected occupation of New Orleans by the French in accordance with the Treaty of Madrid (following the secret Treaty of Ildefonso) was "felt like a light breeze by the Indians."[15] The President believed that with the hope of French protection, the Indians "will immediately stiffen against cessions of land to us. We had better do at once what can now be done."[16]

It is possible, therefore, that the trial was planned as much to impress the Indians and facilitate further cessions as it was to bring the defendants to justice. Even if that was the case, and Innes was co-operating in what was a sham trial, he was careful to observe the technicalities of the law. He asked Harrison to forward the original affidavit of a key witness, because a *"Copy of the Affidavit* is insufficient evidence to act upon."[17] The judge assured the governor that when the affidavit was received, warrants would be issued to apprehend the other two suspects, if they had not surrendered by that time. Innes had no doubt that the warrants could be served, "as the Marshal can go in great privacy and take the *Posse* with him."[18] Furthermore, he told Harrison, "particular attention shall be paid to the selection of a Grand Jury[,] and if they find an Indictment against the Criminals[,] to that of the Petit Jury also, as upon these two bodies the conviction of the Criminal depends."[19]

Governor Harrison sent the necessary papers. When the other two suspects had not surrendered by the end of August, Judge Innes issued warrants against them and subpoenas for the witnesses. John Williams, one of the remaining suspects, was taken into custody and held at the Breckinridge County Court House. However, a mob gathered, overpowered the jailer, and let Williams escape. The federal marshal then summoned a guard of nine men, but as they were about to apprehend

[14] Harrison to Innes, Aug. 4, 1802, Innes Papers, Library of Congress, XXI, Pt. i, 1-139.
[15] The president [Thomas Jefferson] to Governor Harrison, Feb. 27, 1803, Carter, ed., *Territory of Indiana*, 92.
[16] *Ibid.*
[17] Innes to Harrison, July 22, 1802, Innes Papers, Library of Congress, XXI, Pt. i, 1-138.
[18] *Ibid.*   [19] *Ibid.*

Williams, he got away again, "in consequence of the vigilance of the people in the neighborhood."[20] As Daveiss later explained, the marshal "was so jeopardized that he has often assured me he would never dare summon a guard of any kind again unless ordered by the secretary [of war]."[21]

This flagrant violation of the authority of the court was a matter upon which Innes and Daveiss were in total agreement. The attorney wrote to Secretary of War Henry Dearborn to support the marshal's claim for payment for the posse and to seek instructions for prosecuting the leader of the mob. Daveiss was very uncomfortable about "the state of the country" and "the sensibility of the people in favor of a man who had *only killed an Indian*."[22]

Judge Innes, also, wrote to Dearborn and told him that obtaining an impartial trial would be difficult and expensive for the government.[23] The judge was willing to go to great lengths, however, because he felt strongly about "punishing flagrant violations of the laws of our country." He continued: "The Indians ought to be convinced that Treaties made with them Shall be held inviolate by punishing the transgressors and thereby prevent that horrid law of retalliation implanted in the breast of Savages from their earliest infancy."[24]

While the judge awaited his answer, the November term of court convened. The grand jury issued presentments against William Hardin, Sr., leader of the rescue mob at Breckinridge County Court House, and three of his accomplices.[25] Later in the month, when Hardin was brought into court in custody of the marshal, Hardin's attorney moved that he be "discharged, the offense presented being only a misdemeanor at common law and not cognizable by this court."[26] Unlike some federal judges of his generation, Innes did not extend federal jurisdiction to common law crimes, and agreed that the court did not have cognizance of the offense, so Hardin was discharged.[27]

[20] Joseph Hamilton Daveiss, "A View of the President's Conduct Concerning the Conspiracy of 1806," ed. Isaac Joslin Cox and Helen A. Swineford, *Quarterly Publication of the Historical and Philosophical Society of Ohio*, XII (1917), 146. Daveiss's memoir, first published in 1807, is hereafter cited as "View of the President's Conduct."

[21] *Ibid.*   [22] *Ibid.*

[23] Innes to the secretary of war, Oct. 14, 1802, Innes Papers, Library of Congress, XXI, Pt. ii, 1-145.

[24] *Ibid.*

[25] DC OB C, Nov. 16, 1802, 327. The sympathies of the mob may be surmised from the fact that Hardinsburg is the county seat of Breckinridge County.

[26] *Ibid.*, Nov. 29, 1802, 412.

[27] In Daveiss's memoirs, he wrote that he had received from General Dearborn instructions written by Attorney General Lincoln on prosecuting Hardin under the

Martin Williams also appeared at this term of the court. The charge against him was continued while his bail was raised to $5,600.[28] Three witnesses who appeared voluntarily were bailed for appearance at the next court for $500 each, and a fourth witness, brought into court in the custody of the marshal, was bailed for $1,000.[29]

The court records are uninformative about what happened next. They report only that on the first day of the March 1803 term, Martin Williams appeared as required. Daveiss made a motion of *nolle prosequi* (that he would not further prosecute) and Williams was discharged. Also dismissed were the four witnesses.[30]

The case may have been dropped because Innes and Daveiss believed that it would be impossible to get convictions even with carefully selected juries. The unusual procedure of bailing witnesses suggests that there was serious question as to whether they could be relied on to appear.[31] It is possible that the whole case was a smokescreen to

---

common law. Daveiss then reminded Dearborn "of the public heat his party had raised about *the common law*," and asked whether the proceedings should be continued. No reply had arrived when the court began, so Daveiss prepared the indictment but informed Judge Innes that he doubted the federal court had jurisdiction. Innes agreed, quashed the charge, and dismissed the defendant. Later, Daveiss received Dearborn's order forbidding him to proceed, on the ground that the offense was a common law matter. Daveiss, "View of the President's Conduct," 146. (Charles Warren referred to Daveiss's account in *The Supreme Court in United States History*, I [Boston, 1926], 435, but erroneously gave the date of the incident as 1807, the year that Daveiss's memoir was published, rather than 1802, as shown in the court records.) Yet I Stat. 112, sec. 23 defined as a federal crime the rescue of "any person who before conviction shall stand committed for any of the capital offenses aforesaid," which included murder on territory under the sole jurisdiction of the national government. Jefferson, although he incorrectly cited sec. 22, noted this provision in his "Observations on the force and obligation of the common law in the United States, on the occasion of Hardin's case, in Kentucky," H[enry] A[ugustine] Washington, ed., *The Writings of Thomas Jefferson*, IX (Washington, D.C., 1854), 485–489. This memorandum discussed the possible conflict between federal statute and state law in interpreting sec. 34 of the Judiciary Act of 1789, but did not include consideration of Article VI of the Constitution as a possible resolution. H. A. Washington dated the "Observations" Nov. 11, 1812, which was probably an error in transcription. The memorandum must have been written ten years earlier, when the case was in progress; Jefferson wrote to Dearborn about the matter at that time. Cf. the president to the secretary of war, Nov. 6, 1802, Carter, ed., *Territory of Indiana*, 75. The original copy of the memorandum printed in Washington's edition has since disappeared and not yet been found. Julian P. Boyd to the author, Jan. 29, 1974; Feb. 14, 1974.

[28] DC OB C, Nov. 15, 1802, 321; Nov. 16, 1802, 337; Nov. 17, 1802, 347.

[29] *Ibid.*, Nov. 16, 1802, 338; Nov. 29, 1802, 413.

[30] DC OB D, Mar. 14, 1803, 103.

[31] There may also have been some doubt about the credibility of the principal witness, Abraham Hiley, who had been brought into court in custody and bailed for $1,000. He was later accused of passing counterfeit money, and was convicted of murder in 1808. He was then sentenced to hang but was pardoned by Gov-

enable Governor Harrison to negotiate the new series of treaties with the Indians. Since this was Harrison's first major assignment as governor, he was particularly intent on accomplishing it. His initial problem was to persuade the chiefs to meet with him. They were understandably skeptical of the governor's intentions, because he was already seeking revision of the "permanent" Treaty of Greenville that had been concluded only seven years earlier. A successful prosecution of white men for killing Indians would certainly have been a useful device to assure the Indians of the good faith of the American government and thereby smooth the way for further cessions.

Harrison was successful with the treaties even though the Williams brothers and Crutchlow were not tried.[32] In September 1802, the governor reached preliminary agreement with the chiefs; at Vincennes in June 1803, the United States received 1,152,000 acres beyond the line established in 1795.[33] He concluded additional treaties with the Kaskaskia Indians in August 1803, and with the Delaware Indians in August 1804. It might be noted that Jefferson did not halt these proceedings, even though the purchase of Louisiana meant that the Americans no longer needed to worry about the French impeding the assimilation of the Indians, or stirring them up.[34]

While the Williams case had been pending in November 1802, the Kentucky District Court was presented with a different kind of criminal charge. The grand jury of that term issued presentments against Asa Combs, and Stephen, Robert, and Daniel Kennedy for having "uttered and published as true, false[,] forged and counterfeit notes of the Bank of the United States," totaling $70.[35] Asa Combs and Daniel Kennedy were brought into court in the custody of the marshal and bail was set at $2,000 for each of them.[36]

---

ernor Harrison. General Court of Indiana Territory, Order Book 1801-1810, 321, 339, 341-345; Francis S. Philbrick, "Law, Courts, and Litigation of Indiana Territory, 1800-1809," *Illinois Law Review*, xxiv (1929), 51.

[32] These suspects' names do not appear again in the Kentucky federal court records, and do not appear at all in the records of the Indiana territorial court.

[33] Dorothy Burne Goebel, *William Henry Harrison: A Political Biography* (Indianapolis, 1926), 84-105.

[34] Jefferson's program for assimilation (or removal, if the Indians resisted with violence) was described with remarkable candor in his letter to Governor Harrison, Feb. 27, 1803, Carter, ed., *Territory of Indiana*, 88-92.

[35] DC OB C, Nov. 16, 1802, 324-326. Forging or counterfeiting certificates, indents, or public securities of the United States was a federal crime punishable by death. i Stat. 112. It is possible that B.U.S. notes were considered public securities despite the fact that the bank was a private corporation (that included the government among its stockholders).

[36] *Ibid.*, Nov. 27, 1802, 409.

Combs was arraigned at the same term and pleaded not guilty. A petit jury acquitted him, and he was discharged.[37] Daniel Kennedy pleaded that he had been ordered to stand trial on the same charge before the Kentucky (state) district court in Lexington. Although Daveiss argued that the plea was insufficient in law to bar the United States from proceeding, Judge Innes ordered that the prosecution against Daniel Kennedy be quashed and that he be dismissed.[38] Writs of *capias ad respondendum* ordering the appearance of the other two defendants remained outstanding at the end of the term.

The charges against Stephen and Robert Kennedy were continued in March.[39] Writs of *alias capias ad respondendum* (reiterating the earlier order to appear) were issued at the next term in July.[40] In November, the charge against Robert Kennedy was abated by his death.[41] This notation was followed by an entry stating that Francis Pierpoint, who had confessed to shooting Robert Kennedy, since dead, was put under a recognizance bond of $1,000.[42] Although the Order Book specified that Pierpoint was under "A Charge of Murder," the bond was only half the amount required in the counterfeiting cases. There was no mention of witnesses, pleadings, or other evidence, nor that the court sought any. In April 1804, when Pierpoint reappeared as required, proceedings were discontinued and he was discharged.[43] Murder was a common law crime, and Pierpoint was probably tried in a state court. In fact, it was unusual for Judge Innes to take any official action at all in the matter.

The outstanding counterfeit charge against Stephen Kennedy was no more successful. An *alias capias* was issued against him at the November term and was followed by a *pluries capias* (still another order to appear) in April.[44] The charge was continued in July and in November, but Stephen Kennedy seems never to have responded. The prosecution was abated in March 1805 by his death.[45]

While the Williams case was ending, and the Kennedy cases were pending, the members of the March 1803 grand jury demonstrated

[37] *Ibid.*, Nov. 30, 1802, 416.
[38] *Ibid.*, Dec. 1, 1802, 427-432.
[39] DC OB D, Mar. 17, 1803, 108.
[40] *Ibid.*, July 4, 1803, 187.
[41] *Ibid.*, Nov. 7, 1803, 229.
[42] *Ibid.*, 305.
[43] DC OB E, Apr. 28, 1804, 85.
[44] DC OB D, Dec. 2, 1803, 461; Apr. 9, 1804, 468.
[45] DC OB E, Mar. 4, 1805, 363. The notations in the Order Books in April, July, and November 1804, and in March 1805, seem to be in error: the name Robert Kennedy is given, instead of Stephen Kennedy, despite the other notations of the former's death.

their political sympathies by attempting to use a Federalist statute against a Federalist. The applicable statute, passed four years earlier, made it a crime to carry on correspondence with a foreign government or to defeat measures of the government of the United States.[46] The law was presumably directed against Republicans (or others) who might interfere with the prowar designs of the Hamiltonian wing of the Federalist party, which were blocked when President Adams's envoys negotiated the Treaty of Morfontaine in 1800. Unlike the alien and sedition acts, the statute remained in force after the Jeffersonians came to power and provided a convenient vehicle for Kentucky Republicans to punish a political enemy.

On March 2, 1803, the Frankfort *Guardian of Freedom* published a letter under the pseudonym "A Western American" which was sharply critical of the alliance with France and of James Monroe, who was then on his way to Paris to negotiate what would become the Louisiana Purchase. The writer charged that Monroe was not to be trusted, and predicted that he would acquiesce in the recent withdrawal by Spain of the grant of deposit at New Orleans. This "Western American," like others before him, believed that the eastern states could not compete with the West and intended to keep the frontier economically and politically dependent, and he advocated secession from the Union and independence for Kentucky.

But there was a crucial difference between this writer and those impatient men who had made similar suggestions in 1794: he was a Federalist, and they had been Republicans. The political identification of most Kentuckians had not changed in the intervening nine years. In 1803 there was peace with the Indians, the excise was repealed, there seemed at last to be a reasonable prospect of obtaining New Orleans—and, most important of all, Jefferson was president and Monroe was *his* man. Under these circumstances, to advocate secession and to criticize the government seemed to many people to be seditious. Furthermore, it was against the law. A mob of indignant Kentuckians marched to the newspaper's office, demanded to know the identity of the letter writer, and burned him in effigy.[47] The federal grand jury promptly brought a presentment against the offender, Francis Flournoy, for "tending to excite a spirit of discord, discontent, or schism among our citizens," and asserted that his letter constituted "unlaw-

[46] 1 Stat. 313 (Jan. 30, 1799).
[47] William Elsey Connelley and E[llis] M[erton] Coulter, *History of Kentucky*, ed. Charles Kerr, 1 (Chicago, 1922), 431-435.

fully commencing a written correspondence, *indirectly*, with the French government."[48] A *capias ad respondendum* was issued to insure his appearance at the next term.

Both the Republican judge and the Federalist attorney for the district must have appreciated the ironies of the situation, but fortunately for Flournoy and freedom of the press they both refused to exploit this opportunity to exacerbate the political animosities of the state. Fortunately, also, the matter became moot within a month. In April the French unexpectedly offered to sell all of the Territory of Louisiana to the United States. There was no question in the minds of Kentuckians about the president's wisdom in accepting the offer. Protests by Spain were greeted in Kentucky by a determination to march on New Orleans, if necessary, to secure possession.[49] Flournoy and his letter soon seemed unimportant. The presentment was not mentioned in the Order Book for July; at the November term, it was dismissed on the motion of the United States attorney.[50]

During the first fifteen years of the court, only two criminal charges resulted in jury convictions, and no capital charges were tried. (The only distillers who had been found guilty of criminal charges by petit juries were John Mannen, who had used pistols to obstruct service of a warrant, and Elias Pleu.) Martin Williams and Francis Pierpoint had been released, one to go free, the other probably to be tried in a state court. Judge Innes did not expand his authority in criminal cases and was not eager to be a "hanging" judge. Indeed, the only known criticism he ever made of English legal processes was about the severity of punishments in capital cases.

In this regard, Innes thought that one of the great benefits of the Revolution was "the mild and rational Penal System now in force."[51] He contrasted the English system unfavorably, listing the ten acts that constituted treason and their maximum punishments (hanging, disemboweling, beheading, drawing and quartering, and burning). He thought that the limited and specific definition of treason in the United States was greatly superior, as were the prohibitions against forfeiture of estate and corruption of blood. "This distinction," he pointed out,

---

[48] DC OB D, Mar. 14, 1803, 94-102.

[49] Connelley and Coulter, *History of Kentucky*, I, 430.

[50] DC OB D, Dec. 2, 1803, 458. Daveiss's motion may well have been inspired by his political affiliation: he would certainly have been reluctant to prosecute another Federalist for criticizing the government. Flournoy's letter was republished in 1806 in an effort to discredit Daveiss for his partisanship. John Wood to Henry Clay, Oct. 9, 1806, Hopkins and Hargreaves, eds., *Clay Papers*, I, 244.

[51] Grand jury address, Innes Papers, Library of Congress, xviii, 2-123.

"confines the Offence wholly to the Culprit and does not extend to punish the innocent . . . neither does it heap up affliction upon the afflicted."[52] He also praised the protections that the constitutional amendments afforded to those accused of crimes: the rights to counsel, to witnesses, and to information of the charge. "They are the result of cool deliberation dictated by the principles of humanity, they are benefits which arise from a free Government founded on the Rights of Mankind."[53]

In a counterfeit case in 1804, a situation arose that tested Innes's principles. The July grand jury indicted Christopher Irvine and William Alcorn for counterfeiting and passing six notes of the Bank of the United States. (Four were $100 notes; two were $50 notes.) Alcorn, who apparently could not raise bail, was committed to the Franklin County jail. Irvine was put under a $10,000 bond to appear in September.[54] A special session of the court was held that month to try the cases. Irvine failed to appear, and the United States attorney moved for a writ of *scire facias* to compel the appearance of Irvine's sureties. Issuance of the writ was suspended by the judge until the next term of the court so that Irvine's sureties might produce him.[55]

Meanwhile, Alcorn was led to the bar in the custody of the marshal and pleaded not guilty. But after a three-day trial he was convicted by a petit jury.[56] In passing sentence, Judge Innes expressed his belief in the deterrent effect of "exemplary punishment."[57] Yet, he added, the prisoner was a poor man with a large family, and "to mult [mulct] you in a large sum would tend to injure your innocent family and would be unimportant toward increasing the funds of the Government."[58] Instead, he sentenced Alcorn to five years at hard labor in the state penitentiary, a punishment that would appear to work an even greater injury on his family than any monetary penalty.

Irvine's sureties produced him in November, and trial was set for the following March.[59] When he did not appear on the appointed day, the court declared him in default and issued writs of *scire facias* against his sureties.[60] Once again they produced him, and in July at a "Special

[52] *Ibid.*   [53] *Ibid.*

[54] DC OB E, July 3, 1804, 91-106; July 4, 1804, 122; July 9, 1804, 156. Irvine deposited $5,000; two sureties each deposited $2,500.

[55] *Ibid.*, Sept. 27, 1804, 220.   [56] *Ibid.*, 224.

[57] Draft of sentencing statement, Innes Papers, Library of Congress, XXVII, Pt. i, 8-54.

[58] *Ibid.* The draft indicates that Innes considered but rejected fines of "a small sum" and "the sum of $5."

[59] DC OB E, Nov. 5, 1804, 235; Nov. 7, 1804, 237; Nov. 8, 1804, 239.

[60] *Ibid.*, Mar. 18, 1805, 416.

District Court of the United States" held concurrently with the regular term, Irvine was tried.[61]

After four days of testimony, the judge announced that the government's evidence was "not the best legal testimony that might have been produced" and was insufficient to support and maintain the issue.[62] The case was not permitted to go to the jury, which was discharged after Daveiss entered a *nolle prosequi*. Over objections of his counsel, Irvine was committed to jail while the court considered a motion by Daveiss that he wished to prepare a new indictment. The next day Judge Innes ruled that another prosecution for the same offense was not sustainable in law after a *nolle prosequi* had been entered, and the defendant was discharged.[63] The following March, Irvine and his sureties were assessed costs: 12.40\frac{1}{10}$ for the writ of *scire facias*, and $15.61 for the cost of the prosecution.[64]

The Irvine trial was followed by the most famous of all criminal charges brought in the Kentucky federal courts during this period: Daveiss's abortive prosecution of Aaron Burr. The federal attorney had little love for any Republicans, and none at all for the man who had been vice-president during Jefferson's first term. Daveiss had adopted his middle name in honor of Alexander Hamilton, and he hated the man he considered Hamilton's murderer.

But more than memories were behind Daveiss's actions. Burr visited Kentucky in May 1805, and again in August, and his visits left in their wake a flurry of mysterious preparations and rumors. Burr and his associates advertised for large quantities of pork, flour, horses, cattle, and guns; contracted for boats; and recruited dozens of men for six months' unspecified service. Daveiss doubted both explanations of Burr's plans: either that he was planning a settlement in the Louisiana Purchase, or that he was hiring men to work on a proposed canal around the Falls of the Ohio who would be paid in lands that Burr claimed.[65] As an attorney who had clients indirectly involved with

[61] DC OB F, July 1, 1805, 47; July 2, 1805, 59; July 11, 1805, 109.

[62] *Ibid.*, July 15, 1805, 119.

[63] *Ibid.*, July 15, 1805, 119; July 16, 1805, 123.

[64] *Ibid.*, Mar. 10, 1806, 292.

[65] In 1795, Spanish Governor Carondelet had granted 1,200,000 acres along the Ouachita River to Felipe Neri, Baron de Bastrop, on condition of settlement. Settlement was never begun and a patent was never issued. It was against American policy to validate such claims when the territory was acquired in the Louisiana Purchase. The claim had passed through several hands before Burr, with borrowed money, purchased a portion of it, but it had not been registered with the territorial land office. Burr could not have failed to recognize how speculative a venture this was, and whether he intended to use the area as a staging ground or as a cover for other activities is uncertain. Thomas Perkins Abernethy, *The Burr Conspiracy* (New York, 1954), 22, 73-77.

the land in question, Daveiss knew how fragile Burr's claim was.[66] Daveiss also questioned the loyalty of Burr's friends in Kentucky, most of whom were Republicans, and some of whom had been identified with earlier episodes of the Spanish conspiracy.[67]

By January 1806, Daveiss was convinced that Burr planned to seize New Orleans, force the dismemberment of the West because of its dependence upon the mouth of the Mississippi, and with domestic manpower and foreign support conquer Mexico and establish a western empire with himself at its head. As Daveiss saw Burr's priorities, "Mexico was the first object, the Mississippi the second, and the Ohio the completion of the scheme."[68]

Daveiss soon decided that the president should know what was going on, and began a correspondence describing his suspicions about treason in high places.[69] When the president encouraged him to be specific, Daveiss named Judge Innes, Governor Harrison, Congressman John Fowler, General John Adair, Henry Clay, John Breckinridge, and General Wilkinson as persons who were involved.[70] To get more details, Daveiss traveled from his home at Yellow Banks (Owensboro) to St. Louis, and later to Louisville.[71] As the weeks passed into months, Daveiss wrote that a plot of major proportions, like the Cataline conspiracy, was afoot. But to his intense frustration, Jefferson did not reply from April until September.[72] When he did write, he assured Daveiss that his letters were being kept among private papers, instead of in official files. But the president was vague about any action that he or the government might take, and Daveiss was not assuaged. He did not know that Jefferson was sufficiently concerned to send John

[66] Bastrop became indebted in Kentucky to Charles P. S. Wante (among others), who was Daveiss's client, and transferred various land claims to him. Both Daveiss and Henry Clay were involved in complicated litigation arising from Bastrop's activities, and both doubted the value of his assignments. Henry Clay to William Taylor, Mar. 8, 1803, Hopkins and Hargreaves, eds., *Clay Papers*, I, 101, 110n. Although the judges had been divided on the issue, a suit involving one of these assignments was finally dismissed in 1810 on the ground that the federal court did not have jurisdiction. *Banks* v. *Bastrop*, Circuit Court Order Book B, Dec. 7, 1807, 45; *ibid.*, June 6, 1810, 365. (Hereafter cited as CC OB.) Justice Todd testified to the weakness of Burr's claim at the trial in Richmond. Abernethy, *Burr Conspiracy*, 257.

[67] Abernethy, *Burr Conspiracy*, 88, 94.

[68] Daveiss, "View of the President's Conduct, 98.

[69] The letters, written Jan. 10, Feb. 10, Mar. 5, Apr. 5, and Apr. 21, are described *ibid.*, 53-154.

[70] Jefferson to Daveiss, Feb. 15, 1806, Paul Leicester Ford, ed., *The Writings of Thomas Jefferson*, VIII (New York, 1897), 424; Daveiss, "View of the President's Conduct," 68.

[71] Abernethy, *Burr Conspiracy*, 91, 95.

[72] Jefferson to Daveiss, Sept. 12, 1806, Ford, ed., *Jefferson Writings*, VIII, 467.

Graham, secretary of the Territory of Orleans, from Washington through Kentucky with discretionary powers "to consult confidentially with the Governors and to arrest Burr if he made himself liable."[73] What Daveiss did know was that Burr was back again in Lexington, and there seemed substance to persistent rumors that in December, Burr's plan, whatever it was, would be set in motion.

In desperation, Daveiss determined to initiate legal action himself. When the federal court convened for its November term, he submitted a deposition charging that Burr had been and was now "engaged in preparing, and setting on foot, and in providing and preparing the means, for a military expedition and enterprise . . . making war upon the subjects of the King of Spain."[74]

The attorney moved that the court compel the appearance of Burr and other witnesses. Judge Innes proceeded cautiously, aware of the political implications of the case and of the requirements of due process. Later in the day the first in a series of hand-delivered notes was exchanged between the judge and the attorney.[75] The judge was concerned because he did not "know of any law which authorizes *the Court* to exercise a right of inquiry previous to a trial."[76] He reminded the attorney of the Fifth and Sixth Amendments, of the provisions for criminal charges in the Judiciary Act of 1789, and of the rules of the court regarding grand juries. He thought that the charge must be brought by someone other than Daveiss, "i.e., by some person having actual knowledge."

The "caution and circumspection" urged by Innes seemed to Daveiss to be mere legal quibbling. He argued that he thought probable cause was a sufficient reason for the court to act. Daveiss needed the compulsory processes of the court to insure the appearance of Burr and other witnesses and wanted to keep Burr in custody until they could attend. Innes remained unconvinced that this was proper, and in a second message he suggested that it would be false imprisonment to hold Burr until Daveiss's witnesses appeared. Innes concluded: "This . . . is a strong reason why there should be stronger evidence greater than suspition at the time of issuing a Warrant."[77] But Daveiss, while admitting that buying arms and engaging men were not in themselves

[73] Abernethy, *Burr Conspiracy*, 86.
[74] DC OB G, Nov. 8, 1806, 65-71; Daveiss, "View of the President's Conduct," 153.
[75] Daveiss's notes and Innes's drafts of his replies are in Innes Papers, Library of Congress, xviii, 2-76 to 2-81.
[76] Innes to Daveiss, Nov. 5, 1806, *ibid.*, 2-76.
[77] Innes to Daveiss, Nov. 6, 1806, *ibid.*, 2-79.

offenses, still persisted in asserting that doing either *"as a preparation for an expedition, is an offence."*[78]

Two days later the judge reached his decision and announced it by the unprecedented method of reading an opinion into the record in open court.[79] He repeated the questions raised by Daveiss in their private correspondence and restated his own answers. There were, he pointed out, only four kinds of proceedings available to bring suspects to trial: by application to a judge out of court, by preferring an indictment to a grand jury, by a presentment of a grand jury, and by filing an information.

Innes did not challenge the sincerity of Daveiss's desire to proceed by legal means, but a deposition based upon belief was not legal evidence. The awarding of process had to be predicated upon some act already done, thus giving the court cognizance of the subject and bringing the case before it in a legal posture. The heart of the judge's argument was that:

> The magnitude of this case, not only as it relates to the Community
> —but to the accused, requires that the proceedings be pursued with
> regularity, caution, and circumspection.—If the facts stated in the
> affidavit be true, the project ought to be prevented, and the offender
> punished—yet in doing this, the regular legal steps, pointed out by
> usage or by law, ought to be pursued. If on the other hand the
> accused be innocent, the strong arm of power ought to be confined
> within its proper limits. . . . And on no occasion but *extreme neces-
> sity* ought a Judge to be induced to exercise a power which rests
> on discretion. The law then becomes unknown, and the best Judge
> a Tyrant, because it then depends upon his whim and his caprice.
> It will not then be uniform, but is liable to change with the opinion
> of every Judge.[80]

Judge Innes concluded by reminding Daveiss that there were still two other methods of proceeding. He could apply to the judge out of court and obtain a warrant based upon legal evidence, or he could present evidence to a grand jury which could lead to an indictment.

According to contemporary accounts, Burr was in the courtroom to hear Innes's statement. The former vice-president addressed the court,

[78] Daveiss to Innes, Nov. 6, 1806, *ibid.*, 2-78.
[79] DC OB G, Nov. 8, 1806, 65-71. There are no other full opinions in the Order Books of the district court; those which have been quoted are found in the Innes Papers or in Innes's Opinions. Judge Innes, on this occasion, also instructed the clerk to copy Daveiss's deposition into the Order Book.
[80] *Ibid.*

complimented the judge, and criticized the attorney for interfering in private matters that were none of his business. Disclaiming any illegal activities, Burr said that he would welcome an opportunity to clear himself as soon as possible.[81] Daveiss then moved that the court take official cognizance of the matter, summon a grand jury, and grant subpoenas for witnesses. Judge Innes granted the motion and directed the marshal to summon a grand jury, "without delay."[82]

When the grand jury appeared on November 12, Daveiss announced that he could not prefer an indictment at that time because a key witness could not appear. The witness was Davis Floyd, a member of the Indiana territorial legislature, then in session. Daveiss believed Floyd to be Burr's "quarter master general in all these preparations."[83] While the attorney thought he could still prove "the design and intent," without Floyd he could not prove "the preparation of the means [which] was an indispensible part of the charge to be substantiated."[84] He had to ask that the grand jury be discharged.[85]

According to newspaper accounts, Burr was again in court and again made a public address.[86] He claimed to be disappointed that he had been unable to achieve vindication and asked the judge to have entered on the record the reason the grand jury had been discharged, which was done. Burr then said that although his private business affairs were pressing, he would wait for another opportunity to prove his innocence if Daveiss could get his case prepared reasonably soon. Burr seems to have been quite convincing and to have enjoyed considerable popular support. He had been able to engage two attorneys, one of whom was Henry Clay. But John Rowan, a friend of Daveiss and a Federalist recently elected to the House of Representatives, refused to serve.[87]

On November 25 Daveiss learned that Floyd was in Kentucky and

[81] Connelley and Coulter, *History of Kentucky*, i, 447.

[82] DC OB G, Nov. 8, 1806, 71.

[83] Daveiss to Madison, Nov. 16, 1806, quoted in Daveiss, "View of the President's Conduct," 99.

[84] *Ibid.*

[85] DC OB G, Nov. 12, 1806, 77. Daveiss was apparently correct about Floyd's involvement. He was tried and convicted of a misdemeanor in the Indiana territorial court, and indicted for treason in Richmond, because of his connection with Burr. In August 1807 he was elected clerk by the Indiana territorial legislature, an act that was protested at "a numerous and respectable meeting of the Citizens" of Knox County. "Proceedings of Knox County Meeting" [Jan. 8, 1808], Carter, ed., *Territory of Indiana*, 511-514. Floyd later became a state circuit court judge.

[86] Connelley and Coulter, *History of Kentucky*, i, 448.

[87] *Ibid.*, 449; Rowan to Daveiss, Apr. 18, 1807, Joseph Hamilton Daveiss and Samuel Daveiss Papers, Manuscript Dept., Filson Club, Louisville, Ky.

moved that another grand jury be empaneled. The motion was granted, and a second grand jury ordered for December 2. On the day it was called, the grand jury was sworn, retired, and returned to court. Its foreman announced that it had no presentments, and that the attorney had prepared no indictments.[88]

At this point, Henry Clay took the offensive. Having obtained a statement from Burr unequivocally professing his innocence, Clay protested Daveiss's tactics because they required his client "to be obliged perpetually to dance attendance upon such a charge in that court."[89] Clay particularly objected to the attorney's announced intention of examining witnesses before the grand jury, because there was no precedent for a public attorney to invade the sanctity of the jury room. (Clay was historically correct then, but the practice has since become common both in England and the United States.) His speech anticipated his later reputation as an orator:

> You have heard of the screws and tortures made use of in the dens of despotism, to extort confession; of the dark conclaves and caucuses, for the purpose of twisting some incoherent expression into evidence of guilt. Is not the project of the attorney for the United States, a similar object of terror? . . . I call upon him to produce a single instance where the public attorney has been accustomed to examine the witnesses before the grand jury; to sound the jurors and enter into all their secrets.[90]

Daveiss, playing for time, asked that the grand jury be adjourned until the next day when he would have an indictment prepared. He also moved for an attachment against General John Adair, a witness summoned but not yet present. Innes denied the motion on the ground that the summons had not specified the hour for appearance, but granted it the following day. (It was discontinued when Adair appeared on December 4.) Daveiss preferred an indictment against Adair to the grand jury, but it returned "Not a True Bill" on the charge.[91] Daveiss then preferred an indictment against Burr.

When the grand jury returned to court on December 5, it reported "Not a True Bill" on the charge against Burr. Like everyone else, the jurors knew the importance of their finding and took the unusual step of reading a statement into the Order Book of the court:

[88] DC OB G, Dec. 2, 1806, 230.
[89] *Western World* (Frankfort), Dec. 18, 1806, quoted in Hopkins and Hargreaves, eds., *Clay Papers*, I, 258.
[90] *Ibid.*, 259.
[91] DC OB G, Dec. 3, 1806, 243-261.

We have no hesitation in declaring that having carefully examined and scrutinized all the testimony that has come before us, as well on the charges against Aaron Burr, as those contained in the indictment preferred to us against John Adair, that there has been no testimony before us which does in the smallest degree criminate the conduct of either of those persons, nor can we from all the inquiries and investigations of the subject discover that anything improper or injurious to the interest of the Government of the United States or contrary to the laws thereof is designed or contemplated by either of them.[92]

No one in Kentucky was yet aware of Jefferson's proclamation of November 27, warning against participation in "a military expedition or enterprise against the dominions of Spain," and authorizing the pursuit of persons and the seizure of goods associated with it.[93] Burr's friends held a ball for him in Frankfort: his triumph seemed complete.

While the Republicans celebrated, the Federalists grumbled. Daveiss, especially, criticized the president, saying that his administration was only "milk and water, etc." and the comments were reported to Jefferson.[94] Whether the president was nettled more by Daveiss's criticism or by the fact that he appeared to have been right about Burr's guilt all along, the result for Daveiss was dismissal. For six years Jefferson had tolerated a Federalist as United States attorney in Kentucky, but in April, John Rowan wrote Daveiss to tell him that George Bibb had been appointed to the office.[95] Rowan commented bitterly: "so much for your opposition to Mr. Burr, or your previous vigilance in apprising the Executive of his project."[96] Daveiss considered leaving Kentucky for New York City, but was discouraged from that move by

[92] *Ibid.*, Dec. 5, 1806, 268.
[93] "Proclamation Against Burr's Plot," Ford, ed., *Jefferson Writings*, viii, 481. Albert J. Beveridge, in *The Life of John Marshall*, iii (Boston, 1919), 325, stated that news of the proclamation did not reach western Virginia until about Dec. 10. See also Edwin S. Corwin, *John Marshall and the Constitution* (New Haven, 1919), 38.
[94] Daveiss's remark was probably in more pejorative language. One account is that they were overheard by Philip Caldwell, who had been unfriendly toward Daveiss ever since he had won out in their common courtship of Nancy Marshall. Caldwell told Judge Innes, who wrote to Congressman Thomas Sandford, who in turn passed the letter on to the president. Daveiss, "View of the President's Conduct," 74; John Pope to Daveiss, June 15, 1807, Daveiss Papers, MS Dept., Filson Club.
[95] Bibb's recess appointment, dated Mar. 14, 1807, was confirmed Nov. 18, 1807. Thomas Speed, *History of the United States Courts in Kentucky* (Louisville, 1896), 6.
[96] Rowan to Daveiss, Apr. 18, 1807, Daveiss Papers, MS Dept., Filson Club.

Bushrod Washington who said there were already too many lawyers there.[97] So Daveiss consoled himself by writing his memoirs, detailing his side of the story.

In the end, time and events appear to have vindicated all the principals involved in the Burr affair in Kentucky no matter which side they were on. Judge Innes avoided a charge of arbitrariness and upheld the predictability and tradition of the law by his refusal to sacrifice due process. Henry Clay, although later embarrassed by his own gullibility, provided effective advocacy for his client and a classic warning against the misuse of the office of public attorney.[98] Daveiss was vindicated when Burr was charged with treason and tried in another federal court. Daveiss would also have felt justified by Thomas Todd's evaluation of the situation when he wrote to Innes during the Burr trial that "although it may be doubted whether *Treason* has been committed, no doubt seems to exist as to *Intention*, and that their plans were most diabolical."[99] Jefferson's restraint in the face of repeated warnings from Daveiss (and others) suggests that the president's subsequent moves against Burr, at least until the trial, were neither personal, malicious, vindictive, nor capricious.[100] Burr himself was exonerated by Chief Justice Marshall's strict interpretation of the constitutional definition of treason and the acquittal that followed.[101]

The Burr affair dominated the last term in which Judge Innes presided alone over Kentucky's federal court. In February 1807, a seventh seat was added to the Supreme Court, and Kentucky became part of the Seventh Circuit.[102] The circuit court jurisdiction previously exercised by the district court was transferred to the new circuit court for Kentucky, and the caseload of the district court abruptly diminished.

Grand juries and criminal charges were infrequent in the new circuit court. Judge Innes had long thought that the regular empaneling of grand juries was an unnecessary expense, but while he was the sole federal judge he had apparently been unwilling or unable to limit the discretionary authority enjoyed by the marshal under state law to summon grand jurors.[103] But after Todd joined him during the years 1807

[97] Bushrod Washington to Daveiss, July 6, 1807, *ibid.*
[98] Clay to Col. Thomas Hart, Feb. 1, 1807, Hopkins and Hargreaves, eds., *Clay Papers*, I, 273.
[99] Todd to Innes, Sept. 27, 1807, Innes Papers, Library of Congress, XVIII, 2-93.
[100] Cf. Charles Warren, *Supreme Court*, I, 301-315.
[101] Robert K. Faulkner, "John Marshall and the Burr Trial," *Journal of American History*, LIII (1966), 247-258.
[102] II Stat. 420.
[103] Innes to Breckinridge, Dec. 27, 1801, Breckinridge Family Papers, XXI, 3559.

to 1816, grand juries were convened only three times, when the federal attorney was prepared to prefer charges.

The first of these occasions came in May 1807, when Ephraim Hubbard was indicted on a charge that was never specified in the court's records.[104] Hubbard was able to outstall the writs issued by the court. The *capias ad respondendum* issued in May was followed by an *alias capias* in November, and then by a *pluries capias* a year later. Finally, in May 1809, the government's attorney moved that the prosecution be abated, apparently because of the death of the defendant.[105]

Meanwhile, in November 1808, Andrew Mitchell, a mail carrier, and Richard Berry were indicted by a grand jury for "breaking open and robbing the mail of the United States and feloniously taking therefrom [bank] notes . . . to the amount of $400."[106] Both of the accused pleaded not guilty, and were brought to trial a week later.

Mitchell was tried first. As the jury was adjourned from day to day, the jurymen were permitted to retire to a room in a private house, arranged by the marshal with the recorded consent of the defendant.[107] After six days of testimony, Mitchell was found guilty of unlawfully opening the mail, but not guilty of embezzling a letter or taking away the bank notes. His attorneys moved that judgment not be rendered against him because the jury had found him not guilty of "the gist of the issue," and because the indictment was faulty in three particulars. The judges agreed, and the defendant was discharged.[108]

The Berry trial followed immediately and proceeded similarly. It lasted even longer (nine days) during which the jury retired to a room in another private house with the recorded consent of the accused. But Berry's jury found him guilty. Sentencing was postponed until the next term of the court, and Berry was bailed for $8,000.[109]

The Innes Papers reveal that the postponement was granted in order to give Berry an opportunity to apply for a pardon. The judges, four of the jurymen, and "five hundred other persons" supported the request. Their petitions indicate that it was based on Berry's former reputation and, according to the judges' statements, a general belief that the evidence upon which Berry had been convicted had been "only presumptive" and circumstantial.[110] The day for sentencing ar-

[104] CC OB A, May 12, 1807, 41; Nov. 2, 1807, 48; CC OB B, Nov. 9, 1808, 135.
[105] *Ibid.*, May 2, 1809, 187.   [106] CC OB B, Nov. 7, 1808, 131.
[107] *Ibid.*, Nov. 15, 1808, 149.
[108] *Ibid.*, Nov. 21, 1808, 157; Nov. 29, 1808, 167.
[109] *Ibid.*, Nov. 23, 1808-Dec. 5, 1808, 160-172.
[110] Copies of the petitions are in Innes Papers, Library of Congress, xxi, Pt. ii, 1-227 to 1-230.

rived before the president's answer, and Berry was given two years at hard labor and costs. This was a mild sentence for the time, because robbery of the mail involving theft of bank notes usually brought the maximum penalty, ten years' imprisonment.[111] Berry evidently served some weeks of the term before news that the pardon had been granted reached Kentucky.[112]

The final criminal charge prosecuted during the period under discussion came at the last court held by Innes and Todd together. In November 1815, a grand jury indicted Dennis Brashear, an assistant postmaster, for feloniously concealing and embezzling a letter that contained a $50 bank note drawn on the Kentucky Insurance Company. Brashear surrendered himself and pleaded not guilty, and two days later his trial began. It lasted for three days, when the jury acquitted him, and he was discharged by the court.[113]

The paucity of government causes brought in the circuit court during these nine years contrasted vividly with the greater variety of cases and the greater number of suits prosecuted earlier in the district court. It is doubtful that the relative absence of such criminal charges in the circuit court was "a great proof of the Virtue of the Inhabitants of this Western District," as Judge Innes had confidently assumed a generation earlier.[114] It is more likely that the limited caseload resulted from the repeal of the internal revenue laws, the small number of actions defined by Congress as federal crimes, and the refusal of the federal judges in Kentucky to extend federal jurisdiction to common law crimes.

Yet if there were fewer criminal cases in the circuit court than there had been in the district court, the spirit in which they were processed remained the same. Judge Innes had set high standards during the years before 1807, and the pattern continued after Justice Todd came on the bench. Together, they compiled a notable record. In the Kentucky federal courts there were no convictions for political crimes. The independence of grand juries was maintained. Bail was regularly granted to the accused. The defendant was discharged when there

111 Cf. Leonard D. White, *The Federalists: A Study in Administrative History* (New York, 1948), 430; Leonard D. White, *The Jeffersonians: A Study in Administrative History, 1801-1829* (New York, 1951), 310. The crime had been considered so serious that the original penalty, provided in 1 Stat. 232 (1792), was death.
112 CC OB B, May 12, 1809, 211; Stephen Pleasanton to Innes, June 21, 1809, Innes Papers, Library of Congress, XXI, Pt. ii, 1-231.
113 CC OB D, Nov. 6, 1815, to Nov. 14, 1815, 262-283.
114 Draft of address to a grand jury, *ca.* 1784, Innes Papers, Library of Congress, XVIII, 2-25.

was a fatal variance in an indictment. The judges joined in petitioning for pardon when a conviction was based upon circumstantial evidence. The only obvious departure from English practice was the extension of criminal trials over many days, a practice that probably better protected the rights of defendants than did the briefer one- or two-day trials required in England during this period.

The government won a relatively low percentage of its criminal cases between 1789 and 1816 in Kentucky. This was not necessarily a result of the judges' adherence to due process, but a product of several factors. First, petit jurors simply refused to convict their neighbors who were accused of violating the internal revenue laws, because those violations were not seen as criminal actions. Second, a fairly high proportion of defendants died before their cases came to trial, because life expectancy was low and mortality rates were high in that generation. Third, Kentucky's location was important because the accused who did not wish to stand trial could easily disappear in the ubiquitous and expanding frontier country, and the government did not have the means to pursue them.

In one of the internal revenue cases, Judge Innes wrote that "penal laws are to be construed Strictly against the Citizen and favorably for him . . . [and] the same line of decision is to be observed in criminal prosecutions."[115] But it was not only the criminal provisions of the internal revenue laws that were interpreted narrowly, and not only the protections for accused distillers that were interpreted broadly. All persons accused of crimes in the Kentucky federal courts were protected by the safeguards that had been developed in England over the centuries, and were now incorporated in the American Constitution. From 1789 to 1816, the federal judges in Kentucky consciously and consistently upheld the standards that had distinguished the long history of the doctrine of due process of law.

[115] *U.S.* v. *Jones*, draft opinion, Innes Papers, Library of Congress, xxvii, Pt. i, 8-75.

CHAPTER SEVEN

Private Civil Suits in the Courts

THE caseload of the federal courts in Kentucky from 1789 to 1816 was divided into three approximately equal parts. In one-third of the cases, the United States was plaintiff or accuser; and because the federal government was responsible for enforcing federal internal revenue acts and federal criminal statutes, these cases are not unexpected. Another third of the cases involved disputes over land. This portion of the docket was predictably large because of the extensive litigation that resulted when settlement preceded survey and land grants were issued both by Virginia and by Kentucky. But the final third of the caseload, made up of other private civil suits, reflects a surprisingly prominent role for these federal courts. That so large a number of litigants chose to bring suit in them when their state courts had concurrent jurisdiction suggests that, at least in Kentucky, the lower federal courts were much more necessary and respected than has generally been assumed.

This private caseload comprised common law issues that came under federal jurisdiction because of the constitutional provision authorizing federal jurisdiction in controversies between citizens of different states. This "diversity jurisdiction" was granted to federal circuit courts by section 11 of the Judiciary Act of 1789. (As mentioned previously, the district court in Kentucky had circuit court jurisdiction until 1807, after which Kentucky had a circuit court similar to those of the seaboard states.) The bases of diversity of citizenship, however, are difficult to pinpoint in most of these cases. Surprisingly, the clerks of the court did not uniformly specify the residence of litigants in the Order Books, although seemingly less essential matters such as formal pleadings were included in the otherwise terse records. Diversity must be deduced from other internal evidence. For example, some of the litigants can be identified as merchants of other states or nations. In other cases, the final judgment awarded by the court often noted the relative value of currency issued by other states, which indicates that the contested obligations had been incurred between a Kentucky resident and a person who lived outside Kentucky. The circuit court cases that were included in the Complete Record always specified residence, and litigants in those suits were always citizens of different states, or foreign plaintiffs suing Kentuckians, or claimants to land granted by

149

different states. Judge Innes's written opinions, also, occasionally alluded to diversity factors. Finally, both Innes and Todd were keenly aware of the limited extent of federal judicial authority, and it is extremely unlikely that they would have heard cases that did not appear to come under their constitutional and statutory jurisdiction.

In the Kentucky federal courts between 1789 and 1816 there were 699 private suits, excluding injunctions and land cases.[1] Considering the variety of grievances that must have been sustained by the litigants, and the number of forms of action available in contemporaneous practice, it is perhaps surprising that only three forms of action were used extensively: case, covenant, and debt.[2] The total absence of assumpsit and trover, which were commonly used in that period, and the scarcity of trespass cases, suggests that the judges had unusual standards for categorizing. They seem to have viewed debt (and to a lesser extent, covenant) as a catch-all for all contract actions, and case as a catch-all for all tort actions (those involving injuries or civil wrongs). This aspect of the courts' practice marks a strange departure from the judges' general adherence to English precedents, and it is unexplainable on the basis of evidence currently available.

It is also sometimes difficult to know the correct form of action for a particular case because of inconsistent labeling. A suit might be called "Covenant" at one term of the court and "Debt" at another, yet in the end there was only one judgment.[3] (The single judgment distinguished these suits from others that were duplicated under different forms of action because of the limitations then imposed on the kinds of complaints that could properly be combined. In cases reflecting such limitations on joinder, the two actions ran a parallel course, and judgments were separately rendered for each, sometimes at different terms.) Probably some of the confusion about the forms of action was the result of errors made by the clerks when they transcribed their hastily written notes into the Order Books some time after the event. The inconsistency is significant principally because it explains why there cannot be absolute precision in the totals given for the forms of

[1] Land cases are discussed in Chapter Eight.
[2] These terms are defined in the glossary, Appendix E.
[3] For examples of actions labeled covenant at one term and debt at another, see *Warren* v. *Fuqua*, District Court Order Book E, Nov. 19, 1804, 285; District Court Order Book F, Mar. 21, 1805, 6 (hereafter cited as DC OB); and *Cock's Representatives* v. *Jouitt, ibid.*, July 14, 1806, 456; Circuit Court Order Book A, Nov. 19, 1807, 128. (Hereafter cited as CC OB.) For examples of suits labeled covenant at one term and case at another, see *Barksdale* v. *Carr*, DC OB B, June 18, 1800, 376; DC OB C, June 5, 1802, 307; *Taylor* v. *Edwards*, DC OB D, Mar. 22, 1803, 134; *ibid.*, July 12, 1803, 229.

action. But in the clerks' defense, it should be noted that often dozens of suits were heard in a single day, and hundreds in a single term.[4] Still, any quantifying is inevitably inexact when a particular suit was successively labeled "Debt," "Covenant," "Case," "Debt," "Covenant," "Debt,"—only to be dismissed after ten docketings, making it impossible to determine the proper action from an interpretation of the judgment.[5]

The problems of analyzing the Kentucky docket multiply when comparing it with other contemporary federal courts, because the validity of all statistical data is doubtful. None of the numerical totals given in any source can be confirmed by another. For example, in 1802 Secretary of State James Madison submitted a revised report on the number of suits instituted in the lower federal courts through June 1801, which stated that Kentucky had docketed 870 of the nation's 8,358 federal cases.[6] The accuracy of his report has been challenged on the ground that it was a political document that was designed to demonstrate that the inferior courts were superfluous by under-reporting the number of cases.[7] Although the figures reported for Kentucky were certified by Clerk Thomas Tunstall and supported by Judge Innes, they are far greater than the 587 cases recorded in the Order Books. Tunstall and Innes, of course, may have been inflating their totals in order to demonstrate the importance of their court and their work.[8] But notations in the Order Books allude to actions taken in the clerk's office, and it is likely that many cases were handled there, and never

[4] Notes made by the clerk from July 1799 through March 1801 illustrate how easily such confusion could occur. United States District Court, Memorandum Book of Thomas Tunstall, Manuscript Dept., Filson Club, Louisville, Ky.

[5] See *Finlay* v. *Pope*, DC OB C, Nov. 26, 1802, 399; DC OB D, Mar. 21, 1803, 129; *ibid.*, Mar. 26, 1803, 182; *ibid.*, July 9, 1803, 224; *ibid.*, Nov. 12, 1803, 360; DC OB E, July 3, 1804, 108; *ibid.*, Nov. 5, 1804, 228; *ibid.*, Mar. 7, 1805, 372; DC OB F, July 3, 1805, 65; *ibid.*, Mar. 8, 1806, 285; DC OB G, July 18, 1806, 500.

[6] A "List of Suits Decided and Depending in the Courts of the United States" was transmitted by Madison to President Jefferson, who submitted it to Congress Feb. 26, 1802. Walter Lowrie and Walter S. Franklin, eds., *American State Papers, Miscellaneous: Documents, Legislative and Executive of the Congress of the United States*, i (Washington, 1834), 319-325.

[7] Julius Goebel, Jr., *Antecedents and Beginnings to 1800*, in Paul A. Freund, ed., *The Oliver Wendell Holmes Devise History of the Supreme Court*, i (New York, 1971), 569-573. (Hereafter cited as *Antecedents and Beginnings*.)

[8] Lowrie and Franklin, eds., *American State Papers, Miscellaneous*, i, 320. Madison had earlier reported 200 fewer private suits instituted in Kentucky, 179 fewer decided, 21 fewer depending; 98 fewer government suits instituted, and 228 fewer decided. *Ibid.*, 325. Innes believed that the errors could be traced to the Federalists who opposed his handling of internal revenue cases. Harry Innes to John Breckinridge, Jan. 14, 1802, Breckinridge Family Papers, Manuscript Division, Library of Congress, xxi, 3611. See Chapter Five, n. 96.

151

were recorded on the docket. If that is true, the Kentucky federal courts had an even greater caseload than the present study, based upon the Order Books, can demonstrate.[9]

Differences in classification systems make it even more difficult to compare caseloads. A study of the Ohio federal courts in this era states that there were only 61 cases heard in that district court from 1803 to 1807, and only 267 cases in that circuit court from 1807 to 1820.[10] Obviously the number of cases was much smaller than in Kentucky, despite the fact that Ohio's population was growing so fast that it surpassed Kentucky's by 1820.[11] But most of the district court cases in Ohio are described simply as "actions for money," and the circuit court cases only as "involving titles to land." In the absence of more precise categories, it cannot now be known either whether the forms of action used in Ohio resembled those used in Kentucky, or to what degree the dockets resembled each other.

Similarly, a survey of all the lower federal courts from 1789 to 1801 lists only three states with a greater number of equity cases than was found in this study.[12] However, the common law cases quantified include suits in which the United States was a party—making impossible any comparison between the number of private suits in the caseloads.[13] Finally, none of the statistics presented agree either with Madison's report or with those of the Kentucky Order Books.[14] And other multi-court studies have inquired only into the origin of cases carried to the United States Supreme Court, which was a small proportion of the total number of lower court cases.[15] Still, the thrust of available data

[9] Cf. Lowrie and Franklin, eds., *American State Papers, Miscellaneous*, I, 320, with my Appendix A and Appendix C.

[10] Irwin S. Rhodes, "The History of the United States District Court for the Southern District of Ohio," *Cincinnati Law Review*, XXIV (1955), 1-17.

[11] *Historical Statistics of the United States* (Washington, D.C., 1961), 13.

[12] Dwight F. Henderson, *Courts for a New Nation* (Washington, D.C., 1971), 87, 119.

[13] *Ibid.*, 73, 116, 147.

[14] Nor do they agree with figures sent by Innes to Breckenridge, which are also at variance with the Order Books. The small number of cases in Tennessee reported *ibid.*, 112, 113, may have been due to the reputation of Judge McNairy. Innes believed that the business of the Tennessee District Courts would not grow "unless *Wisdom* could be added to the Court in this state." He said that at the fall term 1801, only 76 cases were heard in West Tennessee and 27 in East Tennessee, while 555 had been heard in Kentucky. (The Kentucky Order Books record only 283 cases.) Innes's version may have been related to his petition for an increase in salary. Innes to Breckenridge, Dec. 27, 1801, Breckenridge Family Papers, XXI, 3559.

[15] John P. Frank, "Historical Basis of the Federal Judicial System," *Law and Contemporary Problems*, XIII (1948), 3-28; Goebel, *Antecedents and Beginnings*, 802-813.

suggests that the Kentucky federal courts were among the busiest in the nation, even though they did not hear any of the admiralty or maritime cases that constituted an important component of federal jurisdiction in the seaboard states.[16]

In any event, the quantity of cases in the Kentucky federal court did not affect the conventional character of their disposition. Common law actions, especially, were handled in a manner consistent with English procedure as the judges understood it. Each form of action possessed its own distinctive pleadings and implementing writs. Default judgments were not uncommon, but when facts were in dispute there were trials by juries and assessment of damages by those juries. Sometimes litigation continued term after term until the requirements of proper notice had been observed and defendants given an opportunity to appear and present evidence. Even apparently simple cases at law were carried on the Order Books for years; in some instances, as long as the average suit in chancery dealing with land.

The court consistently maintained traditional standards of due process. For example, when depositions were scheduled, the adverse parties were carefully informed of the time and place and the commissioners who would preside.[17] In the early years, those chosen as commissioners were evidently known to the court, at least by reputation (as in the case of persons such as Andrew Jackson), or were officials whose office determined their suitability (such as the mayor of Philadelphia). As time went on, the naming of specific commissioners was occasionally superseded by designating "any Justice of the Peace" as commissioner, until this became the usual practice.

In addition, the court usually observed the limitations on jurisdiction imposed by the Constitution and the statutes. Judge Innes declined jurisdiction in a suit brought by one citizen of Great Britain against another because he could find nothing in the Constitution that granted jurisdiction to federal courts when both parties were aliens. He pointed out that the courts of the United States "are limited in their Jurisdiction by the Constitution and the laws of Congress [and] can exercise no Jurisdiction but what is specially given to them and cannot assume a Jurisdiction by construction."[18]

---

[16] Henderson, *Courts for a New Nation*, 88, 119, 147; Goebel, *Antecedents and Beginnings*, 596-607.

[17] Sec. 30 of the Judiciary Act of 1789 regarding depositions and notice is discussed in Chapter Four.

[18] *Bailiff* v. *Tippin* in [Harry Innes], "Cases in the Court of the United States for the District of Kentucky, from its first Organization to the year 1806 Inclusive," United States Court for the Western District of Kentucky, Louisville, 161-164

Innes was a Jeffersonian strict constructionist to the core, even in circumstances that were personally difficult for him. In 1806 his friend Thomas T. Davis was jailed in Mercer County and applied for a writ of *habeas corpus*. Davis claimed that his recent appointment as judge of Indiana Territory gave him the right to immunity from arrest in civil cases, but Judge Innes declined to issue the writ.[19] He observed that "no law can abridge a right which is given, nor can one be created by law which is not provided for in the Constitution." That document exempted only members of Congress from arrest under certain circumstances. Innes suggested that perhaps state judges could order Davis's release because they were not as constrained as federal judges. But he found "no Common Law powers under the Constitution and laws of the United States except such as are expressed in the laws relative to the judicial courts." He repeated that "the people of the United States of America, have formed a confederated government, have delegated certain powers to that government as expressed in the constitution and all rights claimed under it must be derived from it."[20]

Innes had an appreciation of the logic of the federal judicial system that is perhaps surprising for an Antifederalist who saw political issues from the perspective of Kentucky. For example, a defendant who pleaded *nil debet* (that he owed nothing) on a judgment obtained by his creditor in a Virginia state court was firmly rebuked. Judge Innes quoted the full faith and credit clause of the Constitution (Article iv, section 1) and the Judiciary Act of 1789, and stated that the Kentucky federal court would respect Virginia's court records and judicial proceedings. He also cited a case that had been decided similarly in

---

(1802). (Hereafter cited as Innes Opinions.) Two years later, however, the Supreme Court in *Mason et al.* v. *The Blaireau* (2 Cranch 240) ruled that federal courts would entertain suits where all parties were aliens if none of them objected.

[19] *Thompson* v. *Davis*, Innes Opinions, 465-470 (1806). Davis had been jailed for failure to comply with the judgment of the district court in Washington, D.C. in a suit for debt. Earlier, when Davis had been in Congress, he made inquiries for Judge Innes at the Treasury Department on the question of recovering entry fees on stills that had not been entered, and on complaints that may have been made by United States attorney for the Kentucky District, William Clarke. Davis also supported in Congress a proposal urged by Judge Innes for establishing a circuit court for Kentucky. Denial of the *habeas corpus* did not end their friendship; the two men corresponded while Davis was judge in Indiana. Thomas T. Davis to Charles Lee, Feb. 25, 1800, Harry Innes Papers, Manuscript Division, Library of Congress, xxvii, Pt. i, 8-3; Oliver Wolcott to Davis, Feb. 25, 1800, *ibid.*, xxi, Pt. i, 1-89; Davis to Harry Innes, Feb. 28, 1800, *ibid.*, xxvii, Pt. i, 8-2; Innes to Davis, July 20, 1807, *ibid.*, xxi, Pt. ii, 1-213.

[20] *Thompson* v. *Davis*, Innes Opinions, 465-570 (1806). Section 14 of the Judiciary Act of 1789 prohibited federal judges from issuing writs of *habeas corpus* when the prisoners were not in federal custody. 1 Stat. 73.

the Pennsylvania federal circuit court, asserting that if that case had not been so clear, or the judgment so "satisfactory," it would have been carried to the United States Supreme Court.[21]

This sensitivity to the requirements of federal jurisprudence led Innes to reach decisions consistent with contemporary Supreme Court cases, although he did not quote them. This is seen especially in debt cases. The large number docketed in the Kentucky federal courts suggests that many Kentuckians shared "an opinion which prevailed among a great number of the Citizens in Virginia that the Debts due to the British Subjects contracted before the war would never be collected by compulsory measures."[22] In July 1804 Innes curtly dismissed this argument as a "matter of opinion only," and upheld the validity of a British merchant's claim. If he knew of it, it is rather surprising that he did not cite the Supreme Court decision in *Ware* v. *Hylton* (1796), which would have reinforced his own.[23]

But in the collection of small debts owed to British merchants Innes may have extended the power of his court beyond its proper limits. In many of these cases, the court ignored section 11 of the Judiciary Act of 1789, setting $500 as the minimum "matter in dispute" required for circuit court jurisdiction.[24] To the extent that this jurisdictional minimum denied British creditors access to the federal courts, it con-

[21] *Freeland* v. *Lynch, ibid.,* 436-439 (1805). The Pennsylvania case was *Armstrong* v. *Carson's Executors,* 2 Dallas 302 (1794). Innes evidently studied Dallas's Circuit Court Reports; he cited *Maxwell's Lessee* v. *Levy,* 2 Dallas 381 in his draft opinion for *Jacobs* v. *Brown,* Innes Papers, Library of Congress, xxviii, 9-22. A receipt among his papers indicates that he bought the New York term reports, but no citations from them have been found. Statement of Account from J. and D. Maccoun, Lexington, Feb. 28, 1807, *ibid.,* xxi, Pt. ii, 1-205.

[22] *Lightfoot's Executor* v. *Cunningham and Co.,* Innes Opinions, 326-328 (1804).

[23] Innes may have considered *Ware* v. *Hylton,* 3 Dallas 199, a weak opinion because it struck down a 1777 Virginia statute that had been repealed in 1787, conditional upon the British relinquishing the western posts and paying for captured slaves. The British agreed to the former in Jay's Treaty (1794), but their failure to agree to the latter rankled with Virginians (and former Virginians in Kentucky). Nevertheless, the statement of the supremacy of federal treaties in *Ware* v. *Hylton* was relevant to Innes's case, and was the issue governing his assumption of jurisdiction in the small debt cases of British merchants described below. Innes received Volume 2 of Dallas's Reports where Supreme Court cases were included with Pennsylvania Circuit Court cases. It seems likely that Innes also received Volume 3, which was published in 1799. For the Virginia statutes, see William Waller Hening, *The Statutes at Large: Being a Collection of all the Laws of Virginia From the First Session of the Legislature, in the Year 1619* (New York, 1809-1823), ix, 337-380; *ibid.,* xii, 528.

[24] The district court jurisdiction, also held by the Kentucky court, was irrelevant because i Stat. 73 sec. 9 limited district courts to cases arising from admiralty and maritime jurisdiction, petty crimes, federal penalties and forfeitures, charges against consuls and vice-consuls, and alien tort actions.

155

flicted with the provision of the British treaty of 1783, reiterated in the treaty of 1794, that "Creditors . . . shall meet with no lawful impediment to the Recovery . . . of all bona fide Debts." The Constitution did not provide the answer to this problem, because Article vi granted equal supremacy to federal laws made in pursuance of it, and to treaties—a logical impossibility, as the question raised by these debt cases illustrates. Innes resolved the conflict by following the most recent enactment: the treaty of 1794. His decision was consistent with the principle, familiar to him in common law, that the most recent precedent governs.[25]

Innes's decision may also have been based upon his conviction that the intention of the framers of the judiciary act should always be taken into account. It is possible that he thought that Congress could not have intended to bar recovery of debts owed to foreign merchants, no matter how small they were, because the collection was required by treaty. "In considering a Statute," Judge Innes wrote in one opinion, "it is always necessary to keep in View the Intention of the Legislature as far as it can be ascertained."[26] On another occasion he referred to "the Spirit and Intention of the Law" as a standard of construction.[27] He usually advocated construing statutes narrowly, but he wrote that the "Intention of the Legislature is to be regarded in Cases of Ambiguity."[28] It is ironic that this Jeffersonian concern for the intention of the legislature may have led Judge Innes to a Federalist position on the supremacy of the federal government and its treaties where the debts due to the British were involved.

As a result of Innes's interpretation, many British merchants collected small amounts that in other federal jurisdictions probably were uncollectable. For examples, James Smith & Co. got judgment for $50.43 on a debt dating from 1772, and $11.33 on a debt dating from 1778.[29] Another British merchant, Peter Murdock, docketed more suits than any other single plaintiff in the court (with the exception of the

[25] Article vi states that "This Constitution, and the Laws of the United States which shall be made in Pursuance thereof; and all Treaties made, or which shall be made, under the Authority of the United States, shall be the supreme Law of the Land." It is conceivable, but less likely, that Innes thought that the statement of treaty supremacy plus the two treaties outweighed the statement of statutory supremacy and the single statute. In any event, choosing the most recent enactment is a principle followed also in modern legal practice.

[26] *Trimble* ads. *Estill*, Innes Opinions, 130-132 (1800).

[27] *Dickinson* v. *Few*, *ibid.*, 267-273 (1803).

[28] *Lynch* v. *Payne*, *ibid.*, 207-222 (1802).

[29] *James Smith & Co.* v. *Flowers*, DC OB B, Mar. 15, 1799, 64; *James Smith & Co.* v. *Devin*, *ibid.*, July 13, 1799, 123.

United States). Murdock brought thirty-seven actions in debt, all but two of which came to judgment during this period. The original debts in many of these cases were under $500, and the judgments were for far less. In twenty-five of these cases, judgments were between $100 and $499; ten others were under $100. One was only $15.39; another was $18.50. The calculation of interest in the judgments indicates that one of the debts dated back to 1769, and ten others were contracted between 1774 and 1777. Still, even with interest charges added, these cases did not approach the jurisdictional amount.[30] The smallness of some of these debts is particularly noteworthy when it is remembered that according to the usage of the period, the plaintiff sued for the total amount of debt, even when some payment had been made on it. As an illustration of this, one suit for $73.35, on which the defendant was allowed $62.82 credit for payments made, had a balance of only $10.53 in the judgment.[31]

Nor do the contemporary limitations on joinder explain the discrepancies between these debts and the jurisdictional amount. In modern practice, a creditor would group all debts of a single debtor in one suit, even when the debts had been contracted at different times. In the early Kentucky federal court, however, each debt required a separate suit. For example, in November 1803, Archibald and Alexander Henderson Co. (a British trading company) brought three suits for debts originating at different dates, against Isaac Murphey. Each suit involved $30.70, and judgments for these amounts went for the plaintiff. Even if the suits had been combined, the total of $92.10 falls far short of $500.[32]

The court also waived the statute of limitations on these cases, and it was not at all uncommon for a plaintiff to docket a suit twenty or thirty years after the debt had been contracted. In March 1800, a defendant pleaded that "lapse of time" barred the plaintiff's action. The court, however, overruled the plea, and it is clear that this was consistent with other rulings.[33]

But it is evident that waiving the jurisdictional amount was a policy pursued by Judge Innes only while he sat alone on the Kentucky federal bench. There were no judgments for such small amounts after

[30] See, for examples, *Peter Murdock and Co. v. Barbee*, DC OB E, July 9, 1804, 148; *Peter Murdock and Co. v. Arnold*, DC OB D, July 12, 1803, 231.
[31] *James Donald and Co. v. Montgomery*, DC OB A, Mar. 13, 1798, 188; *ibid.*, Mar. 14, 1798, 190.
[32] *Archibald and Alexander Henderson Co. v. Murphey*, DC OB D, Nov. 16, 1803, 378, 379.
[33] *James Smith and Co. v. Caldwell*, DC OB B, Mar. 28, 1800, 345.

157

Thomas Todd joined him upon the creation of the Seventh Circuit Court in 1807. After that date, also, the number of dismissals "for want of jurisdiction" jumped markedly and included some debt cases that had been on the docket for years.

Most of the law cases docketed in the Kentucky federal courts did not require careful interpretations of the Constitution, treaties, federal and state statutes, or legislative intent. The vast majority were handled so routinely that opinions were unnecessary. Innes wrote only three dozen full opinions for common law issues, but these, and others issued for other suits, are enough to illustrate the philosophy upon which the court based its decisions, even though they constitute a small proportion of the total. Unless title to land was involved, the opinions of of the Kentucky federal courts were much more likely to rest upon English legal scholars or reports than they were to depend upon contemporary American sources. There were, in any event, fewer of the latter than of the former. And although the Kentucky judges may have misconstrued English precedents and handed down individualized versions of English law, they did so within the framework of formal pleadings, ancient forms of action, traditional due process—and rigid discipline.

It was not accidental that the character of the proceedings was unbending and unchanging during the years Innes sat on the bench. He jealously guarded his right to govern his court as he believed proper, and considered that one of the important privileges he enjoyed when he was the only federal judge in Kentucky was that of promulgating the rules of procedure.[34] In civil as in criminal cases, he asserted his determination to regulate the practice in his court, "provided always that the said Rules and Regulations be not repugnant to the Laws of the United States." He explained that he doubted that even section 34 of the Judiciary Act of 1789 extended to "the mode and manner in which a suit should be commenced and prosecuted," because "the State law is the rule of decision in cases arising under them, but not the rule of Practice."[35] When Todd joined the bench in Kentucky in 1807, the character of the court was well established, and he showed no wish to change it. The formality of this character may be illustrated by examining the disposition of the private actions at law, according to categories.

The rarest of the common law actions unrelated to land was the venerable form of action of trespass, which charged the defendant

[34] *Thompson* v. *Davis*, Innes Opinions, 468 (1806).
[35] Draft opinion, Innes Papers, Library of Congress, xxvii, Pt. i, 8-52.

with committing an unlawful act directly injuring the plaintiff. It is surprising that trespass cases appeared at all, because they were much more likely to fall under state, rather than federal, jurisdiction. Assault and battery accompanied the charge in two of the five federal trespass cases. Although the pleadings were extensive and contained exaggerated rhetoric, they were unspecific except for naming litigants and dates, and do not explain why these cases were on the docket. (The plaintiffs were not, apparently, revenue agents.)

The first of the trespass cases was docketed in March 1799, and came to trial at the following July term, when the jury found that the plaintiff had sustained damages in the amount of $20. Like many of the debt cases, the amount in controversy was far below the jurisdictional amount specified by the Judiciary Act of 1789. Strangely enough, there were no more trespass cases until May 1812, when a second suit was initiated. Two more cases were brought in May 1814, and one in May 1815. (A study of the federal statutes does not indicate any changes in federal law that would account for the reemergence of this form of action.) One of the five was dismissed; the other four were accompanied by jury trials. Three of the judgments went for the plaintiffs, the remaining one for the defendant.

Another form of action at law which developed from trespass was trespass on the case. (This was sometimes referred to as "Action on the Case" in the Complete Record, and was noted simply as "In Case" in the Order Books.) This charged an indirect injury to the plaintiff by the defendant, which was usually the financial damage sustained when the defendant failed to pay for "goods, wares, and merchandise" sold and delivered by the plaintiff. In the stilted language of the Order Books, this was expressed as the "nonperformance of the assumpsit aforesaid." Because of the limitations on joinder, a suit in case was sometimes coupled with another suit brought simultaneously by the same plaintiff against the same defendant, either in covenant or in debt.[36] This duplication of suits in two forms of action indicated that the court was careful about maintaining the distinctions between the forms of action. (It also meant that the fees charged by the court would be doubled for the unsuccessful suitor.)

In case, also, there were judgments for amounts under the $500 jurisdictional amount before 1807. But at the November 1808 term, after Todd had joined the bench, litigants in one suit agreed that the amount in dispute was under $500, and the court dismissed the suit

[36] For example, see *Glassell* v. *Jones* (debt), DC OB C, June 20, 1800, 385; *Glassell* v. *Jones* (case), *ibid.*, June 20, 1800, 386; *ibid.*, June 23, 1800, 410.

on the ground that it did not have jurisdiction.[37] There were no suits under the jurisdictional amount after that. The judgments in this form of action were strikingly uniform: all but one of the forty-three actions in case that went to trial resulted in decisions for the plaintiffs.[38]

Another form of action was covenant, which dealt with matters that today would come under contract law. Covenant and debt were closely related because both were used to enforce agreements. Originally they were mutually exclusive: debt was used where a specific sum of money was involved, covenant where other forms of obligation had been breached. By the late eighteenth century, covenant had generally come to include a breach of a promise to pay a fixed sum of money, recorded in a document under seal. This development may account for some apparent confusion in the Kentucky federal court records, because two judgments were exactly like debt judgments, and may have been termed covenant in error.[39] In other instances, the defendant produced a surety, a procedure more commonly followed in debt.[40] Evidently Judge Innes narrowly interpreted the circumstances under which covenant cases could be brought.[41] This may explain why there were only 62 covenant cases during the period (compared with 510 debt cases), and why 27 percent were dismissed. Only one action in covenant (but none in case or trespass) was carried to the United States Supreme Court.

Detinue was another form of action historically related to debt. Detinue was employed when a plaintiff charged a defendant with wrongfully detaining movable property and refusing to return it, and there were six such cases in these court records. The movable properties in three of the cases were slaves; in one, slaves and horses; and in the remaining two, horses alone. The use of detinue in Kentucky marked a departure from contemporary English practice. In England, detinue disappeared long before it was forbidden in 1833, because it required wager of law as a method of proof. (Wager of law was an ancient procedure by which the defendant produced eleven neighbors who, as compurgators, swore that they believed him, and thereby denied the plaintiff's claim.) Wager of law was not used in America,

[37] *Porter* v. *Estill*, CC OB B, Dec. 10, 1808, 185.
[38] The exception was *Reed* v. *Estill*; CC OB B, May 23, 1811, 510.
[39] In *Winters* v. *Hall*, the defendant acknowledged owing $30.40, with interest since 1798, DC OB F, Mar. 9, 1806, 277. In *Russel* v. *Moore*, the judgment was $500, with interest from 1795, DC OB E, Mar. 11, 1805, 382.
[40] *Winters* v. *Barr*, DC OB A, Mar. 19, 1793, 34; *Meeker* v. *Edwards*, DC OB C, Nov. 23, 1801, 138; *Heugh* v. *Ralston*, DC OB F, July 8, 1806, 422.
[41] *Wilson* ads. *Heathcote & Dall*, Innes Papers, Library of Congress, xxi, Pt. i, 13-10.

and detinue in the Kentucky courts was handled like other common law issues, with petit juries to find the facts.

Another peculiarity of detinue contributing to its rarity was that the defendant could satisfy a judgment against him by choosing to keep the chattels and pay damages, or by choosing to return the chattels even though they were injured. These alternatives were so often unsatisfactory to the plaintiff that trover had generally superseded detinue elsewhere. (Trover is similar to modern "conversion": improperly converting the assets of another to one's own use.) But in the Kentucky federal courts there were no trover cases during the years under examination, and this in itself is a major and surprising difference from the practice of other American and English courts during the period.

Detinue cases were few in number, but two of them were among the most actively litigated suits in the court. These were brought by Samuel Willison, "next friend" (husband) of Rebecca Willison, against Jonathan Taylor and Jacob Spiers. (Married women could not sue in their own right.) The defendants had bought slaves from Mrs. Willison's father, from whom she had been estranged because of her marriage. Willison claimed that the slaves belonged to his wife because they were the children of a female slave who had been given to her by her grandmother a decade before the Revolution. The suits were initiated in November 1800, and were heard at least once at almost every term of the court for the next eleven years, while the parties presented an impressive amount of parole and written evidence. (These cases were similar to suits in chancery with their depositions, wills, accounts, valuations, and other pertinent records, and the evidence recorded in the Order Books revealed much more information than was usual in law cases.) There were five jury trials: jurors were withdrawn from the first three (indicating hung juries), and the fourth awarded the slaves to the plaintiff. The defendants then carried the case on a writ of error to the United States Supreme Court, which remanded it back to the Kentucky court on the ground that the judge had failed to instruct the jury that no gift of a slave was valid under Virginia law unless the deed was recorded.[42] (The Willisons had claimed that the record could not be produced because of the destruction accompanying the Revolutionary War.) With those instructions, a fifth jury in 1811 finally awarded the slaves to the defendants. The jury also awarded the defendants their costs, which were considerable.[43]

[42] *Willison* v. *Spiers*, 4 Cranch 398 (1808).
[43] Henry Clay was the Willisons' attorney. In 1820 he submitted a bill to her executor for $66.66⅔ for attorney's fees still owed him and $378.80 which he

Few common law issues continued so long or were so active; most were concluded within a few court terms. This was particularly true for debt cases. But the most significant fact about the debt cases was their volume: there were 510 actions for debt, more than 22 percent of the total of 2,290 cases in the courts. Collectively, these cases yield evidence about many related matters.

For example, it is clear that there was a great deal of risk in lending money. The form used for the promissory notes of the period reflected this by obligating the borrower for double the amount he borrowed. A typical note was worded: "I, John Doe, do promise to pay to Richard Roe $100.00 on or before the 4th day of May, 1794, to which payment I do bind myself, my Heirs, Executors, and Administrators in the Penal Sum of $200.00." (Even Judge Innes, whose reputation and financial stability must have been superior to those of many borrowers, had to sign such an agreement in a promissory note executed in 1776.)[44] This form also explains why judgments in debt cases were frequently halved in the Kentucky federal courts. Despite the language of the notes, the judges evidently believed that the borrower should pay only the actual amount of the debt (plus costs and damages, when these were awarded), and not the penal (double) amount, even though the defendant was legally bound for that. These judgments suggest that the federal court in Kentucky was not unsympathetic to debtors, at least during these early years.

The problems of collection are also illustrated by the frequency with which many different plaintiffs initiated separate suits against a single defendant at a particular term of the court. In such instances it was evident that the credit of the defendant had become doubtful, and all his creditors hurried to obtain judgments while there was still property upon which liens could be placed.[45]

Debt suits are notable, also, because as a group they were completed quickly. If the plaintiff waived a writ of inquiry (which called for jury trial), it was possible to conclude the case on the same day it was docketed. In the 41 cases for which writs of inquiry were waived,

had advanced for costs. Henry Clay to Eldred Simkins, June 20, 1820, James F. Hopkins and Mary W. M. Hargreaves, eds., *The Papers of Henry Clay*, II (Lexington, Ky., 1961), 871.

[44] The money was borrowed from Thomas Tunstall. Innes Papers, Manuscript Dept., Filson Club, Louisville, Ky.

[45] The only comparable grouping of cases in the records of these courts occurs in an opposite manner in ejectment cases. One plaintiff in ejectment often docketed several separate suits against various defendants at one time, in an attempt to remove all the allegedly illegal occupants of land to which he had a claim.

summary judgments for the plaintiffs were rendered immediately. When defendants acknowledged their debts, as they did in 114 cases, judgments usually came during the term at which the suit was initiated or at the succeeding term. Any debt suit was abated upon the death of the defendant, for an action of debt did not lie against heirs or devisees in Kentucky, in spite of the wording of the promissory notes and section 31 of the Judiciary Act of 1789.[46] (The executors or administrators of a deceased creditor could, however, sue his debtors.) Even defended debt cases rarely continued beyond a year or two, although one was carried on the docket for over twenty years, a circumstance that Judge Innes deplored in an opinion.[47] Debt cases involving partnerships were likely to continue longer than suits against individuals because of the requirement that each member of the partnership must be sued separately for the total amount of the debt.[48] The mere act of filing suits often brought immediate results: in 9 of the dismissed suits, the records report that agreement had been reached. The same reason probably accounted for the 31 cases that were discontinued on motion of the plaintiffs.

If the debtor chose to defend the charge, he could post bail for his appearance, or (as in the government's debt cases against distillers) he could produce another person who "came into Court and undertook for [the defendant] that if he shall be cast in the action aforesaid he shall satisfy and pay the condemnation of the Court or render his body to prison in discharge of the same or on failure thereof that he will do it for him."[49] Yet only one instance has been found where a surety was jailed upon the failure of the defendant.[50] And every one of these contested cases eventually went to a jury. But their findings show that despite the rhetorical protestations in the pleadings, defenses were almost invariably *pro forma*: of the 236 trials, only 5—2.1 percent—resulted in decisions for the defendants. In the others, the juries

[46] Section 31 stated: "That where any suit shall be depending in any court of the United States, and either of the parties shall die before final judgment, the executor or administrator of such deceased party who was plaintiff, petitioner, or defendant, in case the cause of action doth by law survive, shall have full power to prosecute or defend any such suit or action until final judgment."

[47] *Horner* v. *Singleton*, draft opinion, Innes Papers, Library of Congress, XXVII, Pt. i, 8-130.

[48] See *North and Haskins* v. *Pigman and Crow*, originally directed against Pigman in March 1805. Judgment against him was rendered in DC OB F, July 10, 1805, 107, and the case was then directed against Crow until it was discontinued in Oct. 1811.

[49] *LeClair* v. *Hambleton*, DC OB A, Dec. 16, 1794, 77. The formal pleading was always noted in debt cases, as described in Chapter Five.

[50] *Wilkins* v. *Ayers*, DC OB B, Nov. 18, 1800, 477.

included in their findings the amount of the debt, the damages (generally one cent), and the interest that had accrued. Then the judges declared when the debt might be discharged by a lesser amount. This was half the debt if the penal amount had been contracted, or whatever remained after deducting payments made on the principal. The judges also regularly added costs, which included fixed fees for the attorneys as well as for the court.

The overwhelming proportion of judgments for plaintiffs in debt cases suggests that judgment debtors, then as now, were usually what are colloquially referred to as deadbeats. And the amounts of money they owed was sometimes very large—well worth the expense and trouble of paying a lawyer and filing suit. Except for the small debts owed the British merchants, most cases were over the jurisdictional minimum of $500, and some were far in excess of that amount. For examples, *Watkins* v. *Wilson* involved a debt of $5,000; *Joynes* v. *Owen*, of $7,500; and *Wante* v. *Vanpradelles* was a suit for $24,000. All of these amounts were halved in the final judgments, but whether they were ever paid is not known.[51]

The judgments in many of these cases provide information about the relative value of contemporary currencies. Whenever juries found for the plaintiffs, especially during the first decade of the court, the judge frequently stated the amount owed in the currency of the state where the debt had been contracted, together with its equivalent in Virginia or Kentucky currency. Not until 1799 was the equivalent amount in United States dollars regularly given. It is clear from these records that federal currency did not entirely supplant state currencies, many of which were paper money, until some time after the adoption of the Constitution and the establishment of a federal currency. The fears of debtors that state currencies would be repudiated or worthless is shown to have been needless.[52]

Groundless too, at least in Kentucky, was the fear that the federal courts would favor out-of-state litigants in cases coming under diversity jurisdiction.[53] The disposition of the cases shows that if there

[51] DC OB E, Nov. 19, 1804, 283; CC OB C, May 9, 1814, 412; DC OB E, Nov. 27, 1804, 323.

[52] This was one of the reasons for opposition to the Constitution in North Carolina and other states, according to James R. Morrill, *The Practice and Politics of Fiat Finance: North Carolina in the Confederation, 1783-1789* (Chapel Hill, N.C., 1969), 96-99; and E. James Ferguson, *The Power of the Purse: A History of American Public Finance, 1776-1790* (Chapel Hill, N.C., 1961).

[53] Innes himself had feared this, as reported in Chapter Two. Charles Warren believed that favoritism was a consequence of the 1842 *Swift* v. *Tyson* decision, but because Innes and Todd followed state decisional law and state statutes (ex-

was any favoritism, it was toward plaintiffs—who were probably as often Kentuckians as non-Kentuckians. The statistics in Table 1 illustrate this conclusion: 74.6 percent of all decisions in law cases unrelated to the revenue acts or to land went for the plaintiffs. The figure climbs to 81.3 percent when one adds the cases discontinued on motion of the plaintiffs, presumably because the defendants settled out of court. And when cases did go to juries, they found for the plaintiffs 96.7 percent of the time, probably as a result of the judges' instructions. The court did quash, dismiss, and nonsuit plaintiffs in 13.7 percent of the total number of docketed law suits. But it must have become increasingly obvious to plaintiffs as time went on that if the court would accept their cases, if their lawyers handled them in the manner that the judges considered proper, if they themselves lived long enough, and especially if their causes went to trial, the chances were overwhelming that, sooner or later, they would gain the redress they sought.

The statistical data are summarized in Table 1.

TABLE 1

Disposition of Private Law Cases by Form of Action, 1789-1816

	Case	Covenant	Debt	Detinue	Trespass
Juries for plaintiff	42	16	231	3	3
Juries for defendant	1	0	5	3	1
Defendant acknowledged charge	15	7	114	0	0
Plaintiff's case discontinued	10	1	31	0	0
Summary judgment for plaintiff	0	0	41	0	0
Plaintiff nonsuited	2	3	8	0	0
Case quashed	0	0	6	0	0
Case abated	3	3	6	0	0
Case dismissed	24	17	35	0	1
Cases pending in 1816	19	15	33	0	0
	116	62	510	6	5

These statistics illustrate what was certainly one of the major reasons why plaintiffs in Kentucky chose to sue in the federal courts whenever

cept in *Green* v. *Biddle*, as reported in Chapter Eight), that had no precedents in Kentucky during this period. Charles Warren, "New Light on the History of the Federal Judiciary Act of 1789," *Harvard Law Review*, xxxvii (1923), 83-91. See also Charles Warren, *Supreme Court in United States History*, i (Boston, 1926), 633-651, and the discussion of Warren's misunderstanding about the reputation of the federal courts in Kentucky in Chapter One, n. 27.

they could, rather than in the state courts. They usually had a choice, of course, because most of the jurisdiction given the lower federal courts was concurrent with the state courts. The law was probably the same in both sets of courts in Kentucky, because both Judge Innes and Justice Todd scrupulously followed state decisional law, as required by section 34 of the Judiciary Act of 1789. The expense was also the same, because the judiciary acts required that federal courts follow the costs prescribed for the state courts. But it is doubtful whether any other courts could match the probabilities for success that the federal judges in Kentucky could provide to plaintiffs in law cases.

This examination of the private caseload of the Kentucky federal courts has shown that the large number of cases docketed cannot be explained on the basis of usurpation of suits that more properly belonged in state courts, nor on any evidence of a bias favoring non-residents. But the courts did have one other outstanding characteristic, in addition to their decisional support for plaintiffs, that probably distinguished them from their competitors and doubtless contributed to their reputation and popularity.

In the consistency of their procedures and in their notable devotion to the spirit and formalities of English legal tradition, the Kentucky federal courts must have seemed remarkable. There is abundant evidence that the courts operated in an atmosphere that rose above the primitive conditions of the frontier. From their very beginning, these courts were managed with confidence and certainty by judges who clearly believed in what they were doing. Their rigid adherence to traditional forms, which was especially noticeable in the common law cases, must have marked their courts as places of predictability and stability in an otherwise uncertain and changing world. The caseload demonstrates that at least in Kentucky, the lower federal courts were perceived as popular and necessary institutions even in the adjudication of private actions unrelated to land. This finding suggests that what actually happened in the early inferior federal courts, and what is believed to have happened, may be two quite different matters.

CHAPTER EIGHT

Land Cases in the Courts

THE excessive litigation over land in Kentucky has long made that state notorious, and has given it a reputation for contentiousness that early court records show was well deserved.[1] Almost half the private suits docketed in the federal courts from 1789 until 1816 dealt with land: 712 cases out of a total of 1,515. The frequency of these conflicts is reflected also in state court records, and early volumes of *Kentucky Reports* are dominated by decisions on competing land claims.

There are several reasons for this large number of lawsuits. From the very beginning, provisions regarding the distribution of the land were complicated, confusing, and sometimes contradictory. Survey rarely preceded settlement in Kentucky, and never in the period covered by this study. None of the early settlements was established on land that had previously been surveyed, a factor that led to infinite confusion.[2] Furthermore, the technology of surveying was very primitive, and the laws made demands of the surveyors that they could not fulfill. Finally, the system of registering surveys and entries was exceedingly inadequate and inefficient.

The earliest land claims in Kentucky derived from Virginia which, while still a colony, chartered land companies and issued individual land warrants. The land companies came first. Among the best known and most important of these was the Ohio Company, organized in 1747, which was granted 200,000 acres in the Ohio valley on both sides of the river. Although its success was limited by the harshness of life on the frontier and the hostility of the Indians, it was soon followed by similar ventures. Land hunger and speculative fever led to formation of the Mississippi Company headed by George Washington; the Loyal Company headed by Dr. Thomas Walker and John Lewis; and

---

[1] Humphrey Marshall, *History of Kentucky* (Frankfort, Ky., 1824), I, 150-153; Lewis N. Dembitz, *Kentucky Jurisprudence* (Louisville, Ky., 1890), 152-185; Charles Warren, *The Supreme Court in United States History*, I (Boston, 1926), 219, 636; Paul W. Gates, "Tenants of the Log Cabin," *Mississippi Valley Historical Review*, XLIX (1962), 3-9.

[2] The only part of Kentucky surveyed before entry or settlement was the Jackson Purchase, acquired from the Indians in 1818. Dembitz, *Kentucky Jurisprudence*, 165. The laws of both Virginia and Kentucky provided for entry before survey, as will be seen below. Lewis N. Dembitz, *A Treatise on Land Titles*, I (St. Paul, Minn., 1895), 68.

the Transylvania Company headed by Judge Richard Henderson. These companies obtained vast acreages in what was then western Virginia, and through propaganda encouraged penetration of the wilderness.

Most of the initial individual land claims derived from military warrants authorized by George III in a proclamation dated October 14, 1763, rewarding his subjects for services rendered in the French and Indian War. These military warrants, issued by royal governors, entitled former colonial officers of the British army to a specified quantity of land (from 50 to 5,000 acres, depending on rank) to be located "on the western waters."[3] Men who had served in colonial forces also applied for military warrants, but it was uncertain whether their claims for land had legal status equal to those of the royal army's veterans.[4] All these warrants would seem to have been in conflict with the more famous proclamation issued only one week earlier that reserved the land west of the Appalachian watershed for the Indians. But the conflict between the two proclamations was resolved in favor of Anglo-American settlement. The auditor general of North America issued an opinion in 1766 stating that the Proclamation of October 7, 1763 did not void prior land grants (including those of the companies), and the royal governors apparently extended his ruling to include grants issued after that date.

Land-hungry pioneers pushed across the mountains, following trails marked out by such men as Thomas Walker, Christopher Gist, and Daniel Boone. Others traveled down the Monongahela and Ohio Rivers, a route that was easier but more dangerous because of the exposure to Indians in the valley. The encounters were frequent and bloody, yet the Indians were forced to cede hunting rights in what would become Kentucky at the conclusion of Lord Dunmore's War in 1774. Later, as was typical, hunting rights were expanded by Anglo-American interpretation and actual settlement to mean total cession. The Indians, of course, did not agree to this expansion at their ex-

[3] The Royal Proclamation of Oct. 14, 1763 was repeated in *Gist* v. *Robinett*, the first land case docketed in the federal court, and in the pleadings of every successive chancery suit in which the claim derived from the proclamation. It may also be found in early compilations of Kentucky statutes. For example, District Court Order Book A, June 14, 1795, 83 (hereafter cited as DC OB); William Littell, *The Statute Law of Kentucky: With Notes, Praelections, and Observations on the Public Acts*, I (Frankfort, Ky., 1809), xiii.

[4] Thomas Perkins Abernethy, *Western Lands and the American Revolution* (New York, 1959), 84.

168

pense, and the tenacity with which they tried to resist the tide of new immigrants is well known.[5]

But land hunger proved stronger than fear of Indians, and by 1779 an estimated 20,000 people had settled in Kentucky. So many of these were quarreling among themselves over their claims to land that the state of Virginia was forced to make two major efforts to resolve the controversies. The first was the appointment of a land commission, whose members journeyed to Kentucky and reviewed more than 1,400 claims—an average of 17 a day. After six months they confirmed 1,328 of them (representing 5,415 square miles, approximately one-eighth the area of the state), declared their work completed and the conflicts resolved, and returned to Virginia.[6] Seldom has a public commission been more industrious, optimistic, or naive.

Virginia's second method to resolve the land controversies was to enact a lengthy and comprehensive land statute.[7] It specified four steps for securing title to a specific tract of land: obtaining a warrant, making an entry, surveying the land, and returning the survey and entry to the land office. When all of these steps had been properly completed, a patent to the land was to be issued. Unfortunately, this law also failed to resolve conflicts, and may actually have created more, because each of the steps created its own series of problems and led to further controversies. An analysis of each step illustrates some of these difficulties.

People who fell in any of several categories could apply to the governor and obtain a land warrant, specifying a particular number of acres to be located on the vacant and unappropriated lands of the commonwealth. The first group of people eligible were veterans, who could apply for military warrants. A second group were those who brought immigrants (excluding convicts) into the West, who could apply for warrants based upon "importation rights." A third group were actual settlers who built dwellings and cleared land, who could

---

[5] The federal court records a generation later frequently referred to deaths or injuries at the hands of Indians when litigants failed to appear. An example of Indian protest against the greediness of Kentucky settlers as late as 1793 is found in "Speeches of John Baptist de Coigne, Chief of the Wabash and Illinois Indians, and Other Indian Chiefs," Saul K. Padover, arr., *The Complete Jefferson* (Freeport, N.Y., 1969 [orig. publ. 1943]), 452.

[6] Samuel M. Wilson, *The First Land Court of Kentucky 1779-1780* (Lexington, Ky., 1923), 43-67.

[7] William Waller Hening, *The Statutes at Large; Being a Collection of all the Laws of Virginia from the First Session of the Legislature, in the Year 1619*, x (New York, 1823), 35-65; Littell, *Statute Law of Kentucky*, I, 392-464.

apply for "preemption" warrants. (Those who had built a dwelling and raised a crop before 1778 could claim up to 1,400 acres.) After 1781, poor people could obtain a warrant on credit. Anyone who did not fall into any of the preceding categories could buy a treasury warrant upon payment of forty pounds for each 100 acres.[8]

The law gave first priority to those who had settled in Kentucky before 1778, and second priority to military warrants.[9] Treasury warrants were objects of wild speculation and limited applicability. For examples, the Henderson grant was barred to settlement other than that arranged through the Transylvania Company; and the land between the Green River, the Ohio River, and the Tennessee River was set aside for military warrants.

It was not difficult to obtain warrants. They were issued with extravagant generosity and with complete disregard for the total number of acres involved. The process begun by royal governors was continued by state governors after the Revolution. (Military warrants were given to veterans of the Virginia and Continental armies, authorizing entries in amounts of land ranging from 100 to 5,000 acres, depending on rank.) Other kinds of warrants were also freely issued. It seems clear that the governors of late eighteenth-century Virginia viewed the West as an area of unlimited expanse, and no one ever bothered to add up the total amount of land specified in the warrants. It is quite likely that the total acreage of the land warrants greatly exceeded the entire area of Kentucky.[10] And it is certain that the acreage of the warrants exceeded the amount of good land in particularly desirable locations. Therefore, even the first step required by the 1779 law carried with it great problems for the future.

[8] St. George Tucker estimated that £40 in Virginia currency was the equivalent of $2 in United States currency. This meant that Virginia lands sold for "the hundredth part of the price at which the lands belonging to the United States" (on the opposite side of the Ohio River) were sold. If his estimate was accurate, the bargain price itself contributed to speculation. St. George Tucker, ed., *Blackstone's Commentaries: With Notes of Reference, to the Constitution and Laws, of the Federal Government of the United States; and of the Commonwealth of Virginia,* II (Philadelphia, 1803), app. D, 68. Preemption warrants for 1,400 acres cost even less, for although the first 400 acres cost $2.25 an acre, the additional 1,000 acres cost only $40.

[9] Abernethy, *Western Lands,* 224, 251; Patricia Watlington, *The Partisan Spirit: Kentucky Politics, 1779-1792* (New York, 1972), 18.

[10] Gates, in "Tenants of the Log Cabin," *MVHR,* XLIX (1962), 4, quotes George M. Bibb as having said that thousands more land warrants had been issued by Virginia than there was land available. Virginia and Kentucky eventually issued a total of 143,228 different land grants. Willard Rouse Jillson, *The Kentucky Land Grants* (Louisville, Ky., 1925), 12.

The second step also held hazards. The holder of the warrant (or his agent) selected the land he wanted and made an entry with the surveyor of the county in which the land lay, stating the number of acres allotted in the warrant and contained in the tract, and describing "as near as may be the particular location." This entry was to be based upon "proper allusions to known objects, which shall serve as indices to the particular tract of land," and the description was supposed to be clear enough to apply "certainly to one identical tract, and not uncertainly to two or divers."[11]

These allusions, or calls, led to the development of the doctrine of notoriety, which stated that the reference points had to be ones that were generally recognized—and recognizable—by other persons besides the claimant who were in the vicinity at the approximate time of the entry. In other words, if the entry described a grove of cherry trees, a fordable place in a creek, a certain cabin, or a neighbor's property line (and any entry might contain at least this many calls), all of these must have been generally known in the neighborhood by these designations, in their stated relative positions, at the time of the entry. For such an entry to hold up in court, there could be no other similar grove of cherry trees near the site, no other such fordable place in the creek, no other cabin, no other property line with which the allusions might be confused. Furthermore, whenever the entry was challenged (and this might occur many years later), it was necessary to produce persons who could verify the notoriety of the calls at the time of the entry. Given the dispersal and the mobility of people in this era, and the mortality rates of the period, locating witnesses and obtaining depositions could be as formidable a task as any other step in the complicated process. But even when such witnesses were found, their testimony was often challenged. Much of the material contained in depositions gathered for cases in chancery arising in the Kentucky federal courts dealt with the alleged and challenged notoriety of features described in entries. Especially before 1807, advisory juries were commonly used in the federal courts to determine the facts relating to notoriety. This use of juries was a practice recognized by the Supreme Court, and accepted by it as a useful procedure in the Kentucky courts' attempts to settle the controversies.[12]

[11] George M. Bibb, *Reports of Cases at Common Law and in Chancery Argued and Decided in the Court of Appeals of the Commonwealth of Kentucky*, I (Frankfort, Ky., 1840), 16. (IV *Kentucky Reports*.)

[12] *Marshall* v. *Currie*, 4 Cranch 172 (1807). Reasons for using advisory juries in these cases are discussed below.

After an entry had been presented to the county surveyor, a potential landowner was at the mercy of that officer, his deputies, and the nearly impossible colonial (and, later, state) laws. For example, a Virginia act of 1772, which remained in force after independence, required surveyors "to return all their new surveys and protract and lay down their plats by the true and not by the artificial or magnetic meridians."[13] Since the available instruments registered the magnetic meridian, surveyors needed either training in astronomy or accurate information regarding the degree of variation of the needle from the true meridian to correct their measurements, in order to comply with the law. Such information about variations was published from time to time in newspapers by persons with astronomical instruments in the East, but a considerable sophistication in mathematics was needed to convert this data for use in the West.[14] Furthermore, the passage of time was an additional variable, especially when a later survey rested upon an earlier one, and the facts of the older survey had to be established.

Unlike Virginia, Kentucky did not require examinations or particular qualifications for surveyors, and this had a devastating effect upon the accuracy of their surveys. One of the first statutes passed in the new state specified "that no previous examination shall be necessary to authorize the governor and senate to make the appointments of surveyors."[15] With some important exceptions, most of the land in the state was surveyed by Kentucky-appointed men, because surveying was such a dangerous occupation before 1794. (It was not until the Battle of Fallen Timbers that surveyors could move throughout the state without fear of Indian attack in unsettled areas.) Furthermore, the Kentucky surveyors were not only likely to be untrained or poorly prepared, they also were political appointees, a factor that doubtless had its effect upon their work. Any surveyor who wished to keep his job was tempted to turn in surveys beneficial to those responsible for his appointment. There was little turnover for any reasons other than

[13] Littell, *Statute Law of Kentucky*, i, 389.

[14] Even educated surveyors could make serious errors. In Kentucky the best known is the southern boundary of the state, which was supposed to be at 36°30' from near Abingdon, Virginia, west to the Tennessee River. The line was run in 1779 and 1780 by a party headed by Dr. Walker and Colonel Henderson, who were probably more sophisticated than most surveyors of the period. Nevertheless, the boundary was marked from six to ten miles north of the intended latitude. Jillson, *Kentucky Land Grants*, 11.

[15] Cf. this provision of the 1792 Kentucky statute with that of the 1779 Virginia law requiring surveyors to be licensed by the College of William and Mary. Littell, *Statute Law of Kentucky*, i, 62, 409.

political ones, for surveyors held office during good behavior.[16] Theirs was a very lucrative position, because they collected fees regardless of the inaccuracy of their work, and the more surveys needed, the more money was made. It was also a profitable occupation because of the opportunities provided for staking out good land unclaimed, or poorly defended, by others. Colonel Thomas Marshall and Humphrey Marshall, for example, are believed to have made their fortunes by taking advantage of information acquired through their work as surveyors.[17]

And most of the assignments were not uncomplicated. The early surveys often rested upon natural landmarks (such as rivers, salt licks, springs, or hills), and the quantity of land was computed from these calls. Any shift in the surface might make computation inaccurate, any impenetrable area might make staking off impossible. When cabins were built, previous surveys might be rendered obsolete. A survey that included a cabin was required to be in a square, with lines due north and south, including the cabin at the intersection of the diagonals. Quantity was then computed from that reference point. The possibilities for conflicts in surveys were seemingly endless. Yet all these conflicts had to be resolved by the courts, working from crude drawings submitted by surveyors and the testimony of witnesses regarding notoriety of calls. The federal court records were filled with orders for surveys and resurveys, some of which were accompanied by instructions that were later changed and required another series of surveys. Such orders, of course, postponed judgment, and land cases involving surveys were continued on the dockets for years.

The primitive technology of surveying, the lack of professionalism of the surveyors, inadequate information about the sites, and inapplicable instructions by the court all added up to incredible confusion. It is not surprising that a legal scholar who was knowledgeable both about Kentucky jurisprudence and American land laws commented that "the Kentucky surveyors, unless by accident, were never correct in their bearings," and thus this third step in gaining title was regarded as a major hurdle for the wary and unwary alike.[18]

Because the fourth step required that the entry and the survey be returned in time to the land office, almost as much depended upon the

[16] *Ibid.,* 61.

[17] Similarly, Joseph Hamilton Daveiss's extensive patents in what later became Daviess County and in adjacent areas were based upon a caveat initiated by surveyor John Handley who, because of his professional position, knew of defects in a previous survey. *Wilson* v. *Mason,* 1 Cranch 45 (1801).

[18] Dembitz, *Kentucky Jurisprudence,* 171.

surveyor's sense of responsibility as upon his competence. The 1779 Virginia statute required that surveys be made, marked upon the ground, and the plat and notes returned to the land office within twelve months after entry. This time limit was the usual standard in Kentucky, although statutes providing extensions (especially for persons under disability, such as infants, captives, those of unsound mind, and married women) were passed as late as 1811. The applicability of such an extension had to be proved if claimed; otherwise, the twelve months standard prevailed. If, therefore, the surveyor neglected to make the survey in time, or marked it inadequately, or failed to return the plats and notes within the applicable time limit, the entry was lost—through no fault of the claimant.

Requiring the return of the plats and notes to the land office was intended to prevent multiple or overlapping claims, but in fact it did not do so because there was no accurate or adequate map of all of Kentucky upon which surveys could be marked. The hand-drawn maps were descriptive but not exclusive, and it was entirely possible for the same tract to be entered and surveyed by two or more claimants who knew nothing of each other. An advisory jury reported to the court in 1804 "that more than one entry and survey has been made on almost all the good land in the State of Kentucky."[19] Furthermore, all the claimants might hold evidence of completion of the fourth step: the issuance of the patent upon return of the entry and survey. As a result, although legally "a patent issued under the Great Seal of the Commonwealth imports absolute verity," patents actually were issued with an astonishing disregard for previous or rival entries and surveys, and often to several different people for the same land.[20]

By 1814, Henry Clay complained that "our lands in Kentucky are frequently covered by two or three or more original patents granted by the State."[21] This shingling characteristic was still a problem as late as 1890, when Lewis N. Dembitz wrote:

Little if any vacant land is left in Kentucky; much has been patented more than once, and more than twice. There is no check by regular subdivision, and neither the county surveyor nor the Register of the Land Office can know officially whether land of which the survey or grant is asked has not been patented before. Many

19 DC OB E, Nov. 29, 1804, 334.
20 Dembitz, *Kentucky Jurisprudence*, 175.
21 Henry Clay to William H. Crawford, May 10, 1814, James F. Hopkins and Mary W. M. Hargreaves, eds., *The Papers of Henry Clay*, ɪ (Lexington, Ky., 1959), 898.

174

patents have been taken out only to give color of title, so as to carry the effect of possession under the limitation laws. . . . It is believed that in one county (Breathitt) more than twice the area has been listed for taxation, claimants being willing to strengthen the color of title thus at the expense of a trifling State tax.[22]

Obviously, obtaining a patent to land did not secure it, and yet this step was often treated as an end in itself. An agent who acted for the absent holder of a military or treasury warrant and was able successfully to locate a tract, make entry, secure a survey, arrange for the return of the survey and entry, and finally to gain the patent, generally was paid a portion of the land as his fee. In cases arising from warrants issued before Kentucky became a state, the fee was one-half the land. For approximately the next decade, the fee was reduced to one-third the land; at the end of the period under discussion, it was sometimes one-fourth the land. This was a considerable contingency fee, but it probably reflected fairly accurately the risk involved.

This risk was believed to be worth the trouble because often thousands of acres of land were at stake. Even securing a doubtful patent was useful, because it gave color of title and provided a basis for litigation. (Competing claims, called "interferences," were common in the federal court records.) Everything connected with land policy and land laws, and their administration, seems in retrospect to have provided grounds for litigation. The land laws of Virginia and Kentucky may have been intended to secure land for their citizens simply, efficiently, justly, and permanently, but the hundreds of land cases in the Kentucky courts, federal and state, reflect the number of times the system broke down. Whether the justice delayed in the lengthy course of this litigation meant justice denied is a question that cannot be answered with certainty. What is certain is that it must have been difficult for anyone to maintain his right to land without a considerable investment in lawyers' fees and in legal processes.

The 712 land cases in the Kentucky federal courts from 1789 until 1816 were brought under one of four designations: "In Ejectment," "On a Writ of Right," "On a Caveat," or "In Chancery." The first two were common law actions; the second two were proceedings in equity.[23] The basis for choice among these four depended upon whether the

---

[22] Dembitz, *Kentucky Jurisprudence*, 185.
[23] There were also three cases "On a Writ of Dower," excluded from the discussion below because they involved widows' rights and were handled routinely. The issues raised in those suits were only peripherally related to land.

patent had been issued; the dates of the entry, survey, return, or patent; and questions of occupancy, inheritance, and descent.

An action in ejectment was commonly brought by the holder of a senior (earlier) patent against the holder of a junior (later) patent who was in possession of the land, or against an occupier of the land who held no patent. In the period under study, 282 such cases were brought, involving a far greater number of litigants. (All of the heirs might be grouped with the plaintiff; all of the tenants in possession might be grouped as the defendants, although sometimes they were sued separately.) If all the steps leading to issuance of the senior patent had been accomplished according to law, judgment went for the plaintiff. If there had been defects along the way, judgment went for the defendant. But the latter alternative seldom occurred because, as in other common law cases in the court, jury findings usually went for the plaintiff, although plaintiffs were not always victorious. Of the cases that were terminated, 17 percent were abated, dismissed, or nonsuited—all results which theoretically benefited the defendants. Four cases were carried to the Supreme Court, two on certification, and two on writs of error. (These will be discussed below.) Four other suits were remanded to the state courts, for undiscovered reasons, and thirty-three were discontinued on motion of the plaintiff or acknowledgment by the defendant. Table 2 shows these results.

TABLE 2

Disposition of Ejectment Cases, 1789-1816

Judgment for plaintiff (after trial)	88
Judgment for defendant (after trial)	3
Defendant acknowledged charge	10
Dismissed	16
Discontinued	23
Nonsuit	6
Remanded to state courts	4
Abated	4
Pending at end of period	128
Total	282

Although the purpose of ejectment was the simple one of proving title, the means provided were exceedingly complicated. True to its commitment to tradition, the federal court required rigorous adherence to the convoluted fictions and pleadings that for centuries had dis-

176

tinguished this form of action. The plaintiffs and defendants were initially called by alliteratively contrasting names, and their actual identity was revealed only in subsequent pleadings at a later stage of the proceedings.[24] The intricate verbal formulae included letters from fictitious persons known as "Casual Ejectors," and letter-perfect pleadings that were repeated, each in its proper order, for every case. No deviations were permitted, and no shortcuts were tolerated. Furthermore, all of these matters were carefully written out in the otherwise succinct Order Books of the court. The extraordinary amount of time and energy consumed by these fictional devices represented considerable effort by the clerk, but the rigidity of the procedures made his labor unenlightening. The circumstances that must have distinguished one case from another are totally obscured, as every action proceeded exactly like every other action in ejectment, and presumably exactly like the thousands that had preceded it. The only variables were the names of the litigants (when these were revealed), and the different points at which default might be established, or at which the issue was joined.

Ejectment actions occasionally reached judgment much sooner than land cases brought under other procedures. Default judgments (probably reflecting the widespread squatter occupancy of the period) could result at the term following the initial docketing. Even when the defendants appeared, the issue might be joined, trial held, and judgment rendered within three or four terms of the court, an unusually rapid termination for any case of any kind in these courts. Some ejectment cases, however, extended over many years, and there was great variation in the time required for completion of these suits. Indeed, a large proportion of the ejectment actions never came to judgment. By 1816, 128 cases were pending, but many of these had been inactive for years. Probably the mere filing of the suit often accomplished the desired result and made further litigation unnecessary. The defendants in these instances may have been squatters without color of title, or they may have been persons who, for financial or other reasons, chose not to defend. Court action was troublesome and expensive, and it may have been easier to move on, into the expanding frontier.

The other action at law in the Kentucky land cases was the writ of right, which was used to settle disputes between litigants by deter-

[24] Usually these were the familiar John Doe and Richard Roe, or John Den and Richard Fen, but sometimes the attorneys exercised their ingenuity and litigated cases in the names of Richard Peaceable and Henry Troublesome, Samuel Seekright and Solomon Spendall, Elder Grant and Void Claim, suggesting a bias toward the plaintiffs.

mining who had the better right of possession, rather than by establishing the abstract right of the demandant.[25] Both parties held patents (legal titles) and the question of the better right involved matters of descent or inheritance.

Writs of right also had distinguishing terminology and pleadings that obscured the different circumstances of the cases. In this action, a demandant (instead of a plaintiff) sued a tenant (instead of a defendant), and pleadings continued until the mise (instead of the issue) was joined. Fortunately, the original way of determining who had the better right, trial by battle, had long since been superseded by trial by jury. The request for jury trial was expressed by the parties putting themselves "on the assizes." Petit juries, the court's version of the English grand assizes, were then called to find the facts.

Eight persons brought seventeen writs of right during the period to 1816. The results of these cases were mixed. Three were abated by death (two of the tenants, and one of the demandants), and a fourth was abated because the tenant pleaded nontenure. One "assize" found for the demandant, another for the tenant, and judgments followed accordingly. The remaining eleven suits were still pending in 1816.

Even rarer were the dozen suits brought "on a Caveat," preventing issuance of a patent until title was determined. This equity proceeding was the most common of all procedures used in contemporary cases reported from the Kentucky Court of Appeals, but it constituted a very small proportion of the cases in the Kentucky federal courts.[26] (It is possible that the greater caseload of the federal courts is explainable, in part, by the greater variety of relief available there during this period.) At least one caveat was brought in the federal district court by counsel who hoped to secure relief on the grounds of a minor but not irreconcilable difference between the Virginia statute and the Kentucky statute: the former specified four circumstances under which a

[25] The clearest contemporary discussion of the conditions governing writs of right found so far is Justice Story's opinion in *Green* v. *Liter,* 8 Cranch 229 (1814).

[26] James Hughes, *A Report of the Causes Determined by the Late Supreme Court for the District of Kentucky and by the Court of Appeals in which Titles to Land Were in Dispute* (Cincinnati, 1869) (I *Kentucky Reports*); Achilles Sneed, *Decisions of the Court of Appeals of the State of Kentucky from March 1, 1801 to January 18, 1805 Inclusive* (Cincinnati, 1869) (II *Kentucky Reports*); Martin D. Hardin, *Reports of Cases Argued and Adjudged in the Court of Appeals of Kentucky from Spring Term 1805 to Spring Term 1808, Inclusive* (Frankfort, Ky., 1810) (III *Kentucky Reports*); Bibb, *Reports of Cases . . .* (IV-VII *Kentucky Reports*).

caveat might be brought but the latter had no similar restriction.[27] In caveat cases as in others, the judges in the Kentucky federal courts consistently quoted section 34 of the Judiciary Act of 1789 and followed the state statutes and decisions that were properly applicable. Under the Compact with Virginia, rights deriving from Virginia were decided according to Virginia law; the judges followed Kentucky law in rights deriving from Kentucky.

The decrees in caveat cases were mixed. Four went for the plaintiffs, two for the defendants, two were dismissed, and four were pending in 1816. Three cases were carried to the Supreme Court, and will be discussed below.

A much more common use of equity procedures for determining land ownership was the large number of cases brought in chancery. Although it has often been asserted that there was very little equity practiced in the United States during this early period, the federal court records show that this was not true in Kentucky.[28] The 401 chancery suits were a sizable proportion of the total number of private cases, and furthermore, these chancery actions were not law cases masquerading as equity. Many were initiated after judgment in ejectment in order to recover through equity some interest impossible to gain through common law, while others were filed after a grant had been issued.[29]

One aspect of these chancery suits that was unusual was Judge Innes's frequent use of advisory juries, although this was not without

[27] *Caldwell* v. *Waters and Handley* (1806) in [Harry Innes], "Cases in the Court of the United States for the District of Kentucky, from its first Organization to the year 1806 Inclusive," United States Court for the Western District of Kentucky, Louisville, 255. (Hereafter cited as Innes Opinions.)

[28] Roscoe Pound, review of Walter Wheeler Cook, *Cases and Other Authorities in Equity, Harvard Law Review*, xxxvii (1923), 396-399; William F. Walsh, "The Growing Function of Equity in the Development of the Law," in *Law: A Century of Progress 1835-1935* (New York, 1937), 153; Richard H. Field and Benjamin Kaplan, *Materials for a Basic Course in Civil Procedure* (Mineola, N.Y., 1968), 305. These assumptions are based on a belief that most American judges were ignorant of English equity procedures before the work of Chancellor James Kent and United States Supreme Court Justice Joseph Story. An important corrective is Stanley N. Katz, "The Politics of Law in Colonial America: Controversies over Chancery Courts and Equity Law in the Eighteenth Century," in Donald Fleming and Bernard Bailyn, eds., *Law in American History*, Perspectives in American History, v (Cambridge, Mass., 1971), 257-285.

[29] A caveat could be filed after survey but before the grant was issued; a suit in chancery only after completion of all the steps required by law including the issuance of the patent. Draft opinion, *Wilson* v. *Mason*, Harry Innes Papers, Manuscript Division, Library of Congress, xxvii, Pt. i, 8-116.

179

English precedent. English chancellors sometimes asked the advice of juries in the complementary (and often competing) courts of law, and used it at their discretion. Since there was no separation of law courts from equity courts in the federal system, Judge Innes simply consulted similar advisory juries within his single-structured court. These chancery juries were "sworn well and truly to enquire of the facts submitted to them" rather than "to try the issue joined" as were common law juries. Another difference between law juries and chancery juries was that the latter could, and often did, find facts for both parties to the suit, a practice not possible in law.[30]

There are four possible reasons that may explain why Judge Innes so frequently used juries in chancery suits.[31] The first reason is related to his political and legal philosophy. The judge was an ardent Jeffersonian, and it seems likely that he shared Jefferson's conviction that there should be juries in all courts: chancery, admiralty, and ecclesiastical, as well as in common law courts.[32] Jefferson frequently worried about the possible abuse of power by judges and other figures in authority and had an uncommon faith in the wisdom that might be reached by numbers of people. Innes may have had less confidence in the people, but he shared the fear of tyranny by judges, even when he was one of them.[33] His use of chancery juries, like his emphasis on procedural due process and his generosity in granting continuances, helped avoid even the appearance of tyranny or the arbitrary use of power.

[30] As described in Chapter Four, oral testimony was generally required before 1802, but after that, chancery juries relied entirely upon written evidence.

[31] It is clear that although Innes considered that sec. 34 of the Judiciary Act of 1789 required him to follow the decisions of the Kentucky courts in common law cases (except where the Constitution, or federal treaties or statutes provided otherwise), he was not obligated to follow their procedures, although by using advisory juries he was doing so. Kentucky state courts were required by Art. v, sec. 4, first constitution of Kentucky (1792) to empanel juries to find facts in all cases of disputed land titles. This requirement was apparently continued by Art. x, sec. 6, second constitution of Kentucky (1799). *U.S.* v. *Mannen* (1802), Innes Opinions, 170; *Text of Kentucky Constitutions of 1792, 1799 and 1850* (Frankfort, Ky., 1965), 5, 21; Richard Peters, ed., *The Public Statutes at Large of the United States of America, 1789-1873* (Boston, 1850-1873), 1, 73. (Hereafter cited as 1 Stat.)

[32] In a proposed constitution for Virginia that he wrote in 1776, Jefferson provided in Article III that "all facts in causes whether of Chancery, Common, Ecclesiastical, or Marine law, shall be tried by a jury." Even depositions were to be submitted "to the credit of the jury." In a draft of another constitution for Virginia in 1783, Jefferson recommended trials by jury "in all causes depending before any court, other than those of impeachments, of appeals, and military courts." Padover, arr., *Complete Jefferson*, 108, 117.

[33] Note his opinion in the Burr case, Chapter Six.

A second reason for this extensive use of juries in chancery cases may have been that Judge Innes wanted to reduce any suspicion directed at the equity jurisdiction of the federal courts. It has been reported that the post-Revolutionary generation was dubious about the compatibility of chancery courts with the new republic and its democratic aspirations.[34] Any mistrust of the federal chancery jurisdiction would inevitably affect the usefulness and viability of the federal courts. Whatever doubts Judge Innes entertained from time to time about the worth of other branches of the federal government to his state, he certainly wanted to make his court as prestigious and important as possible. With his chancery decrees based upon facts found by juries, it would be difficult to challenge the equity authority of the federal courts in Kentucky.[35]

It seems likely that a third and related reason that Judge Innes used advisory juries in land cases may have been to establish a broader foundation for his decrees than would have been possible had he determined the facts by himself. It is probable that he used "twelve good men and true" as a matter of public policy and personal protection as well as for reasons of philosophy and prestige. Innes must have been acutely conscious of the exposed position he occupied as a single judge, with the lonely responsibility of ruling upon matters of such consequence as the large land claims that were docketed in his court. These cases came into the district court through its circuit court jurisdiction; in other federal circuit courts, responsibility for such decisions was shared between two persons, a Supreme Court justice and a district judge. The use of advisory juries in chancery cases when he sat alone on the bench was, therefore, a sensible protective device for Judge Innes.[36]

An unfriendly remark by Joseph Hamilton Daveiss suggests that this may have been a sensitive issue in Kentucky. The United States attorney for the district wrote that the fact that the Kentucky federal court had "a *single judge*" resulted in "as perfect a judicial despotism . . . as ever military life in civilized nations exhibited."[37] Daveiss's

[34] Charles Warren, "New Light on the History of the Judiciary Act of 1789," *Harvard Law Review*, xxxvii (1923), 99-101 and *passim*.

[35] Mistrust of equity was also reflected in the Judiciary Act of 1789, sec. 30, providing for oral testimony in equity, admiralty, and maritime cases, as well as in actions at common law. (This was discussed in Chapter Four.)

[36] Innes was clearly aware of his vulnerability and once commented on how "disagreeable" it was to be alone on the bench. Harry Innes to John Brown, Mar. 5, 1800, Innes Papers, Library of Congress, xxviii, 9-217.

[37] Joseph Hamilton Daveiss to John Breckinridge, Feb. 25, 1802, Breckinridge Family Papers, Manuscript Division, Library of Congress, xxi, 3679. Daveiss's

attitude was probably widely shared by the Marshalls and other Federalists, especially because they were often litigants in the federal court's most important land cases. And while Innes may not have known the contents of a private letter, he probably was well aware that his political enemies would accuse him of partiality whenever the opportunity arose. It was reasonable for him to try to guard against such a charge. He could not share the bench, but he could share responsibility for determining the facts upon which his decisions rested. And, in fact, chancery juries were seldom used after 1807, when the Seventh Circuit Court was created and Justice Todd joined Innes on the federal court, which further suggests that they were used to protect Innes from criticism.

A final reason why Judge Innes may have used chancery juries in land cases is that he probably wished to guard against any charge that federal diversity jurisdiction favored out-of-state litigants. The expected federal protection against local prejudices and passions might be construed as overprotection for nonresidents, if decisions regularly went for them. One way to assure neutrality was to base decisions on the findings of local juries, so that if some Kentuckians found the facts in land cases, others could not claim that the court favored non-Kentuckians. (The court records provide no evidence that the Kentucky federal courts had any bias toward nonresidents or toward residents.)[38]

The land cases provide abundant evidence of Judge Innes's scrupulous adherence to earlier decisions of the Virginia and Kentucky courts, and his consistency in this area was probably largely responsible for the great number of land cases in the federal court. Both the Order Books and Innes's written opinions frequently cited section 34 of the Judiciary Act of 1789—the so-called "rules of decision" section. He often quoted its mandate, "[t]hat the laws of the several states, except where the constitution, treaties, or statutes of the United States shall otherwise require or provide, shall be regarded as rules of decision in trials at common law in the courts of the United States in cases where they apply."[39]

---

letter expressed his opposition to the expected repeal of the Federalist Judiciary Act of 1801, which had abolished the single-judge district court in Kentucky and replaced it with a circuit court of three judges, one of whom was a Federalist.

[38] As shown in Chapter Seven, in Table 2, and in Appendix B, the great majority of decisions went for plaintiffs, regardless of their residence. Litigation was expensive, and litigants initiated action only when they believed that they had a reasonable chance of success. The quantification of judgments indicates that more often than not the plaintiffs were correct in their decisions to bring suit.

[39] 1 Stat. 73.

Innes's reliance upon state court decisions as well as state statutes stands in marked contrast to the broad construction later given to Justice Joseph Story's 1842 interpretation of section 34 in *Swift* v. *Tyson*. Although Story specifically excluded "rights and titles to real estate and other matters immovable and intra-territorial in their nature" in asserting that federal courts were free to determine general common law principles in contractual and commercial matters where there were no applicable state statutes, later judges extended the *Swift* v. *Tyson* doctrine to justify the development of a general federal common law. In 1938 this trend was reversed in *Erie Railroad* v. *Tomkins*. Writing for the majority of the United States Supreme Court, Justice Louis D. Brandeis recounted the Story opinion and stated that its doctrine had "introduced grave discrimination by non-citizens against citizens" in diversity cases, and was, furthermore, an invasion of the rights of the state.[40] Judge Innes would have agreed. Had he developed a separate federal common law in the land cases, the situation in Kentucky would have been even more chaotic—and the litigation even more voluminous—than it already was.[41]

Another aspect of the court's work that reflected its adherence to state statutes and its responsiveness to local problems was its frequent implementation of the Kentucky occupying claimant statutes. Throughout the period under examination, the court regularly upheld the laws of 1797 and 1812 that provided redress for settlers who had made improvements on land and later lost it in litigation. The common law

[40] Cf. *Swift* v. *Tyson*, 16 Peters 1 (1842) with *Erie Railroad* v. *Tompkins*, 304 U.S. 64 (1938). See also Charles A. Heckman, "The Relationship of *Swift* v. *Tyson* to the Status of Commercial Law in the Nineteenth Century and the Federal System," *American Journal of Legal History*, xvii (1973), 246-255; Harold M. Hollingsworth, "Comments on Charles A. Heckman's Paper 'The Relationship of *Swift* v. *Tyson* to the Status of Commercial Law in the Nineteenth Century and the Federal System,' and Donald Roper's Paper, 'James Kent and the Emergence of New York's Libel Law,'" *ibid.*, 256-261.

[41] This was pointed out by Thomas Todd while he was a judge on the Kentucky Court of Appeals. He wrote to support repeal of the Federalists' Judiciary Act of 1801 (which had led to the appointment of two additional but unsophisticated judges on the federal bench in Kentucky), saying "the serious mischief which exists in this Country, is the danger of conflicting decisions on our land-claims in the State or Federal Courts. . . . We had better submit our causes to the decision of one Judge who is a cotempary [*sic*] with the law, has been almost an eye Witness to the circumstances which gave rise to a great many claims originating under it—for many years a lawyer at the bar of Courts which were setting principles arising out of it and whose principles and decisions are more in unison with the State Courts, than it is possible, those of additional Judges can be." Thomas Todd to Breckinridge, Feb. 17, 1802, Breckinridge Family Papers, xxi, 3655. This letter was among those seriously misunderstood by Charles Warren, *Supreme Court in United States History*, i, 220, and discussed above, Chapter One, n. 27.

actions of ejectment and writ of right were often followed by an equity proceeding designed to invoke the occupying claimant laws, and suits in chancery were often continued for this purpose. (These procedures were employed in at least thirty-four ejectment cases, three writs of right, and twenty-six chancery suits.) After reaching judgment in the initial land suits, both Judge Innes and Justice Todd regularly suspended issuance of the writ *habere facias possessionem* (to take possession) until the successful litigant complied with the provisions of these statutes. This was long-established practice, accepted both by Kentuckians and by Virginians, and was not questioned until Innes's last term on the bench in December 1815, when the judges' disagreement in *Green* v. *Biddle* brought about a Supreme Court test of the statutes.[42]

The occupying claimant laws were of great importance to owners and occupiers alike. In the extraordinary confusion surrounding warrants, surveys, entries, and patents, it was entirely possible for a settler to have believed himself the legal owner of a tract, to have cleared it, built a house, planted crops and orchards, and then to risk losing everything by an adverse decision in the courts. The occupying claimant statutes provided settlers with color of title an opportunity to claim compensation for improvements. (There was no redress for squatters who did not have a legal paper indicating ownership.) Similarly, a successful claimant could gain compensation for waste of the land and for rents collected by an unsuccessful litigant who had earlier occupied his land. The smaller amount was deducted from the larger, and became part of the court's final decree. In order to determine these amounts, the federal judges appointed commissioners to make valuations and to report their assessments to the court.[43] These commissioners' reports reveal something about the way Kentuckians lived during this period and how one land case differed from another —matters that are obscured by the formal pleadings. Houses, fences, cattle, crops, and orchards are listed and valued, as is the amount of land cleared, and the length of time the occupant had lived on it. What can only be surmised is the difficulty with which improvements had to be begun all over again, years after an initial settlement had

[42] The Virginia statute of 1661 (13 Car. 2 cap. 70) is reprinted in Littell, *Statute Law of Kentucky*, I, 641, immediately preceding the 1797 Kentucky statute.

[43] Gates, in "Tenants of the Log Cabin," *MVHR*, XLIX (1962), 12, states that local juries made these evaluations, a procedure which may have been followed in the state courts. In the federal courts, however, no more than seven commissioners, identified by name, always performed this service.

been made. Almost all suits in chancery took a long time to reach completion. The original litigants might be old or dead before the final disposition of the land was made. Many of the land cases which were followed by the application of the occupying claimant laws continued on the Order Books of the court for decades.

And even after judgment by the Kentucky federal courts, litigation might extend even longer when large amounts of land were involved and litigants took their cases to the United States Supreme Court. Preparations were made to carry thirty-nine of the land cases heard in the Kentucky federal courts before 1816 to the high court. Six of these never reached decision; some were dismissed because counsel failed to appear; and others were dropped, presumably because the parties decided to accept the decision of the lower court. But between 1801 and 1822 the Supreme Court ruled on thirty-three Kentucky land cases.[44]

Seven of these were "certified" to the Supreme Court because the judges were divided on questions of law. Sometimes the question involved the jurisdiction of the court, a common problem because policy was unclear during the early years of the federal court system. In the cases arising in Kentucky, the Supreme Court always ruled that the lower court did have jurisdiction, thereby reflecting that broad view of federal authority generally attributed to the Marshall court. Sometimes the Kentucky judges were unsure about the propriety of accepting the processes and records of other courts or about hearing cases where the residence of all the litigants had not been specified in the pleadings. The Supreme Court recommended acceptance of the former and remanded the latter for amendments to the pleadings. One of the questions certified was whether the occupying claimant laws were in violation of the Compact with Virginia, and the later decision by the Supreme Court that the statutes were invalid made *Green* v. *Biddle* the most famous land case from Kentucky during this era.[45]

Most of the land cases were carried to the Supreme Court on writs

[44] Gates's statement (*ibid.*, 19) that "no cases had been appealed to the federal courts before 1819" is somewhat misleading. Few cases of any kind were appealed to the Supreme Court in this period because the area of appeal was very limited: the cases from the Kentucky federal courts were usually carried to the high court on certification or on writs of error. *Green* v. *Biddle* (the occupying claimant case) was certified to the Supreme Court in 1815, although it was not heard until 1821. *Green* v. *Biddle*, Circuit Court Order Book D, Dec. 2, 1815. (Hereafter cited as CC OB.)

[45] *Green* v. *Biddle*, 8 Wheaton 1 (1821). Gates states that the ruling was ignored in Kentucky and in later federal land policy. "Tenants of the Log Cabin," *MVHR*, XLIX (1962), 24-31.

of error. (A writ of error petitioned the high court to reexamine matters of law in the record, but not matters of fact.) The matters of law that were questioned involved interpretation of the complicated provisions of the Virginia land law of 1779 and subsequent Kentucky statutes. From the bench in Washington came rulings requiring new surveys, calculating the validity of prior claims, defining the distinctions between seisin and occupation, or stating that land had been properly surveyed but improperly entered or properly entered but improperly surveyed. In most of these cases, it is difficult to find a pattern of decision on the part of the Supreme Court. On the basis of the facts given, it seems as likely that the Court would affirm as reverse the Kentucky courts. Furthermore, several opinions noted the confused state of land titles in Kentucky and expressed the reluctance of the distant Supreme Court to reverse decisions of a local court, reflecting a general conviction that such matters should be determined by persons familiar with the state laws and their traditional interpretation. In one such opinion, Chief Justice Marshall cautioned against challenging the principle upon which decisions had been based:

> It is impossible to say how many titles might be shaken by shaking the principle. The very extraordinary state of land title in that country has compelled its judges, in a series of decisions, to rear up an artificial pile from which no piece can be taken, by hands not intimately acquainted with the building, without endangering the structure, and producing a mischief to those holding under it, the extent of which may not be perceived.[46]

However, despite such assertions of judicial self-restraint, the Supreme Court did reverse the lower court on fifteen occasions, while upholding it only eleven times. But the opinions in these cases do not reveal that the Supreme Court was basing its judgments on principles different from those employed in the Kentucky courts. Interestingly, five of the reversals included a factor that may have been more relevant: the participation, either as litigants or as counsel, of persons who were relatives or political allies of Chief Justice John Marshall or of the Marshall family in Kentucky.[47] And in none of these cases did the chief justice disqualify himself; in fact, he even wrote the opinions for three of the five reversals in which he had at least an indirect in-

[46] *Bodley and Hughes* v. *Taylor*, 5 Cranch 191 (1809).
[47] *Bodley and Hughes* v. *Taylor*, 5 Cranch 191 (1809); *Marshall* v. *Currie*, 4 Cranch 172 (1807); *Wilson* v. *Mason*, 1 Cranch 45 (1801); *Taylor and Quarles* v. *Brown*, 5 Cranch 234 (1809); *Thompson* v. *Colston*, 2 Wheaton 336 (1817).

terest. (One opinion was written by Justice Johnson and one by Justice Washington.)

This failure of the chief justice to recuse himself stands in marked contrast to the behavior of his colleagues in Kentucky. Both Judge Innes and Justice Todd regularly abstained from considering causes in which they were interested. Usually the circumstances leading to their disqualifications are difficult to determine, because the court records offer no explanation and reasons must be discovered in other evidence. But, for example, Judge Innes did not sit in *Lewis* v. *McFarland*, because he had been asked to be an executor of the will of the father-in-law of the plaintiff. Nor did Innes sit in *Jones* v. *Netherland*, because his wife's deceased former husband had been a creditor of the defendant. Justice Todd abstained in *Matson* v. *Hord* and *Finley* v. *Lynn*, as did Innes in *Frazier and Vowles* v. *Craig*, and in *Thompson* v. *Colston*, although their reasons are unknown. Yet whatever Innes's interest in the latter suit, it probably was not as great as that of Chief Justice Marshall who did sit: Rawleigh Colston was his brother-in-law and his partner in the earlier purchase of the Fairfax lands in Virginia.[48]

This insensitivity of Chief Justice Marshall to possible conflicts of interest is revealed in other significant land cases. Marshall presumably heard and voted on *Marshall* v. *Currie*, a case in which his first cousin Humphrey Marshall was both plaintiff and attorney. In the opinion delivered by Justice Johnson, it is clear that the court overruled the findings of an advisory jury in chancery, a striking example of judicial activism.[49] The opinion acknowledged the use of juries in Kentucky chancery practice, but stated that "[t]his court is not uninfluenced by an anxiety to save the early estates acquired in that country." It was, perhaps, an understandable anxiety, but it might have been more to the point to have acknowledged that that anxiety was heightened when the early estates were claimed by Marshalls.[50]

[48] W[illiam] M[cClung] Paxton, *The Marshall Family* (Cincinnati, 1885), 51.

[49] Marshall's entry was dependent upon a call in an entry which stated that a certain beech tree had been marked "D.L." in 1784. The defendant argued that this marking was not sufficient to enable others to notice it, because the beech stood in a grove of beeches, and there was no proof that the marking was generally known to be there at that date. Using the doctrine of notoriety, an advisory jury had found this fact for the defendant, and the Kentucky court had awarded the disputed land to him. 4 Cranch 172 (1807).

[50] The transitory nature of the early estates was commented upon by a descendant of Justice Todd. Charles S. Todd stated that at Isaac Shelby's death (43 years after he had established himself "upon the first settlement and preemption granted in Kentucky"), "he was the only individual in the state residing upon his own settlement and preemption; death; removals to the new states or better bills having dispossessed all of the early settlers. . . . This fact illustrates the migratory

187

The chief justice himself wrote the opinion for *Wilson* v. *Mason*, in which Joseph Hamilton Daveiss, Humphrey Marshall's closest political ally, represented the Wilson claim. The Supreme Court's award to Wilson (reversing the Kentucky District Court) brought Daveiss 30,000 acres, and two years later he married Nancy Marshall, the sister of the chief justice.[51]

This proved, however, to be the only case arising from Kentucky where the final opinion involved more than interpretation of the land laws. Counsel for the Mason claim argued that under the Compact with Virginia, land rights acquired under Virginia authority were to be decided according to the Virginia statute of 1779. That law had specified that writs of error could not be taken in cases of caveat, and therefore the United States Supreme Court could not review the decision of the federal court in Kentucky (which had ruled for Mason). But Marshall denied this limitation and pointed out that the Constitution

> gave jurisdiction to the federal courts in controversies between citizens of different States. The same constitution vested in this court an appellate jurisdiction in all cases where original jurisdiction was given to the inferior courts, with only "such exceptions . . . as the congress shall make." . . . Nor is there . . . any exception . . . which would exclude the case of a caveat from its general provisions. If then, the compact between Virginia and Kentucky was even susceptible of the construction contended for, that construction could only be maintained on the principle that the legislatures of any two States might, by agreement between themselves, annul the constitution of the United States.[52]

---

character of the people and the great uncertainty of land claims." Charles S. Todd, "Sketch of the Life of Isaac Shelby" (1873), Todd Family Papers, Manuscript Dept., Filson Club, Louisville, Ky.

[51] Mason's entry, one of the earliest claims based upon the 1779 statute, was dated Oct. 27, 1780. The land was surveyed in 1783, and the plat and notes were returned in September and October of that year. Wilson's surveyors (John Handley and Christopher Greenup), believing that there were defects in Mason's survey, made an entry in April 1783 for 40,926 acres that included Mason's 8,300 acres, and in March 1784 filed a caveat challenging the issuance of a patent to Mason. Mason filed a cross caveat, and the cases were heard in the Kentucky District Court from July 1798 until June 1800, when Innes upheld Mason's claim. This decision was challenged by a writ of error, and the case was carried to the Supreme Court, where Daveiss argued for the Wilson claim. The Supreme Court decided for him in the November 1801 term—not an unusually long lapse of time from the beginning of a land case to its conclusion. 1 Cranch 45 (1801).

[52] *Ibid.*

This opinion, delivered in John Marshall's first term as chief justice, would be followed by many others reflecting a broad interpretation of federal judicial power and national supremacy. But the Supreme Court's decisions on other Kentucky land cases appear to have been influenced by matters other than political and legal philosophy, even though the relationships involved were sometimes more subtle. A chancery suit brought by Griffin Taylor and Tunstall Quarles against John Brown in the Kentucky court was dismissed in March 1806, after four jury trials. (Judge Innes could not remove himself from his friend's case because he was the only judge, but presumably the advisory juries protected him from suspicion of partiality.) The dismissal was reversed by the Supreme Court in 1809, after the case was argued for the complainants by John Rowan. Rowan was a prominent Kentucky Federalist who had carried Humphrey Marshall's attempt to impeach Innes to the House of Representatives during the preceding year.[53]

Even the husband of Judge Innes's stepdaughter learned to choose his counsel by affiliation. Thomas Bodley gained a Supreme Court order reversing the Kentucky court and ordering a more advantageous survey after his case was argued by Humphrey Marshall.[54]

The consistent effectiveness of the chief justice's connections suggests that the outcomes of other cases taken to the Supreme Court may have been determined, at least in part, by relationships that are now difficult if not impossible to trace. The question of conflict of interest has rarely been raised against members of the nation's highest court. But the answer, like so many others, may be found in long-overlooked records.

This surprising reason for an otherwise inexplicable pattern of appellate decisions tends to overshadow other findings emerging from the study of this portion of the Kentucky federal court docket. As has been shown, the Order Books alone yield unexpected evidence even about the land cases, the best known part of the courts' work. The very size of the caseload demonstrates that many plaintiffs preferred their federal courts over their state courts. The number of chancery suits suggests that the judges were not unsophisticated; their attention to traditional pleadings and their generosity in granting continuances show a notable devotion to due process and a conscious avoidance of hasty or arbitrary judgments. The use of juries indicates a broader

[53] *Taylor and Quarles* v. *Brown*, 5 Cranch 234 (1809).
[54] *Bodley and Hughes* v. *Taylor*, 5 Cranch 191 (1809). The case was argued before the Supreme Court at the February terms in 1806, 1807, and 1809. Marshall was counsel, with Hughes, at the 1807 hearing.

189

participation in decision reaching than has been suspected, and the frequent citation of state statutes and of decisions of the state Court of Appeals illustrates a responsible awareness of the necessity of avoiding conflicts between the federal courts and the state courts. Finally, the consistent application of the occupying claimant laws proves that until 1816 the federal courts in Kentucky were sympathetic with the problems of settlers who might otherwise have suffered from the effects of an extraordinarily inefficient and complicated land law.

If the Kentucky federal courts favored the wealthy, it was principally because it was only they who could afford the court costs and attorneys' fees attendant upon extensive litigation. The number of lawsuits is evidence of the many conflicts resulting from the laws, and also points to the difficulties of retaining possession of good land without the services of experienced attorneys. The tendency of Kentuckians to litigate made land ownership virtually impossible for anyone without a good lawyer, and it appears that sometimes it was important to choose counsel on the basis of their connections on the Supreme Court, as well as their skill.

Conclusion

THE Order Books of the early federal courts in Kentucky appear to be among the least enlightening of American public records. Although they were written in English, their language is nearly incomprehensible. Only a rare word or phrase links the past with the present; classical pleadings and forms of action that have long since fallen into disuse tend to obscure whatever was going on. But when the proceedings are deciphered, the caseload recreated and rearranged, two interwoven histories begin to emerge.

The first and more obvious is a hitherto hidden legal history which has been discussed in earlier chapters. However, the topical organization of those chapters has fragmented and tangled the strands of a second and more subtle history: the chronicle of the political factors that profoundly influenced the work of the courts and perhaps also the jurisprudence practiced there.

Many of these political factors resulted from an ineluctable dichotomy between the perceptions and priorities of those who lived in the West and of those who worked in the nation's capital. This division was present when the Constitution was written and continued throughout the following generation, although its force decreased as time went on. For example, the court which is the focus of this study was not initially believed to be either necessary or desirable by many Kentuckians, including the man who was to dominate it for the next twenty-seven years. But Congress wanted an outpost of federal judicial authority on the frontier. The court was not expected to have much business, and it was not part of the seaboard circuit system where most of the federal caseload would probably lie. But the Kentucky federal court soon played a sensitive role in balancing local and national interests, and it eventually became a very busy place. It achieved prominence, however, by a circuitous route. Ironically enough, it gained acceptance by protecting the people from the consequences of ignoring unpopular federal statutes. Having proven its usefulness, the court then took advantage of the opportunities provided by an increasing caseload to expound familiar principles and to produce predictable results. As the years passed, it became the most visible link between the people of this western state and their national government.

Establishing the court's legitimacy to its constituents was a considerable challenge in the beginning because few Kentuckians had a national perspective. They viewed situations and events from a place that was isolated from the center of their government by hundreds of miles and a mountain chain. Their problems were clear and immediate: subduing the native Americans who opposed them, converting the wilderness into farmland, and getting their agricultural surplus to markets. A government that did not help in these areas was of little use on the frontier. These westerners believed in their legal equality with the East and in their right to survive and prosper. But they knew that despite an astounding growth in their numbers, they remained a small proportion of the American people. And they doubted that the eastern majority would protect them whenever there was a conflict between regional interests.

Meanwhile, over the mountains, the elected and appointed representatives of the people worked to establish a more perfect Union. There was no certainty then that the Constitution would provide a more durable frame of government than had the Articles of Confederation, but the ultimate success of the War for Independence depended upon these leaders' ability to maintain the confidence and trust of the people while they resolved the challenges confronting the nation. Among the problems competing for their attention were establishing the national credit, funding the debt, achieving international respect but avoiding entangling alliances and war, balancing sectional interests, and implementing theoretical principles while knowing that every choice constituted a precedent that might influence the future.

One of the immediate questions facing these officials was how best to raise money to pay for the war debts of the states and the protection of the frontiers. A head tax would fall heavily upon the poor and on slaveowners, higher tariffs would inhibit trade, and a land tax would be impossible to administer, given the millions of acres to be surveyed and evaluated. Congress finally agreed with Secretary of the Treasury Hamilton that the simplest and most expedient measure would be an excise on distilled products. On this question as on others, it was hard to achieve consensus because of the members' own varying convictions, talents, motives, and experiences. But decisions had to be made, and once they were, those early public servants were not very tolerant of criticism, much less opposition. The rewards of public service rarely compensated for the bleakness of their bachelor-boarding house lives, and they considered their critics both parochial and ungrateful.

It is, therefore, not surprising that even Washington, whose prestige lent credibility to the executive branch, had difficulty finding people

192

willing to accept government positions and keeping those who did faithful to the public interest. His secretary of war was distracted by personal interests at crucial moments, and was said to be incompetent in managing his western responsibilities. His talented secretaries of state and the Treasury disagreed on almost every abstract issue and its practical manifestation. The Congresses of the day were peopled by senators and representatives imbued with the theory of deputy representation but who were prevented from consulting with their constituents by the primitiveness of transportation and communication. The federal judiciary was sometimes ignored and the authority of the Supreme Court was challenged. Washington himself wanted desperately to retire from public life and resume his career as a farmer, but he saw revolution abroad and feared it at home. He gambled, briefly, on using force in Pennsylvania, hoping to end violence and gain compliance with the internal revenue laws. But he knew, although he did not admit it publicly, how little effect that demonstration had on others in the West.

Kentuckians, especially, were not intimidated by the government's actions in Pennsylvania. Having at last achieved statehood, they were busy sorting out the implications of federalism and making a living on land whose ownership was often uncertain. Courts were absolutely essential to their security because settlement had preceded survey, and a complicated land law inherited from Virginia made titles difficult to establish and seemingly impossible to maintain. In the year of the Whiskey Rebellion, the highest state court overturned the findings of an earlier land commission and rendered thousands of titles suspect. But that decision provided an unexpected opportunity for the Kentucky federal court, which had a previously little-used concurrent authority in many land cases, to demonstrate its usefulness.

The federal court was governed by Harry Innes, a Virginia-trained judge with vast experience in local land laws. He was a man his neighbors could trust. Like many of them, he had been an Antifederalist, and for a decade after the adoption of the Constitution he continued to doubt whether the government it established had sufficient value for the people of his region. Like them, he was suspicious that navigation of the Mississippi might be sacrificed to eastern commercial interests, that insufficient resources and planning were committed by the United States to end the depredations of the Indians, and that the internal revenue acts placed an unfair burden on Kentucky's most exportable product. But he was, in addition, a practical person. He accepted appointment to the federal bench and retained the office even after he was offered the highest post in the state judiciary, probably because the federal salary was greater and more certain than the state one. He organized the court, promulgated rules, admitted attorneys, convened grand juries, and heard a few cases, conscientiously following the archaic niceties of the English legal tradition—while serenely ignoring the most broadly applicable federal statute, the law imposing a tax on whiskey. In any event, there was no one to prosecute for the United States, a circumstance that did not trouble Innes at all. So he presided over a growing civil caseload, carefully continuing controversies term after term, while the overriding political questions worked themselves out.

The Kentucky Federalists, many of whom were related to Thomas Marshall by blood or marriage (and thereby also to his prominent son John) criticized Innes for being autocratic and fumed about the inactivity in the federal court, and with some justice. But their persuasiveness was limited because their position was most publicly and most abrasively argued by Humphrey Marshall, a man whom it was easy to dislike. He took on the Jeffersonian establishment of the state, one by one, but instead of converting them to their duty he only made them more certainly Republican. Just as the whiskey tax symbolized the difference between national and local priorities, so Humphrey Marshall symbolized the insensitivity of the Federalists to what was then a loyal but deeply skeptical opposition.

By 1794, silent civil disobedience against the internal revenue acts gave way to mass public meetings against the national administration for negotiating with the English instead of the Spanish. Some prominent Kentuckians, emboldened by the victory over the Indians at Fallen Timbers, even contemplated seizing what the government had failed to secure by marching on to New Orleans. This was a project that the French were pleased to encourage, but it might well have embroiled the nation in a European war. Toward the end of the year, Washington's cabinet at last became thoroughly alarmed by the possible consequences of the disaffection of these westerners. After returning from Pennsylvania, the president decided to send Pinckney to Spain to secure navigation of the Mississippi by treaty, and to send Judge Innes's brother to Kentucky to prevent the frontiersmen from taking matters into their own hands. Both missions were eventually successful, but positive results of the Spanish treaty were slow to be realized. The stubborn Kentuckians continued to withhold both their commitment and their taxes from the national government, even after the appointment of a federal attorney who tried to prosecute them. Washington

194

retired to Mount Vernon, exhausted and embittered, leaving the un-resolved mistrust of Kentucky in the hands of his successor.

John Adams had the advantage of eight years of national stability but the disadvantage of being unable to inspire personal loyalty. He had never been first in the hearts of his countrymen, least of all to westerners. Despite his distinguished service to the nation during and after the Revolution, he was seen as a regional and factional figure who was of but not for the people. He could not depend upon the allegiance of his own cabinet, much less that of the opposition, who failed, he thought, to appreciate the degree to which France was threatening national autonomy. Temperamentally Adams had always found it difficult to accept disagreement, and he considered domestic dissent a threat to national survival. In that spirit he signed the alien and sedition acts in 1798. The latter, especially, seemed to Jefferson-ians to threaten basic principles of the Constitution, and in Kentucky and Virginia they countered with Resolutions. Adams's tendency to equate Federalism with patriotism hastened the maturing of political parties, and led opponents to view semi-reformist measures like the Judiciary Acts of 1801 as partisan ploys. Their suspicion was reinforced in Kentucky by Adams's handling of appointments to the new western circuit bench. He reassigned the experienced district judges of Ken-tucky and Tennessee, both Jeffersonians, to the circuit court, but de-nied them the higher salaries and titles of other circuit judges. He also appointed as their nominal superior a man whose chief distinctions were his Federalism and his relationship (by marriage) to the Mar-shalls.

The constellation of these national and local events directly affected the federal court in Kentucky. Distrust of the state courts, combined with confidence in Innes's experience, brought an increasingly heavy caseload. But perhaps the judge's most important contribution was his management of William Clarke, the determined but careless federal attorney. Innes refused to let Clarke convict ordinary farmers of crimi-nal charges when their only crime was evasion of the revenue laws, or to conduct a witch hunt against prominent Jeffersonians. The attorney may have had the statutes on his side, but the people had the judge on theirs. Eventually, under pressure from the Treasury Department, a *modus vivendi* was agreed upon: Clarke could bring civil charges for debt (the taxes owed the government)—but he was required to have incontrovertible evidence and to obey scrupulously the formali-ties of the English legal tradition. Because it was difficult for him to do either of these things, the internal revenue laws were only a little

195

more effectively enforced during Adams's administration than they had been during Washington's. Furthermore, the threat to proper implementation of section 34 of the Judiciary Act of 1789, posed by the midnight appointments of two judges unfamiliar with state land laws, seems to have inspired an outpouring of appreciation for Innes. After the dust had settled, a surprising number of plaintiffs chose to bring their cases in his court.

Many Kentuckians did not come unequivocally into the Union until after the election of Jefferson. He was their president, perhaps even more than Washington had been. He seemed to understand and appreciate their problems as few other easterners did. Some knew, and others suspected, that it was Jefferson who had secretly framed the Kentucky Resolutions against the sedition act. He certainly recognized what a profound irritant the whiskey tax presented and promised to support its repeal. Hundreds of distillers in Kentucky responded by acknowledging their obligations to the United States for the first time, although the statute was by then ten years old. (Because the attendant fines and forfeitures were remitted by Jefferson's secretary of the Treasury, the distillers' acquiescence was important principally because it constituted a *pro forma* recognition of the supremacy of federal law over local resentments.) Jeffersonians in Congress also restored the federal courts to the *status quo ante* Adams; for Kentucky this meant that the unsophisticated "imported" judges departed, and once again Innes ruled alone on their important land cases. The following year, the administration purchased Louisiana and settled forever the questions of navigating the Mississippi and using New Orleans as a port of deposit. And halfway through his second term, Jefferson got legislation that created a new seventh seat on the Supreme Court, to be filled by a westerner who would sit on new circuit courts in Kentucky, Tennessee, and Ohio. Unlike Adams, Jefferson consulted widely with people from the area and acted upon their advice. He then chose Thomas Todd, Innes's cousin and protégé, and by so doing consolidated Kentucky's allegiance to himself and his party.

About the same time, Innes's warfare with Humphrey Marshall (and therefore the Kentucky Republicans' warfare with the Kentucky Federalists) was reaching a climax. Innes's role in two concurrent but unrelated events brought matters to a head. The first was when Innes blocked the efforts of federal district attorney Joseph Hamilton Daveiss (another Federalist and Marshall brother-in-law) to indict Aaron Burr for treason. Burr thereupon left Kentucky and proceeded downriver. But when he was seized two months later and taken to Richmond for trial, it appeared that Innes had at best been naive, or at worst protecting a traitor. The second event was when a Kentucky legislative committee found that Benjamin Sebastian, an associate of Innes, had been receiving a pension from Spain in return for cooperation in trying to secure the secession of Kentucky. During the investigation, Innes revealed that a decade earlier he and George Nicholas, too, had been approached by the Spanish, but they had not reported the overture to the administration. This revelation convinced the Kentucky Federalists that Innes and his allies had been engaged in a "Spanish conspiracy" of some twenty years' duration. Innes escaped censure, but the legislature recommended that the House of Representatives inquire whether he should be impeached.

Innes fought to preserve his position through Wilson Cary Nicholas, a Virginian who was a surviving brother of George Nicholas. Wilson Cary Nicholas, in turn, consulted with the president. Jefferson was only casually acquainted with Innes, but he knew both Nicholas brothers well. Wilson Cary Nicholas had been invited to Monticello with Madison and Monroe to draft the Kentucky Resolutions, and he had been entrusted with seeing that they reached Kentucky and, through the good offices of George Nicholas, were introduced in the Kentucky legislature (by John Breckinridge).[1] Now Nicholas had to prevent Innes's impeachment in order to preserve his deceased brother's reputation. Although the mechanics of the Innes-Nicholas-Jefferson strategy remain hidden, the results are suggested by the vote of the House. Enough Republicans' votes were secured that Kentucky Federalist John Rowan's motion to establish a committee of inquiry was lost with the adjournment of Congress.

For some time after the failure of the impeachment attempt, national politics seem to have had less influence on the Kentucky federal courts than they had earlier. (The feud between the Republicans and Federalists shifted to the state court system, where Innes and Todd brought libel suits against Humphrey Marshall.) But the day of acquiescence in national policies was still not at hand for all Kentuckians. When Congress passed new internal revenue laws to pay for the War of 1812, it soon became clear that there were some westerners who remained unreconciled to whiskey taxes. This time, however, the federal district court supported the government and promptly pursued the errant distillers. It took a few terms and some instructive

[1] Thomas Jefferson to Wilson Cary Nicholas, Aug. 26, 1799, Papers of Thomas Jefferson in the Collections of the Massachusetts Historical Society, Boston, given by Thomas Jefferson Coolidge.

judgments, but the lesson was learned—and a second Whiskey Rebellion never materialized in Kentucky.

These federal courts did not need federal statutes to enforce in order to keep busy, because the private caseload remained heavy and active. Land cases alone equaled internal revenue suits in number, and there were almost as many other private controversies as land cases. All together, more than two thousand people brought their causes to the Kentucky federal courts for adjudication during the period covered by this study. Although Innes had his own notions about the proper use of English forms of action, and Todd apparently disagreed about the extent of federal jurisdiction, when it came to judgments their patterns were remarkably consistent. The quantification of these judgments shows why plaintiffs brought so many cases to the federal courts when the state courts had concurrent jurisdiction. It was evident that if the federal judges accepted a case, the plaintiff at law was almost certain, eventually, to win, and the complainant in chancery to gain what was sought. Losing defendants, who had to pay judgments, court costs, and legal fees, were unlikely to risk more money by carrying their cases further—unless, of course, they had connections in Washington.

Only forty-four defendants did take that risk, but some of them had connections of the first order. They, or their attorneys, were related to the chief justice himself. And John Marshall, unlike Harry Innes or Thomas Todd, did not regularly excuse himself from such cases. Whether he did or not, the Marshall court generally upheld the lower court's decisions in protecting property rights. But sometimes it was particularly protective of the interests of the ubiquitous Marshall family, at the expense of others who had won their cases in the lower courts in Kentucky.

Untangling the strands of kinship and alliance leaves the federal courts in Kentucky appearing baldly political and renders their neutrality suspect. But the fundamental political decisions made by the Kentucky judges were not necessarily partisan ones. Innes and Todd believed that crimes were defined by violence, that contracts should be honored, that debts should be paid (even when the creditors were British merchants), and that the dispossessed should be compensated. Property rights might be balanced, but they would be honored. These were the principles the judges upheld by the authority of their court —and therefore of their government. In Kentucky, the results of the War for Independence were limited to ending the suzerainty of Great Britain: this was a limited revolution. (English legal forms, were, of

198

course, admirably suited for this purpose.) And Innes also believed that if the experiment in republicanism was to survive, the republic must demonstrate its concern and prove its value to its skeptical western constituents before unpopular statutes could or would be enforced.

That first generation of Kentuckians must have observed what historians may deduce from the evidence: that the attorneys who could appeal to the precepts and principles preferred by the court were the ones most likely to win their cases. The lawyer's legal strategy was essentially a political art, but it was confined within the value system that the judges upheld and the community accepted. Even the restrictions of classical pleadings and the rituals of ancient procedures did not deter the court from promulgating its own view of what the law was and should be. The federal courts in Kentucky manifest in microcosm Justice Oliver Wendell Holmes's classic assertion:

> The life of the law has not been logic; it has been experience. The felt necessities of the time, the prevalent moral and political theories, intuitions of public policy, avowed or unconscious, even the prejudices which judges share with their fellow-men, have had a good deal more to do than the syllogism in determining the rules by which men should be governed. The law embodies the story of a nation's development through many centuries, and it cannot be dealt with as if it contained only the axioms and corollaries of a book of mathematics.[2]

Beyond the sampled statutes, isolated cases, personal memoirs, factional accounts, and most importantly, beyond the obscurantism of forgotten formalities, lies the legal history of the early republic—in evidence contained in the records of the courts themselves. Only when they have all been studied can the role of the judiciary be accurately evaluated. The records of the first federal courts in Kentucky suggest that these long-overlooked inferior courts provided a significant link between an otherwise distant government and its citizens by promulgating a familiar and predictable law and by interpreting public policies in ways that secured the national experiment in self-government.

[2] O[liver] W[endell] Holmes, Jr., *The Common Law* (Boston, 1881), 1.

Private Case Docket of the Federal Courts in Kentucky

District Court, December 1789-November 1800
Circuit Court, May 1801-May 1802
District Court, November 1802-November 1806
Circuit Court, May 1807-November 1815

Court Term	Common Law Cases[1]		Chancery Suits[2]		Judgments During Term	Pending at End of Term	Total New Cases
	NEW	OLD	NEW	OLD			
1789 Dec.	0	0	0	0	0	0	0
1790 Apr.	0	0	0	0	0	0	0
1790 June	0	0	0	0	0	0	0
1790 Sept.	0	0	0	0	0	0	0
1791 June	3	0	0	0	2	1	3
1791 Sept.	4	0	0	0	1	4	7
1792 Mar.	4	3	1	0	6	3	12
1792 Sept.	0	1	0	0	1	2	12
1792 Dec.	0	0	2	1	0	4	14
1793 Mar.	7	0	2	0	1	12	23
1793 June	3	0	3	5	0	18	29
1793 Dec.	11	4	0	1	6	23	40
1794 Mar.	7	8	1	2	4	27	48
1794 July	6	13	3	3	10	26	57
1794 Sept.	2	2	0	0	1	27	59
1794 Dec.	8	3	0	0	0	35	67
1795 Mar.	6	14	1	0	3	39	74
1795 June	2	17	0	0	3	38	76
1795 Sept.	10	15	0	0	8	40	86
1795 Dec.	0	2	1	1	0	41	87
1796 Mar.	1	16	0	2	0	42	88
1796 June	4	10	2	5	3	45	94
1796 Sept.	2	10	3	3	4	47	99
1796 Dec.	6	10	3	2	4	51	108
1797 Mar.	10	16	3	6	12	52	121
1797 June	2	2	1	1	0	56	124
1797 Nov.	10	23	1	7	5	67	135
1798 Mar.	8	23	3	7	6	72	146
1798 July	11	22	4	7	6	82	161
1798 Nov.	6	22	8	9	11	85	175

[1] Includes common law actions of case, covenant, debt, detinue, ejectment, writ of dower, and writ of right.
[2] Includes suits in chancery, caveat, and injunctions.

Court Term	Common Law Cases[1]		Chancery Suits[2]		Judgments During Term	Pending at End of Term	Total New Cases
	NEW	OLD	NEW	OLD			
1799 Mar.	16	21	7	13	7	102	198
1799 July	14	20	3	12	15	105	215
1799 Nov.	14	18	6	15	1	124	235
1800 Mar.	20	37	0	16	17	127	255
1800 June	29	41	11	21	41	129	295
1800 Nov.	30	26	13	29	27	149	338
1801 May	3	2	12	15	1	164	353
1801 Nov.	36	25	16	32	28	194	405
1802 May	20	53	9	40	48	191	434
1802 Nov.	48	48	26	67	34	243	508
1803 Mar.	19	48	2	41	22	251	529
1803 July	20	54	13	42	28	265	562
1803 Nov.	33	52	7	43	32	278	602
1804 Apr.	21	59	7	41	31	290	630
1804 July	26	61	18	43	27	320	674
1804 Nov.	30	58	15	37	32	346	719
1805 Mar.	23	67	8	60	25	388	750
1805 July	31	72	16	55	44	371	797
1805 Dec.	7	4	4	34	10	374	808
1806 Mar.	45	74	30	63	47	406	883
1806 July	32	75	7	59	52	405	922
1806 Nov.	18	72	13	74	39	414	953
1807 May	1	11	5	15	11	414	959
1807 Nov.	48	72	16	111	56	442	1,023
1808 May	2	3	1	9	6	439	1,026
1808 July	8	51	13	85	54	414	1,047
1808 Nov.	5	21	7	19	13	416	1,059
1809 May	29	55	11	73	65	395	1,099
1809 Nov.	10	51	5	58	30	387	1,114
1810 May	23	31	6	58	31	399	1,143
1810 Nov.	25	54	9	42	38	431	1,177
1811 May	18	47	8	37	32	435	1,203
1811 Nov.	15	38	10	27	27	442	1,228
1812 May	33	28	17	33	46	448	1,278
1812 Nov.	16	18	7	16	24	458	1,301
1813 May	13	27	14	21	26	465	1,328
1813 Nov.	10	15	2	5	6	472	1,340
1814 May	31	38	10	33	57	470	1,381
1814 Nov.	42	45	5	15	33	497	1,428
1815 May	31	60	9	30	37	507	1,468
1815 Nov.	39	58	8	24	32	520	1,515
Totals	989		526				

Appendix B

Judgments on Private Suits in Kentucky Federal Courts

District Court, December 1789-November 1800
Circuit Court, May 1801-May 1802
District Court, November 1802-November 1806
Circuit Court, May 1807-November 1815

Court Term	P[1]	D[2]	A[3]	Disc[4]	Dism[5]	Nons[6]	Other[7]	Total
1789 Dec.	0	0	0	0	0	0	0	0
1790 Apr.	0	0	0	0	0	0	0	0
1790 June	0	0	0	0	0	0	0	0
1790 Sept.	0	0	0	0	0	0	0	0
1791 June	2	0	0	0	0	0	0	2
1791 Sept.	1	0	0	0	0	0	0	1
1792 Mar.	6	0	0	0	0	0	0	6
1792 Sept.	0	0	0	1	0	0	0	1
1792 Dec.	0	0	0	0	0	0	0	0
1793 Mar.	1	0	0	0	0	0	0	1
1793 June	0	0	0	0	0	0	0	0
1793 Dec.	5	0	1	0	0	0	0	6
1794 Mar.	4	0	0	0	0	0	0	4
1794 July	7	0	1	0	2	0	0	10
1794 Sept.	0	0	0	0	1	0	0	1
1794 Dec.	0	0	0	0	0	0	0	0
1795 Mar.	2	0	0	0	0	0	1	3
1795 June	1	0	1	0	1	0	0	3
1795 Sept.	7	1	0	0	0	0	0	8
1795 Dec.	0	0	0	0	0	0	1	1
1796 Mar.	0	0	0	0	0	0	0	0
1796 June	3	0	0	0	0	0	0	3
1796 Sept.	2	1	1	0	0	0	0	4
1796 Dec.	3	0	0	0	1	0	0	4
1797 Mar.	10	1	1	0	0	0	0	12
1797 June	0	0	0	0	0	0	0	0
1797 Nov.	3	2	0	0	0	0	0	5
1798 Mar.	5	1	0	0	0	0	0	6
1798 July	6	0	0	0	0	0	0	6
1798 Nov.	9	0	0	2	0	0	0	11

[1] Plaintiff or Complainant.
[2] Defendant.
[3] Abated.
[4] Discontinued.
[5] Dismissed.
[6] Nonsuited.
[7] Remanded to state courts, unless otherwise noted.

Court Term	P[1]	D[2]	A[3]	Disc[4]	Dism[5]	Nons[6]	Other[7]	Total
1799 Mar.	6	1	0	0	0	0	0	7
1799 July	14	1	0	0	0	0	0	15
1799 Nov.	1	0	0	0	0	0	0	1
1800 Mar.	11	1	0	5	0	0	0	17
1800 June	38	3	0	0	0	0	0	41
1800 Nov.	23	4	0	0	0	0	0	27
1801 May	0	0	0	0	1	0	0	1
1801 Nov.	22	1	0	0	5	0	0	28
1802 May	38	1	0	0	7	0	2	48
1802 Nov.	22	1	0	3	8	0	0	34
1803 Mar.	18	0	1	0	2	1	0	22
1803 July	26	0	0	0	2	0	0	28
1803 Nov.	25	0	0	2	4	1	0	32
1804 Apr.	22	5	0	1	2	0	0	30
1804 July	22	0	0	1	2	0	2	27
1804 Nov.	27	0	0	1	3	0	1	32
1805 Mar.	21	0	1	0	2	1	0	25
1805 July	37	1	0	3	2	1	0	44
1805 Dec.	4	1	0	2	1	0	2	10
1806 Mar.	40	0	1	1	2	3	0	47
1806 July	37	3	2	8	2	0	0	52
1806 Nov.	23	0	1	9	4	2	0	39
1807 May	5	1	0	4	1	0	0	11
1807 Nov.	28	1	4	1	8	0	14*	56
1808 May	0	0	0	0	0	0	6*	6
1808 July	14	1	0	0	16	0	23*	54
1808 Nov.	4	1	0	1	3	0	4*	13
1809 May	24	2	2	3	7	1	26*	65
1809 Nov.	10	2	0	0	8	0	10*	30
1810 May	11	1	2	1	9	0	7*	31
1810 Nov.	26	1	0	2	8	1	0	38
1811 May	12	2	0	8	6	2	2	32
1811 Nov.	15	4	0	3	2	2	1	27
1812 May	19	5	0	3	12	4	3*	46
1812 Nov.	18	0	2	3	1	0	0	24
1813 May	19	2	1	1	3	0	0	26
1813 Nov.	3	0	0	2	1	0	0	6
1814 May	31	5	2	1	10	7	1	57
1814 Nov.	14	1	2	2	10	2	2	33
1815 May	22	2	1	0	7	2	3	37
1815 Nov.	17	1	1	0	12	1	0	32
Totals	846	61	28	74	178	31	111	1,329

* Dismissed for want of jurisdiction.

Appendix C

Cases Brought by the United States
in Kentucky Federal Courts

Court Term	New Cases			Total	Judgments			Pend-ing
	CRIMINAL	CIVIL	OTHER[1]		P[2]	D[3]	OTHER[4]	
District Court								
1789 Dec.	0	0	0	0	0	0	0	0
1790 Apr.	0	0	0	0	0	0	0	0
1790 June	0	0	0	0	0	0	0	0
1790 Sept.	0	0	0	0	0	0	0	0
1791 June	0	0	0	0	0	0	0	0
1791 Sept.	0	0	0	0	0	0	0	0
1792 Mar.	0	0	0	0	0	0	0	0
1792 Sept.	0	0	0	0	0	0	0	0
1792 Dec.	0	0	0	0	0	0	0	0
1793 Mar.	0	0	0	0	0	0	0	0
1793 June	0	0	0	0	0	0	0	0
1793 Dec.	0	2	0	2	0	0	0	2
1794 Mar.	0	0	0	2	0	0	0	2
1794 July	0	0	0	2	0	0	2	0
1794 Sept.	0	0	0	2	0	0	0	0
1794 Dec.	0	0	0	2	0	0	0	0
1795 Mar.	1	0	0	3	0	0	0	1
1795 June	0	0	0	3	0	0	1	0
1795 Sept.	0	0	0	3	0	0	0	0
1795 Dec.	0	0	0	3	0	0	0	0
1796 Mar.	0	0	0	3	0	0	0	0
1796 June	0	0	0	3	0	0	0	0
1796 Sept.	0	0	0	3	0	0	0	0
1796 Dec.	2	0	0	5	0	0	0	2
1797 Mar.	4	0	0	9	0	0	1	5
1797 June	0	0	0	9	0	0	0	5
1797 Nov.	0	5	0	14	0	1	1	8
1798 Mar.	1	0	0	15	0	1	1	7
1798 July	3	0	0	18	1	3	2	4
1798 Nov.	12	6	0	36	0	1	0	23

[1] Includes attachments, writs of *fieri facias, scire facias,* etc.
[2] Plaintiff.
[3] Defendant.
[4] Abated, dismissed, discontinued, or nonsuited.

Court Term	New Cases			Total	Judgments			Pending
	CRIMINAL	CIVIL	OTHER[1]		P[2]	D[3]	OTHER[4]	ing
District Court								
1799 Mar.	15	7	0	58	3	0	0	42
1799 July	1	23	0	82	17	4	6	39
1799 Nov.	5	63	0	150	19	1	0	87
1800 Mar.	7	48	3	208	81	5	15	44
1800 June	0	12	4	224	20	9	22	9
1800 Nov.	5	12	3	244	7	1	14	7
Circuit Court								
1801 May	0	0	0	244	0	0	0	7
1801 Nov.	13	161	16	434	30	1	9	157
1802 May	1	51	4	490	45	3	25	147
District Court								
1802 Nov.	10	18	6	524	27	3	10	141
1803 Mar.	1	7	0	532	8	0	5	136
1803 July	0	11	5	548	12	0	1	138
1803 Nov.	1	12	0	561	14	6	8	123
1804 Apr.	0	10	3	574	8	3	3	122
1804 July	2	10	7	593	7	2	2	130
1804 Sept.	0	0	1	594	1	0	0	130
1804 Nov.	0	5	2	601	4	1	8	123
1805 Mar.	0	12	2	615	7	2	3	125
1805 July	0	11	3	629	13	4	1	129
1805 Dec.	0	2	0	631	0	4	0	127
1806 Mar.	0	7	0	638	5	0	2	127
1806 July	0	0	1	639	5	0	23	100
1806 Nov.	0	0	3	642	0	0	7	97
1807 June	0	5	0	5[5]	10	0	2	0[6]
1807 Dec.	0	6	0	11	5	0	0	
1808 July	0	2	0	13	0	0	1	
1808 Dec.	0	2	0	15	2	0	5	
1809 May[7]	0	0	2	17	0	0	3	

[5] The totals in this column refer only to district court cases 1807-1815. The previous total is transferred to that portion of the table containing circuit court cases 1807-1815.

[6] Because the basis for retention of cases in the district court is unclear from the Order Books, pending totals are given in the circuit court portion of the table.

[7] The remaining pages (358-420) of Order Book G are increasingly illegible, and the subsequent quantification may be inaccurate.

Court Term	New Cases			Total	Judgments			Pend-ing
	CRIMINAL	CIVIL	OTHER[1]		P[2]	D[3]	OTHER[4]	
District Court								
1809 Dec.	Met only for adjournment							
1810 May	0	0	1	18	0	0	0	
1810 Dec.	0	5	0	23	0	1	0	
1811 May	0	0	0	23	0	0	0	
1811 Dec.	0	0	0	23	0	0	0	
1812 May	No court held			23				
1812 Dec.	0	0	0	23	0	0	0	
1813 May	No court held			23				
1813 Dec.	No court held			23				
1814 May	1	0	0	24	0	0	0	
1814 Dec.	1	4	0	29	2	0	0	
1815 May	3	20	2	53	20	0	0	
1815 Dec.	6	32	0	91	25	2	3	
Circuit Court								
1807 May	1	1	0	644	0	0	0	92
1807 Nov.	0	0	0	644	0	0	0	93
1808 May	0	4	0	648	0	0	0	97
1808 July	0	0	0	648	0	0	2	96
1808 Nov.	2	0	3	653	1	3	1	91
1809 May	0	6	0	659	4	0	1	91
1809 Nov.	0	0	0	659	0	0	0	91
1810 May	0	0	3	662	7	0	4	84
1810 Nov.	0	12	0	674	11	0	1	88
1811 May	0	0	0	674	4	2	0	82
1811 Nov.	0	1	0	675	3	0	0	80
1812 May	0	0	0	675	1	0	0	79
1812 Nov.	0	0	0	675	0	0	0	79
1813 May	0	1	0	676	0	0	1	79
1813 Nov.	0	0	0	676	0	0	0	79
1814 May	0	0	0	676	0	0	0	80
1814 Nov.	0	1	3	680	3	0	1	83
1815 May	1	1	0	682	1	1	0	87
1815 Nov.	1	0	1	684	1	1	0	95
District Court Cases 1807-1815				91				
			Total	775				

207

Appendix D

Harry Innes's 1785 Book Order[1]

Manchester, 22 November, 1785
Bou[gh]t of John Leitch

	£		
2 Trunks Marked HI/IL No 1 a[nd] 2			
Bacons Abridgment of the Laws, 5 Vol. in			
Russia[n leather binding]	£	8 —	—
Cases in Equity (Time of Talbot)		18	—
Cases in Equity Abridged 2 Vol.	1	16	—
Lord Raymonds Reports of Entries 3 Vol.	4	8	—
Cunninghams Law Dictionary, 2 Vol. 2nd hand	1	18	—
Showers Cases in Parliament		10	6
Vernons Reports, 2 Vol.	1	16	—
[John] Tracey Atkyns Reports 3 Vol.	1	11	6
Burroughs [Burrow's] Reports 5 Vol.	7	1	—
Hales Pleas of the Crown 2 Vol.	1	4	—
Harrisons Chancery Practice, 2 Vol.		12	—
Strange's Reports 2 Vol.	1	1	—
Crown Circuit [Companion]		9	—
Comyns Digest 5 Vol.	7	17	6
Fergusons Civil Society		6	—
Becarea [Beccaria] on Crimes and Punishments		3	—
Montesquieus Spirit of [the] Laws		12	—
Salkelds Reports	1	16	—
Fieldings Works, 12 Vol.	1	16	—
Popes Works and Homer, 15 Vol.	2	5	—
Bible Royal Folio in Russia[n] Leather	2	10	—
Esops [Aesops] Fables by Dodsley		3	—
Robinson Crusoe 2 Vol. Best		6	—
Roderick Random 2 Vol.		5	—
Swin's Champion		—	6
Humphrey Clinker, 3 Vol. in 2		6	—
Dryden's Virgil, 4 Vol. Plates		12	—
Sterne's Sermons 6 Vol. in 2		7	—
Johnson's Dictionary 2 Vol. Folio	4	10	—
Plutarchs Lives 8 Vol.	1	4	—
Catalogue of Law Books		2	6
Forsters [Fosters] Crown Laws		7	—

[1] Harry Innes Papers, Manuscript Dept., Filson Club, Louisville, Ky.

Manchester, 22 November, 1785

Rutherford's Natural Law, 2 Vol.	£		12	—
2 hair Trunks Matted and Corded		1	14	—
Cartage			2	4
	£	59	1	10
Charges, freight, Entry, Searchers fees, W[h]arfage, Shipping, Bills of Lading, prom[ise] of Insrce [insurance]		3	9	7
		62	11	5
15 pr cent	£	9	7	8½
£ 100 14 9½ Currency	£	71	19	1½
40 pr cent Exchange		28	15	1½

Appendix E

A Glossary of Terms Used
in the Kentucky Federal Courts

ABATE: To terminate a suit because of the death of one of the parties.

BILL OF EXCEPTIONS: A statement of objections to the rulings or instructions of the judge, made for the purpose of review by a higher court.

BILL OF REVIVOR: A request to revive a suit after abatement.

CASE: A charge by the plaintiff that he had suffered an indirect injury resulting from action (or inaction) by the defendant. This injury was usually financial damage because of failure by the defendant to pay for "goods, wares, and merchandise" delivered by the plaintiff.

CAVEAT: An equity proceeding, derived from Virginia, warning that a patent to land should not be issued because some required procedure had not been followed, or had not been followed properly, or because there had been an anterior action by the complainant that negated the defendant's action.

CHANCERY: A procedure to gain some equity that could not be gained through the common law actions. In Kentucky, these were land suits often following ejectment cases, sometimes to settle boundary disputes, sometimes to compensate the defeated claimant for his improvements to the land.

COVENANT: A charge that the defendant had broken a legal contract.

DEBT: A charge that the defendant had refused, after demand had been made, to pay money owed to the plaintiff.

DETINUE: A charge that the defendant had wrongfully detained movable property and had refused to return it to the plaintiff. The properties in these cases were slaves and horses.

DISTRAINT (OR DISTRESS) AND SALE: To seize property and sell it, with the proceeds going to pay taxes that the owner has failed to pay.

EJECTMENT: An action to try title to land brought by the holder of a senior patent against the holder of a junior patent, or against an occupier who held no patent.

IN PERSONAM: Proceedings directed against an individual.

IN REM: Proceedings directed against property (e.g., a still).

INFORMALITY: Lack of legal form.

INJUNCTION: A court order to stop the defendant from performing some action.

JUDGMENT DEBTOR: A person against whom judgment was rendered by a court that he owed, but had not paid, a debt.

NIL DEBET: A plea by a defendant that he owes nothing; pleading the general issue in actions of debt.

210

NOLLE PROSEQUI: A motion by the prosecutor that he will not further prosecute the case.

NONSUIT: Termination of a case by the judge when the plaintiff failed to continue, or when the plaintiff failed to substantiate his charge with sufficient evidence.

SUPERSEDEAS: An order to stay execution of a judgment.

TRESPASS: A charge that the defendant had committed an unlawful act directly injuring the plaintiff, sometimes with assault and battery.

UNCERTAINTY: Vagueness.

WRIT OF CAPIAS AD RESPONDENDUM: A command to the marshal to take the defendant, keep him safely, and bring him into court to answer the plaintiff's action. An *alias capias ad respondendum* was a second order reaffirming the first; a *pluries capias ad respondendum* was a third order reaffirming the first. These orders notified the defendant of his obligation to defend the suit and provided for his arrest until he posted security for the plaintiff's claim.

WRIT OF CAPIAS AD SATISFACIENDUM: A command to the marshal to take the defendant, keep him safely, and bring him into court to satisfy the plaintiff's claim. The order provided for the defendant's arrest until he satisfied the judgment of the court.

WRIT OF ERROR: An order commanding a lower court to submit the record of a case to a higher court so that it may review how the law was applied by the lower court judge. Facts found by juries were not reviewable under this writ.

WRIT OF ERROR CORAM NOBIS: An order providing a court the opportunity to correct its own judgment when it was based upon an error in fact.

WRIT OF FIERI FACIAS: An order to secure the amount of money awarded in a judgment from the goods and chattels of the unsuccessful litigant.

WRIT OF HABERE FACIAS POSSESSIONEM: An order to take possession of land after a successful action in ejectment.

WRIT OF RIGHT: A charge that the demandant had a better right to land than did the tenant, because of factors of descent or inheritance.

WRIT OF SCIRE FACIAS: An order to proceed against a surety, or to revive a judgment and secure its execution.

WRIT OF VENDITIONE EXPONAS: An order to the marshal to sell goods or property.

WRIT OF VENIRE FACIAS: An order to the marshal to summon a petit jury.

WRIT OF VENIRE FACIAS AD RESPONDENDUM: An order to the marshal to summon an individual for arraignment.

WRIT OF VENIRE FACIAS DE NOVO: An order to the marshal to summon a jury for a new trial.

I. Manuscript Sources
    A. *Records of the Judicial Branch*
    B. *Records of the Executive Branch*
    C. *Private Papers*
II. Published Primary Sources
    A. *United States Government Documents*
    B. *State and Territorial Documents*
    C. *Private Papers*
III. Newspapers
IV. Legal and Constitutional Histories, Legal Treatises, and
    Casebooks
V. Kentucky Histories
VI. Other Secondary Sources

I. MANUSCRIPT SOURCES

A. *Records of the Judicial Branch*

United States Court for the District of Kentucky
    Order Book A, Dec. 15, 1789-July 13, 1798
    Order Book B, Nov. 19, 1798-Nov. 22, 1800
    Order Book C, Nov. 24, 1800-Dec. 2, 1802
    (Includes United States Court for the Sixth Circuit Order Book, May 16,
      1801-June 5, 1802)
    Order Book D, Dec. 2, 1802-April 13, 1804
    Order Book E, April 13, 1804-March 20, 1805
    Order Book F, March 20, 1805-July 29, 1806
    Order Book G, July 30, 1806-Dec. 11, 1815
United States Circuit Court for the District of Kentucky (Seventh Circuit)
    Order Book A, May 4, 1807-Nov. 24, 1807
    Order Book B, Nov. 25, 1807-May 23, 1811
    Order Book C, May 23, 1811-Nov. 11, 1814
    Order Book D, Nov. 12, 1814-Nov. 4, 1816
United States Circuit Court for the District of Kentucky (Seventh Circuit)
    Complete Record, Book A, 1807
    Complete Record, Book B, 1808, 1809
    Complete Record, Book C, 1810, 1811
    Complete Record, Book D, 1812
    Complete Record, Book E, 1813
    Complete Record, Book F, 1814, 1815
    Complete Record, Book G, 1815

[All Kentucky federal court records listed above are in the custody of the Clerk of the United States Court for the Eastern District of Kentucky, Lexington. They are housed in the Old Federal Building in Frankfort. These records have been microfilmed by the Church of Jesus Christ of Latter Day Saints, and copies of the microfilm are held by the Special Collections Department, Margaret I. King Library, University of Kentucky, Lexington.]

Appellate Case Files of the Supreme Court of the United States, 1792-1831, Records of the Supreme Court of the United States, Record Group 267, National Archives Microfilm Publication M-214, 96 rolls.

[Innes, Harry.] "Cases in the Court of the United States for the District of Kentucky, from its first Organization to the year 1806 Inclusive." [Holographic opinions, bound and labeled on spine *Innes Reports*.] In the custody of James F. Gordon, Judge of the United States Court for the Western District of Kentucky, Federal Court Building, Louisville, Kentucky.

United States Court for the District of Kentucky. Grand Jury Rolls. In the custody of Davis T. McGarvey, Clerk of the United States Court for the Eastern District of Kentucky, Federal Building, Lexington, Kentucky.

United States District Court. Memorandum Book of Thomas Tunstall, Clerk of the United States Court for the District of Kentucky, July Term, 1799. Manuscript Collection, The Filson Club, Louisville, Kentucky.

United States District Court. Order Book. [Mislabeled. Holographic copy of selected Rules and Opinions of the court 1795-1801.] Manuscript Collection, The Filson Club, Louisville, Kentucky.

B. *Records of the Executive Branch*

The following records are in the National Archives, Washington, D.C.:

Records of the Post Office Department, Record Group 28
    Letters Sent by the Postmaster General, 1789-1836, National Archives Microfilm Publication M-601, 50 rolls.

General Records of the Department of the Treasury, Record Group 56
    Internal Revenue, Letters Sent, 1803-1819.
    Internal Revenue Assessors, Duties on Household Goods, 1815-1816.
    Internal Revenue Direct Tax, Correspondence, 1807-1829, file 11713.

Records of the Bureau of Internal Revenue, Record Group 58
    Accounts Current of the Commissioners of the Revenue, 1791-1804, 2 vols.
    Letters Sent by the Commissioner of the Revenue and the Revenue Office, 1792-1807, National Archives Microfilm Publication M-414, 3 rolls.
    Whiskey Rebellion Papers.

General Records of the Department of State, Record Group 59
    Domestic Letters of the Department of State, 1784-1906, National Archives Microfilm Publication M-40, 171 rolls.

Letters of Application and Recommendation, John Adams, 1797-1801, National Archives Microfilm Publication M-406, 3 rolls.

Letters of Application and Recommendation, Thomas Jefferson, 1801-1809, National Archives Microfilm Publication M-418, 12 rolls.

Letters of Application and Recommendation, James Madison, 1809-1817, National Archives Microfilm Publication M-483, 8 rolls.

Miscellaneous Letters of the Department of State, 1789-1906, National Archives Microfilm Publication M-179, 96 rolls.

Records of the Bureau of Indian Affairs, Record Group 75

Letters of Tench Coxe, Commissioner of the Revenue, Relating to the Procurement of Military, Naval, and Indian Supplies, 1794-1796, National Archives Microfilm Publication M-74, 1 roll.

Records of the Office of the Secretary of War, Record Group 107

Letters Received by the Secretary of War, Unregistered Series, 1789-1860, National Archives Microfilm Publication M-222, 34 rolls.

Records of the Solicitor of the Treasury, Record Group 206

Solicitor of the Treasury, Attorneys' Returns, 1821-1830, List of Suits Decided and Pending in the Circuit Court of the United States for the District of Kentucky, file 34508.

Solicitor of the Treasury, Letters Received, United States Attorneys, Clerks of Courts, and Marshals, Kentucky, 1804-1866, file 32092.

Solicitor of the Treasury, Letters Sent, 1820-1830, file 12229.

Assignments of Insolvent Debtors to the United States, Case Papers, 1817-1843, file 23818.

Register of Suits Directed to be Instituted Against Sundry Persons [by the] Solicitor of the Treasury, 1791-1821, file 18182.

Return of Executions Which have been Received by the Marshal, Statement of Executions Issued on Judgments Rendered in Suits on Treasury Transcripts, 1821-1830, file 26889.

C. *Private Papers*

Autographs file (no. 25). Manuscript Collection, Kentucky Historical Society, Frankfort, Ky. (Selected legal papers of Harry Innes.)

Thomas Bodley file (no. 88). Manuscript Collection, Kentucky Historical Society, Frankfort, Ky.

Breckinridge Family Papers. Manuscript Division, Library of Congress, Washington, D.C.

Brown Family Papers. Special Collections Department, Margaret I. King Library, University of Kentucky, Lexington, Ky.

John Mason Brown file (no. 117). Manuscript Collection, Kentucky Historical Society, Frankfort, Ky.

Tench Coxe Papers, Tench Coxe Section, Coxe Papers, Historical Society of Pennsylvania, Philadelphia, Pennsylvania.

Joseph Hamilton Daveiss and Samuel Daveiss Papers, Manuscript Collection, The Filson Club, Louisville, Ky.

William Davies file (no. 223). Manuscript Collection, Kentucky Historical Society, Frankfort, Ky.

Harry Innes file (no. 473). Manuscript Collection, Kentucky Historical Society, Frankfort, Ky.

Harry Innes Papers, Manuscript Division, Library of Congress, Washington, D.C.

Harry Innes Papers, 1750-1810. Manuscript Collection, The Filson Club, Louisville, Ky.

Papers Relating to Harry Innes. Otto A. Rothert, Collector. Manuscript Collection, The Filson Club, Louisville, Ky.

Henry Knox Papers, Massachusetts Historical Society (microfilm), Boston, Massachusetts.

Thomas Jefferson Papers, Library of Congress (microfilm).

Papers of Thomas Jefferson in the Massachusetts Historical Society, Coolidge Collection (microfilm), Massachusetts Historical Society, Boston, Massachusetts.

James Madison Papers, Library of Congress (microfilm).

George Nicholas file (no. 715). Manuscript Collection, Kentucky Historical Society, Frankfort, Ky.

Robert Treat Paine Papers, Massachusetts Historical Society (microfilm), Boston, Massachusetts.

Timothy Pickering Papers, 1758-1829, Massachusetts Historical Society (microfilm), Boston, Massachusetts.

The Political Club, Danville, Kentucky, Records, 1786-1790. Manuscript Collection, The Filson Club, Louisville, Ky.

Winthrop Sargent Papers, 1771-1948, Massachusetts Historical Society (microfilm), Boston, Massachusetts.

Isaac Shelby Papers, Manuscript Collection, The Filson Club, Louisville, Ky.

Todd Family Papers, 1783-1891, Manuscript Collection, The Filson Club, Louisville, Ky.

Thomas Todd file, Manuscript Collection, United States Supreme Court Library, Washington, D.C.

Robert Trimble file, Manuscript Collection, United States Supreme Court Library, Washington, D.C.

Charles Warren Papers, Manuscript Division, Library of Congress, Washington, D.C.

George Washington Papers, Library of Congress (microfilm).

Samuel M. Wilson Manuscript Collection, Special Collections Department, Margaret I. King Library, University of Kentucky, Lexington, Ky.

Oliver Wolcott, Jr., Papers, Manuscript Collection, Connecticut Historical Society, Hartford, Connecticut.

Bennett Young Papers, Manuscript Collection, The Filson Club, Louisville, Ky.

II. PUBLISHED PRIMARY SOURCES

A. *United States Government Documents*

Cranch, William. *Reports of Cases Argued and Adjudged in the Supreme Court of the United States, 1801-1815.* 9 vols. Boston: Little, Brown and Co., 1870.

Dallas, A[lexander] J. *Reports of Cases in the Courts of the United States, and Pennsylvania, 1790-1800.* 3 vols. Boston: Little, Brown and Co., 1870.

Debates and Proceedings in the Congress of the United States, 1789-1824 [*Annals of Congress*]. 42 vols. Washington, D.C.: Gales and Seaton, 1834-1856.

Historical Records Survey. *Inventory of Federal Archives in the States: Federal Courts: Series II, Number 16, Kentucky.* Washington, D.C.: Works Progress Administration, 1939.

Lowrie, Walter, and Franklin, Walter S., eds. *American State Papers, Finance: Documents, Legislative and Executive of the Congress of the United States.* 5 vols. Washington, D.C.: Gales and Seaton, 1834.

————. *American State Papers, Miscellaneous: Documents, Legislative and Executive of the Congress of the United States.* 2 vols. Washington, D.C.: Gales and Seaton, 1834.

Peters, Richard, ed. *The Public Statutes at Large of the United States of America, 1789-1873.* 17 vols. Boston: Little, Brown and Co., 1850-1873.

Wheaton, Henry. *Reports of Cases in the Supreme Court of the United States, 1816-1827.* 12 vols. Boston: Little, Brown and Co., 1870.

B. *State and Territorial Documents*

Bibb, George M. *Reports of Cases at Common Law and in Chancery Argued and Decided in the Court of Appeals of the Commonwealth of Kentucky.* 4 vols. [IV-VII *Kentucky Reports.*] 2d ed. Frankfort: Brown and Hodges, 1840.

Blume, William Wirt, ed. *Transactions of the Supreme Court of the Territory of Michigan 1805-1814.* 2 vols. Ann Arbor, Michigan: University of Michigan Press, 1935.

Carter, Clarence Edwin, ed. *The Territorial Papers of the United States,* Vol. VII, *The Territory of Indiana, 1800-1810.* Washington, D.C.: Government Printing Office, 1939.

Hardin, Martin D. *Reports of Cases Argued and Adjudged in the Court of Appeals of Kentucky from Spring Term 1805 to Spring Term 1808, Inclusive.* [III *Kentucky Reports.*] Frankfort: Johnston and Pleasants, 1810.

Hening, William Waller. *The Statutes at Large; Being a Collection of All the Laws of Virginia From the First Session of the Legislature, in the Year 1619.* 13 vols. New York: R. and W. and G. Bartow, 1809-1823.

Hughes, James. *A Report of the Causes Determined by the Late Supreme Court for the District of Kentucky and by the Court of Appeals in which*

Titles to Land Were in Dispute. [i *Kentucky Reports.*] Cincinnati: W. H. Anderson, 1869.

Journal of the Convention Begun and Held at the Capitol in the Town of Frankfort on Monday the twenty-second day of July in the year of our Lord one thousand seven hundred and ninety-nine. N.p., n.d. Manuscript Collection, Kentucky Historical Society, Frankfort, Ky.

Journal of the First Constitutional Convention of Kentucky Held in Danville, Kentucky April 2 to 19, 1792. Reprint ed. Lexington: State Bar Association of Kentucky, 1942.

Littell, William. *The Statute Law of Kentucky: With Notes, Praelections, and Observations on the Public Acts.* 5 vols. Frankfort: William Hunter, 1809-1919.

Littell, William, and Swigert, Jacob. *A Digest of the Statute Law of Kentucky, Being a Collection of All the Acts of the General Assembly of a Public and Permanent Nature, From the Commencement of the Government to May Session 1822, Also, the English and Virginia Statutes, Yet in Force; Together with Several Acts of Congress. With References to Reports of Judicial Decisions in the Court of Appeals of Kentucky and Supreme Court of the United States.* 2 vols. Frankfort: Kendall and Russell, 1822.

Morehead, C. S., and Brown, Mason. *A Digest of the Statute Laws of Kentucky of a Public and Permanent Nature, From the Commencement of the Government to the Session of the Legislature ending on the 24th February, 1834; With References to Judicial Decisions.* 2 vols. Frankfort: A. G. Hodges, 1834.

Palmer, William P., *et al.*, eds. *Calendar of Virginia State Papers and Other Manuscripts . . . Preserved . . . at Richmond* (1652-1869). 11 vols. Richmond: Rush U. Derr, 1875-1893.

Sneed, Achilles. *Decisions of the Court of Appeals of the State of Kentucky from March 1, 1801 to January 18, 1805 Inclusive.* [ii *Kentucky Reports.*] 2d ed. Cincinnati: W. H. Anderson Co., 1869.

Sutton, R., reporter. *Report of the Debates and Proceedings of the Convention for the Revision of the Constitution of the State of Kentucky, 1849.* Frankfort: A. G. Hodges, 1849.

C. *Private Papers*

Adams, Henry, ed. *The Writings of Albert Gallatin.* 2 vols. New York: Antiquarian Press, 1960.

Bassett, John Spencer, ed. *The Correspondence of Andrew Jackson.* 7 vols. Washington, D.C.: Carnegie Institution of Washington, 1926.

Boyd, Julian P., *et al.*, eds. *The Papers of Thomas Jefferson.* Princeton, N.J.: Princeton University Press, 1950-

Daveiss, Joseph Hamilton. "View of the President's Conduct Concerning the Conspiracy of 1806." Edited by Isaac Joslin Cox and Helen A. Swineford.

Quarterly Publication of the Historical and Philosophical Society of Ohio, XII (1917), 53-154.

Fitzpatrick, John C., ed. *The Writings of George Washington from the Original Manuscript Sources, 1745-1799.* 39 vols. Washington, D.C.: Government Printing Office, 1939.

Ford, Paul Leicester, ed. *The Writings of Thomas Jefferson.* 10 vols. New York: G. P. Putnam, 1905.

Gibbs, George, ed. *Memoirs of the Administrations of Washington and John Adams, Edited from the Papers of Oliver Wolcott, Secretary of the Treasury.* 2 vols. New York: William Van Norden, 1846.

Goebel, Julius, Jr., *et al.*, eds. *The Law Practice of Alexander Hamilton: Documents and Commentary.* 2 vols. New York: Columbia University Press, 1964-1969.

Hopkins, James F., and Hargreaves, Mary W. M., eds. *The Papers of Henry Clay.* Lexington, Ky.: University of Kentucky Press, 1959-

Johnson, Herbert A., *et al.*, eds. *The Papers of John Marshall.* Chapel Hill, N.C.: University of North Carolina Press, 1974-

Kent, William. *Memoirs and Letters of James Kent, LL.D.* Boston: Little, Brown and Co., 1898.

Lipscomb, Andrew A., and Bergh, Albert Ellery, eds. *The Writings of Thomas Jefferson.* 20 vols. Washington, D.C.: Thomas Jefferson Memorial Assn., 1905.

Mays, David John, ed. *The Letters and Papers of Edmund Pendleton, 1734-1803.* 2 vols. Charlottesville, Va.: The University Press of Virginia, 1967.

Padover, Saul K., arr. *The Complete Jefferson.* Reprint ed. Freeport, New York: Books for Libraries Press, 1969.

Rhodes, Irwin S. *The Papers of John Marshall: A Descriptive Calendar.* 2 vols. Norman, Okla.: University of Oklahoma Press, 1969.

Syrett, Harold C., *et al.*, eds. *The Papers of Alexander Hamilton.* New York: Columbia University Press, 1961-

Washington, H[enry] A[ugustine], ed. *The Writings of Thomas Jefferson.* 2 vols. Washington, D.C.: Taylor and Maury, 1854.

Wroth, L. Kinvin, and Zobel, Hiller B., eds. *The Legal Papers of John Adams.* 3 vols. Cambridge, Mass.: Harvard University Press, 1965.

III. NEWSPAPERS

Kentucky Gazette, Lexington, Kentucky, 1793-1816.
The Palladium, Frankfort, Kenutcky, 1798-1803.

IV. LEGAL AND CONSTITUTIONAL HISTORIES, LEGAL TREATISES, AND CASEBOOKS

Abel-Smith, Brian, and Stevens, Robert. *Lawyers and the Courts: A Sociological Study of the English Legal System, 1750-1965.* Cambridge, Mass.: Harvard University Press, 1967.

Ames, James Barr. *Lectures on Legal History.* Cambridge, Mass.: Harvard University Press, 1913.

Association of American Law Schools. *Select Essays in Anglo-American Legal History.* 3 vols. Boston: Little, Brown and Co., 1907.

Aumann, Francis R. *The Changing American Legal System: Some Selected Phases.* The Ohio State University Graduate School Series, Contributions in History and Political Science, no. 16. Columbus: 1940.

———. "The Influence of English and Civil Law Principles upon the American Legal System During the Critical Post-Revolutionary Period." *University of Cincinnati Law Review,* XII (1938), 289-317.

———. "Some Problems of Growth and Development in the Formative Period of the American Legal System, 1775-1866." *University of Cincinnati Law Review,* XIII (1939), 382-445.

Bellot, Hugh Hale. "The Literature of the Last Half Century on the Constitutional History of the United States." *Royal Historical Society Transactions.* 5th Ser., VII (1957), 159-182.

Blackstone, William. *Commentaries on the Laws of England.* Edited by George Sharswood. 4 vols. Philadelphia: Lippincott, 1881.

Blickensderfer, Joseph P. "Problems Concerning Primary Records of Courts." *Law Library Journal,* LII (1959), 338-348.

Bloomfield, Maxwell. *American Lawyers in a Changing Society, 1776-1876.* Cambridge, Mass.: Harvard University Press, 1976.

Blume, William Wirt. "Civil Procedure on the American Frontier: A Study of the Records of a Court of Common Pleas of the Northwest and Indiana Territories (1796-1805)." *Michigan Law Review,* LVI (1957), 161-224.

Boorstin, Daniel J., ed. *Delaware Cases 1792-1830.* 3 vols. St. Paul, Minn.: West Publishing Co., 1943.

Brown, Elizabeth Gaspar. *British Statutes in American Law 1776-1836.* Ann Arbor, Mich.: University of Michigan Law School, 1964.

———. "Frontier Justice: Wayne County 1796-1836." *American Journal of Legal History,* XVI (1972), 126-153.

Chalkley, Lyman. "The Sources, Progress, and Printed Evidences of the Written Law in Kentucky." *Kentucky Law Journal,* XII (1924), 43-57; XIII (1925), 113-139.

Chitty, Joseph. *A Treatise on Pleading: With a Collection of Precedents, Adapted to the Recent Pleading and Other Rules, and With Practical Notes.* 6th ed. 3 vols. London: C. Rowarth and Sons, 1837.

Chroust, Anton-Hermann. "The American Legal Profession: Its Agony and Ecstasy." *Notre Dame Lawyer,* XLVI (1971), 487-525.

———. *The Rise of the Legal Profession in America.* 2 vols. Norman: University of Oklahoma Press, 1965.

Dembitz, Lewis N. *Kentucky Jurisprudence.* Louisville: John P. Morton and Co., 1890.

———. *A Treatise on Land Titles.* 2 vols. St. Paul, Minn.: West Publishing Co., 1895.

Dewey, Donald O. *Marshall Versus Jefferson: The Political Background of Marbury v. Madison.* New York: Alfred A. Knopf, 1970.

Faulkner, Robert K. "John Marshall and the Burr Trial." *Journal of American History,* LIII (1966), 247-258.

Field, Richard H., and Kaplan, Benjamin. *Materials for a Basic Course in Civil Procedure.* Mineola, New York: The Foundation Press, Inc., 1968.

Flaherty, David H., ed. *Essays in the History of Early American Law.* Chapel Hill, N.C.: University of North Carolina Press, 1969.

Frank, John P. "Historical Basis of the Federal Judicial System." *Law and Contemporary Problems,* XIII (1948), 3-28.

Frankfurter, Felix. "Distribution of Judicial Power Between United States and State Courts." *Cornell Law Quarterly,* XIII (1928), 499-530.

Frankfurter, Felix, and Landis, James M. *The Business of the Supreme Court: A Study in the Federal Judicial System.* New York: Macmillan, 1928.

Fleming, Donald, and Bailyn, Bernard, eds. *Law in American History.* Perspectives in American History, Vol. V. Cambridge, Mass.: Charles Warren Center for Studies in American History, 1971.

Friedman, Lawrence M. *A History of American Law.* New York: Simon and Schuster, 1973.

Goebel, Julius, Jr. *Antecedents and Beginnings to 1801.* The Oliver Wendell Holmes Devise History of the Supreme Court of the United States, Vol. I. New York: Macmillan, 1971.

————, and Naughton, T. Raymond. *Law Enforcement in Colonial New York: A Study in Criminal Procedure.* New York: The Commonwealth Fund, 1944.

Goodheart, Arthur L. "Costs." *Yale Law Journal,* XXXVIII (1929), 849-878.

Graham, Howard J. *Everyman's Constitution.* Madison, Wisc.: State Historical Society of Wisconsin, 1966.

Haar, Charles M. *The Golden Age of American Law.* New York: George Braziller, 1965.

Haines, Charles Grove. *The American Doctrine of Judicial Supremacy.* New York: Russell and Russell, 1959.

————. *The Role of the Supreme Court in American Government and Politics 1789-1835.* New York: Russell and Russell, 1960.

Harris, Michael H. "The Frontier Lawyer's Library: Southern Indiana, 1800-1850, as a Test Case." *American Journal of Legal History,* XVI (1972), 239-251.

Harrison, M. Leigh. "A Study of the Earliest Reported Decisions of the South Carolina Courts of Law." *American Journal of Legal History,* XVI (1972), 51-70.

Hart, Henry M., Jr., and Wechsler, Herbert. *The Federal Courts and the Federal System.* Brooklyn, New York: The Foundation Press, Inc., 1953.

Haskins, George L. "Court Records and History." *William and Mary Quarterly,* 3d Ser., V (1948), 547-552.

Heaton, Richard C. "A Study of the Federal Courts for North Dakota." *Dakota Law Review*, IV (1932), 133-174.

Henderson, Dwight F. *Courts for a New Nation*. Washington, D.C.: Public Affairs Press, 1971.

Henderson, Edith Guild. "The Background of the Seventh Amendment." *Harvard Law Review*, LXXX (1966), 289-337.

Hicks, Frederick C. *Materials and Methods of Legal Research*. 3rd rev. ed. Rochester, New York: Lawyers Cooperative Publishing Co., 1942.

Holdsworth, William S. *A History of English Law*. 16 vols. London: Methuen and Co., 1903-1966.

Horwitz, Morton J. "The Conservative Tradition in the Writing of American Legal History." *American Journal of Legal History*, XVII (1973), 275-294.

Howe, Mark, Jr. Review of *Records of the Suffolk County Court, 1671-1680*. *New England Quarterly*, VII (1934), 307-314.

Hurst, James Willard. *The Growth of American Law: The Law Makers*. Boston: Little, Brown and Co., 1950.

————. *Law and Economic Growth: The Legal History of the Lumber Industry in Wisconsin, 1836-1915*. Cambridge, Mass.: Harvard University Press, 1964.

————. *Law and the Conditions of Freedom in the Nineteenth Century United States*. Madison, Wisc.: University of Wisconsin Press, 1956.

Jackson, Richard Meredith. *The Machinery of Justice in England*. 5th ed. Cambridge: Cambridge University Press, 1967.

Johnson, Bradley T. *Reports of Cases Decided by Chief Justice Chase in the Circuit Court of the United States Fourth Circuit 1865-1869*. Introduction by Ferne B. Hyman and Harold M. Hyman. New York: Da Capo Press, 1972.

Johnson, Herbert Alan. "The Prerogative Court of New York, 1686-1776." *American Journal of Legal History*, XVII (1973), 95-144.

Kammen, Michael G. "Colonial Court Records and the Study of Early American History: A Bibliographic Review." *American Historical Review*, LXX (1965), 732-739.

Katz, Stanley N. "Looking Backward: The Early History of American Law." *University of Chicago Law Review*, XXXIII (1966), 867-884.

Kommers, Donald P. "Reflections on Professor Chroust's *The Rise of the Legal Profession in America*." *American Journal of Legal History*, X (1966), 201-213.

Laurent, Francis W. *The Business of a Trial Court: 100 Years of Cases*. Madison, Wisc.: University of Wisconsin Press, 1959.

Law, A Century of Progress, 1835-1935. 3 vols. New York: New York University Press, 1937.

Levy, Leonard W. *Freedom of Speech and Press in Early American History: Legacy of Suppression*. New York: Harper and Row, 1963.

————. *Jefferson and Civil Liberties: The Darker Side*. Cambridge, Mass.: Harvard University Press, 1963.

———. "Liberty and the First Amendment: 1790-1800." *American Historical Review*, LXVIII (1962), 22-38.

Llewellyn, Karl N. *The Common Law Tradition: Deciding Appeals*. Boston: Little, Brown and Co., 1960.

Loyd, William H. "The Surety." *University of Pennsylvania Law Review*, LXVI (1917), 40-68.

Mathis, Doyle. "*Chisholm* v. *Georgia*: Background and Settlement." *Journal of American History*, LIV (1967), 19-29.

Millar, Robert Wyness. "Jurisdiction over Absent Defendants: Two Chapters in American Civil Procedure." *Louisiana Law Review*, LIV (1954), 321-339.

———. "Three American Ventures in Summary Civil Procedure." *Yale Law Journal*, XXXVIII (1928), 193-224.

Miller, John C. *Crisis in Freedom: The Alien and Sedition Acts*. Boston: Little, Brown and Co., 1951.

Mitchell, Broadus, and Mitchell, Louise Pearson. *A Biography of the Constitution of the United States: Its Origin, Formation, Adoption, Interpretation*. New York: Oxford University Press, 1964.

Morgan, Willis D. "The History and Economics of Suretyship." *Cornell Law Quarterly*, XII (1927), 153-171.

Morris, Richard B. "The Current Statesmen's Papers Publications Program: An Appraisal from the Point of View of the Legal Historian." *American Journal of Legal History*, XI (1967), 95-106.

Nelson, William E. *Americanization of the Common Law: The Impact of Legal Change on Massachusetts Society, 1760-1830*. Cambridge, Mass.: Harvard University Press, 1975.

Nettels, Curtis. "The Mississippi Valley and the Constitution, 1815-1829." *Mississippi Valley Historical Review*, XI (1924), 332-357.

———. "The Mississippi Valley and the Federal Judiciary, 1807-1837." *Mississippi Valley Historical Review*, XII (1925), 202-226.

Newmyer, R. Kent. "Justice Joseph Story on Circuit and a Neglected Phase of American Legal History." *American Journal of Legal History*, XIV (1970), 112-135.

———. *The Supreme Court Under Marshall and Taney*. New York: Thomas Y. Crowell, 1968.

Parker, John J. "The Federal Judicial System." *Federal Rules Decisions*, XIV (1954), 361-370.

Peltason, Jack W. *Federal Courts in the Political Process*. New York: Random House, 1955.

Perkins, Rollin M. *Cases and Materials on Criminal Law and Procedure*. 3d ed. Brooklyn, New York: The Foundation Press, Inc., 1966.

Philbrick, Francis S. "Law, Courts, and Litigation of Indiana Territory 1800-1809." *Illinois Law Review*, XXIV (1929), 193-219.

Plucknett, Theodore F. T. *A Concise History of the Common Law*. 5th ed. Boston: Little, Brown and Co., 1956.

223

Pound, Roscoe. *The Formative Era of American Law.* Boston: Little, Brown and Co., 1938.

———. *The Lawyer from Antiquity to Modern Times.* St. Paul, Minn.: West Publishing Co., 1953.

———. "New Possibilities of Old Materials of American Legal History." *West Virginia Law Quarterly,* XL (1934), 205-211.

———. *Organization of Courts.* Boston: Little, Brown and Co., 1940.

———. "The Pioneers and the Common Law." *West Virginia Law Quarterly,* XXVII (1920), 1-19.

———. "The Place of Judge Story in the Making of American Law." *American Law Review,* XLVIII (1912), 676-682.

———. Review of *Cases and Other Authorities in Equity,* by Walter Wheeler Cook. *Harvard Law Review,* XXXVII (1923), 396-399.

———. *The Spirit of the Common Law.* Boston: Marshall Jones Co., 1921.

Records of the Suffolk County Court, 1671-1680. Introduction by Zechariah Chafee, Jr. 2 vols. Boston: The Colonial Society of Massachusetts, 1933.

Rhodes, Irwin S. "The History of the United States District Court for the Southern District of Ohio." *Cincinnati Law Review,* XXIV (1955), 1-17.

Richardson, Richard J., and Vines, Kenneth N. *The Politics of Federal Courts: Lower Courts in the United States.* Boston: Little, Brown and Co., 1970.

Schick, Marvin. *Learned Hand's Court.* Baltimore, Md.: Johns Hopkins University Press, 1970.

Schmidhauser, John R. *The Supreme Court as Final Arbiter in Federal-State Relations.* Chapel Hill, N.C.: University of North Carolina Press, 1958.

Scott, Austin Wakeman, and Kent, Robert Brydon. *Cases and Other Materials on Civil Procedure.* Boston: Little, Brown and Co., 1967.

Simpson, Laurence P. *Handbook on the Law of Suretyship.* St. Paul, Minn.: West Publishing Co., 1950.

Smith, James Morton. *Freedom's Fetters: The Alien and Sedition Laws and American Civil Liberties.* Ithaca, N.Y.: Cornell University Press, 1966.

Smith, Joseph H., ed. *Colonial Justice in Western Massachusetts (1639-1702): The Pynchon Court Record, An Original Judges' Diary of the Administration of Justice in the Springfield Courts in the Massachusetts Bay Colony.* Cambridge, Mass.: Harvard University Press, 1961.

Street, Thomas Atkins. *The Foundations of Legal Liability.* 3 vols. Northport, Long Island, New York: Edward Thompson and Co., 1906.

Surrency, Erwin C. "Federal District Court Judges and the History of Their Courts." *Federal Rules Decisions,* XL (1966), 139-349.

———. "The First Judges of the Federal Courts." *American Journal of Legal History,* I (1957), 76-78.

———. "History of Federal Courts." *Missouri Law Review,* XXVIII (1963), 214-244.

Tucker, St. George, ed. *Blackstone's Commentaries: With Notes of Refer-ence, to the Constitution and Laws, of the Federal Government of the United States; And of the Commonwealth of Virginia.* 5 vols. Philadelphia: William Young Birch and Abraham Small, 1803.

Turner, Kathryn. "Federalist Policy and the Judiciary Act of 1801." *William and Mary Quarterly,* 3d Ser., xxii (1965), 3-32.

————. "The Midnight Judges." *University of Pennsylvania Law Review,* cix (1961), 494-523.

Vaughan, Alden T., and Billias, George Athan. *Perspectives on Early Amer-ican History: Essays in Honor of Richard B. Morris.* New York: Harper and Row, 1973.

Vines, Kenneth N., and Jacob, Herbert. *Studies in Judicial Politics.* Tulane Studies in Political Science, Vol. viii. New Orleans: Tulane University, 1963.

Warren, Charles. *A History of the American Bar.* Boston: Little, Brown and Co., 1911.

————. "New Light on the History of the Federal Judiciary Act of 1789." *Harvard Law Review,* xxxvii (1923), 49-132.

————. *The Supreme Court in United States History.* Rev. ed. in 2 vols. Boston: Little, Brown and Co., 1926.

Wendell, Mitchell. *Relations Between the Federal and State Courts.* New York: Columbia University Press, 1949.

Younger, Richard D. *The People's Panel: The Grand Jury in the United States, 1634-1941.* Providence, R.I.: Brown University Press, 1963.

V. KENTUCKY HISTORIES

Bodley, Temple. *History of Kentucky.* 4 vols. Chicago: S. J. Clarke Publish-ing Co., 1928.

Brown, John Mason. *The Political Beginnings of Kentucky.* Louisville, Ky.: John P. Morton and Co., 1889.

Clark, Thomas D. *A History of Kentucky.* New York: Prentice-Hall, 1937.

Clift, G. Glenn. *Governors of Kentucky 1792-1942.* Cynthiana, Ky.: Hobson Press, 1942.

Collins, Lewis, and Collins, Richard H. *History of Kentucky.* Louisville, Ky.: John P. Morton and Co., 1924.

Connelley, William Elsey, and Coulter, E[llis] M[erton]. *History of Ken-tucky.* Edited by Charles Kerr. 5 vols. Chicago and New York: The Amer-ican Historical Society, 1922.

Cotterill, Robert S. *History of Pioneer Kentucky.* Cincinnati: Johnson and Hardin, 1917.

Crowgey, Henry G. *Kentucky Bourbon: The Early Years of Whiskeymaking.* Lexington, Ky.: University Press of Kentucky, 1971.

Daviess, Maria T. *History of Mercer and Boyle Counties.* Harrodsburg, Ky.: The Harrodsburg Herald, 1924.

Green, Thomas Marshall. *Historic Families of Kentucky.* Baltimore: Regional Publishing Co., 1964 (orig. publ. Cincinnati, 1889).

————. *The Spanish Conspiracy, A Review of Early Spanish Movements in the Southwest: Containing Proofs of the Intrigues of General James Wilkinson and John Brown; of the Complicity Therewith of Judges Sebastian, Wallace, and Innes; The Early Struggles of Kentucky for Autonomy; The Intrigues of Sebastian in 1795-7, and the Legislative Investigation of His Corruption.* Cincinnati: Robert Clarke and Co., 1891.

Jillson, Willard Rouse. *Henry Clay's Defense of Aaron Burr in 1806.* Frankfort, Ky.: n.p., 1943.

————. *The Kentucky Land Grants.* Baltimore: Genealogical Publishing Co., 1971.

————. *Old Kentucky Entries and Deeds.* Louisville, Ky.: Standard Printing Co., 1926.

Kincaid, Robert L. *The Wilderness Road.* Harrogate, Tenn.: Lincoln Memorial University Press, 1955.

Levin, H. *The Lawyers and Lawmakers of Kentucky.* Chicago: Lewis Publishing Co., 1897.

Marshall, Humphrey. *History of Kentucky.* 2 vols. Frankfort, Ky.: George S. Robinson, 1824.

Price, Samuel W. *Biographical Sketch of Joseph Crockett.* Louisville, Ky.: John P. Morton and Co., 1909.

Reprints of Littell's Political Transactions In and Concerning Kentucky; And Letter of George Nicholas to his Friend in Virginia, also General Wilkinson's Memorial. Introduction by Temple Bodley. Louisville, Ky.: John P. Morton and Co., 1926.

Robertson, James Rood. *Petitions of the Early Inhabitants of Kentucky.* Louisville, Ky.: John P. Morton and Co., 1914.

Smith, W. T. *A Complete Index to the Names of Persons, Places, and Subjects Mentioned in Littell's Laws of Kentucky.* Lexington, Ky.: Bradford Club Press, 1931.

Speed, Thomas. *History of the United States Courts in Kentucky.* Louisville, Ky.: Courier-Journal Job Printing Co., 1896.

————. *The Political Club, Danville, Kentucky 1786-1790.* Louisville, Ky.: John P. Morton and Co., 1894.

————. *Records and Memorials of the Speed Family.* Louisville, Ky.: Courier-Journal Job Printing Co., 1892.

————. *The Wilderness Road.* Louisville, Ky.: John P. Morton and Co., 1886.

Todd, Chapman C. "The Early Courts of Kentucky." *The Register of the Kentucky Historical Society,* III (1905), 33-48.

Watlington, Patricia. *The Partisan Spirit: Kentucky Politics, 1779-1792.* New York: Atheneum, 1972.

Wilson, Samuel M. *The First Land Court of Kentucky 1779-1780.* Lexington, 1923.

VI. OTHER SECONDARY SOURCES

Abernethy, Thomas Perkins. *The Burr Conspiracy.* New York: Oxford University Press, 1954.

——. *The South in the New Nation 1789-1810.* A History of the South, edited by Wendell Holmes Stephenson and E[llis] Merton Coulter, Vol. 4. Baton Rouge, La.: Louisiana State University Press, 1961.

——. *Western Lands and the American Revolution.* New York: Russell and Russell, Inc., 1959.

Baldwin, Leland D. *Whiskey Rebels: The Story of a Frontier Uprising.* Pittsburgh, Penn.: University of Pittsburgh Press, 1939.

Bemis, Samuel Flagg. *Pinckney's Treaty.* Rev. ed. New Haven, Conn.: Yale University Press, 1960.

Beveridge, Albert J. *The Life of John Marshall.* 4 vols. New York: Houghton Mifflin Co., 1919.

Borden, Morton. *Parties and Politics in the Early Republic, 1789-1815.* New York: Thomas Y. Crowell, 1967.

Chambers, William Nisbet. *Political Parties in a New Nation: The American Experience, 1776-1809.* New York: Oxford University Press, 1963.

Cooke, Jacob E. "The Whiskey Insurrection: A Re-evaluation." *Pennsylvania History*, xxx (1963), 316-346.

Corwin, Edward S. *John Marshall and the Constitution.* New Haven, Conn.: Yale University Press, 1919.

Dargo, George. *Jefferson's Louisiana: Politics and the Clash of Legal Traditions.* Cambridge, Mass.: Harvard University Press, 1975.

——. *Roots of the Republic: A New Perspective on Early American Constitutionalism.* New York: Praeger Publishers, 1974.

"The Democratic Societies of 1793 and 1794 in Kentucky, Pennsylvania, and Virginia." *William and Mary Quarterly*, 2d Ser., II (1922), 239-256.

Dunne, Gerald T. *Justice Joseph Story and the Rise of the Supreme Court.* New York: Simon and Schuster, 1970.

Eaton, Clement. "A Mirror of the Southern Colonial Lawyer: The Fee Books of Patrick Henry, Thomas Jefferson, and Waightstill Avery." *William and Mary Quarterly*, 3d Ser., VIII (1951), 520-534.

Ellis, Richard E. *The Jeffersonian Crisis: Courts and Politics in the Young Republic.* New York: Oxford University Press, 1971.

Evans, Emory G. "Private Indebtedness and the Coming of the Revolution in Virginia, 1776 to 1796." *William and Mary Quarterly*, 3d Ser., XXVIII (1971), 349-374.

Ferguson, E. James. *The Power of the Purse: A History of American Public Finance, 1776-1790.* Chapel Hill: University of North Carolina Press, 1961.

227

Gates, Paul W. "The Role of the Land Speculator in Western Development." *Pennsylvania Magazine of History and Biography*, LXVI (1942), 314-333.

————. "Tenants of the Log Cabin." *Mississippi Valley Historical Review*, XLIX (1962), 3-31.

Gayarre, Charles [Etienne Arthur]. *History of Louisiana*. 4th ed. 4 vols. New Orleans: F. F. Hansell and Bro., 1851-1903.

Goebel, Dorothy Burne. *William Henry Harrison: A Political Biography*. Indianapolis: Historical Bureau of the Indiana Library and Historical Department, 1926.

Harrison, Lowell H. *John Breckinridge: Jeffersonian Republican*. Louisville, Ky.: The Filson Club, 1969.

Kohn, Richard H. "The Washington Administration's Decision to Crush the Whiskey Rebellion." *Journal of American History*, LIX (1972), 567-584.

Lewis, John D., ed. *Anti-Federalists Versus Federalists*. San Francisco: Chandler Publishing Co., 1967.

Linn, John B., and Egle, William H., eds. *Papers Relating to What is Known as The Whiskey Insurrection in Western Pennsylvania; 1794*. Pennsylvania Archives, 2d Ser., vol. IV. Harrisburg, Pa.: E. K. Myers, 1890.

Main, Jackson Turner. "The Distribution of Property in Post-Revolutionary Virginia." *Mississippi Valley Historical Review*, XLI (1954), 241-258.

Marshall, John. *The Life of George Washington*. 2 vols. Reprint ed., New York: Walton Book Co., 1933 (orig. publ. 1804).

McDermott, John Francis, ed. *The Spanish in the Mississippi Valley 1762-1804*. Urbana, Ill.: University of Illinois Press, 1974.

Miller, John C. *The Federalist Era, 1789-1801*. The New American Nation Series, edited by Henry Steele Commager and Richard B. Morris. New York: Harper and Bros., 1960.

Miller, Perry. *The Life of the Mind in America: From the Revolution to the Civil War*. New York: Harcourt, Brace and World, 1965.

Miller, William. "The Democratic Societies and the Whiskey Rebellion." *Pennsylvania Magazine of History and Biography*, LXII (1938), 324-350.

Morrill, James R. *The Practice and Politics of Fiat Finance: North Carolina in the Confederation, 1783-1789*. Chapel Hill, N.C.: University of North Carolina Press, 1969.

Morris, Richard B. *The Peacemakers: The Great Powers and American Independence*. New York: Harper and Row, 1965.

Nettels, Curtis P. *The Emergence of a National Economy, 1775-1815*. The Economic History of the United States, edited by Henry David *et al.*, Vol. 2. New York: Holt, Rinehart and Winston, 1962.

Paxton, W[illiam] M[cClung]. *The Marshall Family*. Cincinnati: R. Clarke and Co., 1885.

Prince, Carl E. "The Passing of the Aristocracy: Jefferson's Removal of the Federalists, 1801-1805." *Journal of American History*, LVII (1970), 565-575.

Reardon, John J. *Edmund Randolph*. New York: Macmillan, 1974.

Risjord, Norman K. "The Virginia Federalists." *Journal of Southern History*, xxxiii (1967), 486-517.

Rohrbough, Malcolm J. *The Land Office Business: The Settlement and Administration of American Public Lands, 1789-1837*. New York: Oxford University Press, 1968.

Smelser, Marshall. *The Democratic Republic, 1801-1815*. The New American Nation Series, edited by Henry Steele Commager and Richard B. Morris. New York: Harper and Row, 1968.

Van Schaack, Henry C. *Life of Peter Van Schaack, LL.D*. New York: D. Appleton and Co., 1842.

Whitaker, Arthur Preston. "Harry Innes and the Spanish Intrigue, 1794-1795." *Mississippi Valley Historical Review*, xv (1928), 236-248.

————. *The Mississippi Question, 1795-1803: A Study in Trade, Politics, and Diplomacy*. [1934.] Reprint ed., Gloucester, Mass.: Peter Smith, 1962.

————. "New Light on the Treaty of San Lorenzo: An Essay in Historical Criticism." *Mississippi Valley Historical Review*, xv (1929), 435-454.

————. *The Spanish-American Frontier, 1783-1795*. New York: Houghton Mifflin Co., 1927.

White, Leonard D. *The Federalists: A Study in Administrative History*. New York: The Macmillan Co., 1948.

————. *The Jeffersonians: A Study in Administrative History, 1801-1829*. New York: The Macmillan Co., 1951.

Wood, Gordon S. *The Creation of the American Republic, 1776-1787*. Chapel Hill, N.C.: University of North Carolina Press, 1969.

Young, James Sterling. *The Washington Community 1800-1828*. New York: Columbia University Press, 1966.

Index

Adair, John, 74, 139, 143-44
Adams, John, 24, 45, 117, 195
admiralty jurisdiction, 24n
advisory juries, 179-82, 189
Alcorn, William, 137
Antifederalists, 35

Bank of the United States, 24n, 133, 137
Berry, Richard, 146-47
Bibb, George M., 75, 76n, 171
Bodley, Thomas, 44, 189
Brandeis, Louis D., 3, 183
Brashear, Dennis, 147
Breckinridge, John, 35, 37, 71, 139, 197
Brown, James, 69, 71
Brown, John, and Innes, 33, 35-37; and H. Marshall, 43, 46; on Kentucky affairs, 66n, 72n; internal revenue case, 106, 109, 125
Burr, Aaron, 45, 138-45, 196
Bush, Ambrose, 108n, 109, 112, 113

Carondelet, Francisco de, 44
Carrington, Edward, 99n, 101-102, 106-107
case (action at law), 79, 83, 150-51, 159, 165, Glossary
caveat (equity proceeding), 41, 175, 178-79, 188, Glossary
chancery (land cases), 175, 179-85. See also equity
Clarke, William, as U.S. attorney, 72, 73, 195; internal revenue prosecutions, 106-17, 125; as territorial judge, 117
Clay, Henry, as ally of Innes's, 35, 43, 45, 52; and Burr affair, 139, 142-43, 145; as attorney, 161n; on patents, 174
collectors of internal revenue: delinquency among, 26, 102, 114, 121-23, 125; duties and fees, 99-102
Combs, Asa, 133-34

common law, 77-94, 131
Constitution, see United States Constitution
costs, 91-92
covenant (action at law), 79, 83, 84, 150-51, 160, 165, Glossary
Coxe, Tench, 66n, 70, 72, 99-106
Crockett, Joseph, 64
Crockett, Robert, 65
Crutchlow, John, 129-33

Daveiss, Joseph Hamilton, as U.S. attorney, 74-75; and Burr affair, 45, 138-45, 196; and criminal prosecutions, 131-38; and internal revenue cases, 118-22, 125; and Innes, 181; and Jefferson, 25, 144; and stamp act prosecutions, 127-28; and *Wilson v. Mason*, 173n, 188
Davis, Thomas T., 70, 115, 154
Dearborn, Henry, 131-32
debt (action at law), 79, 83-84, 150-51, 155-57, 162-65, Glossary
Dembitz, Lewis N., 78n, 167n, 173-75
detinue (action at law), 83, 160-61, 165, Glossary

ejectment (action at law), 83-84, 87, 175-77, Glossary
equity, 77-83, 85, 87, 90-93

Fallen Timbers, Battle of, 23, 48
Federalist judiciary acts, see Judiciary Acts (1801)
Federalists, 21-23, 35-36, 194
Flournoy, Francis, 135-36
Floyd, Davis, 142
Fowler, John, 139
Frankfurter, Felix, 3-4

Gallatin, Albert, 64-65, 67, 119
Gayoso de Lemos, Manuel, 47-49, 51, 67n
Gillaway, George, 129
Gillaway, James, 129

231

Goebel, Julius, Jr., 8, 118n
grand juries, 95-97, 101, 104-108, 112,
  116, 118. *See also* Innes, Harry,
  grand jury addresses
Greenville, Treaty of, 48, 50, 73n, 125

Hamilton, Alexander, 66n, 72, 99, 102
Hanna, John H., 63
Harrison, William Henry, 117, 129-30,
  132-33, 139
Hubbard, Ephraim, 146
Hunter, James G., 62

Innes, Harry, 31-53; as "A Farmer,"
  38; as Antifederalist, 35; beliefs,
  33-34, 38-40, 193, 198-99; characteristics of, 15, 32, 37; criminal
  prosecutions under, 127-48; early
  life, 31; fears Constitution, 34;
  fights impeachment, 46-47; grand
  jury addresses, 39, 96-97, 108-109,
  136-37, 147; named in Burr affair,
  139; named in "Spanish conspiracy,"
  46; on constitutional interpretation,
  140, 153-55; on internal revenue
  cases, 105, 107-26; on land cases,
  179-90; on management of court,
  81-94, 158; on Sixth Circuit Court,
  54, 56-57; on statistics, 151-52; on
  statutory interpretation, 155-56;
  Spanish contacts, 44, 47-49
Innes, James, 49-50, 103
internal revenue acts, 23, 25, 95,
  97-126, 195-96
Irvine, Christopher, 137-38

Jackson, Andrew, 54-55, 153
Jay, John, 23, 33n, 48
Jefferson, Thomas, and Burr affair,
  139-40, 144-45; and Innes's defense,
  47; correspondence with Innes, 38,
  45n; on Hardin's case, 132n; on
  Indian policy, 130, 133n; on
  internal revenue arrearages, 102-103;
  on juries, 180; on viva voce
  testimony, 83; reputation in
  Kentucky, 26, 35n, 66n, 196
Jones, Thomas, 106, 109-11
Judiciary Act (1789), 19, 140; Section

11, 155; Section 15, 82; Section 16,
  81; Section 30, 82; Section 31, 91,
  163; Section 34, 17, 24n, 84, 158,
  166, 179, 180n, 182-83
Judiciary Acts (1801), 21-24, 54-56,
  195
Judiciary Act (1802), 25, 57
Judiciary Act (1807), 26-27, 58
juries, *see* advisory juries; grand juries;
  petit juries

Kennedy, Daniel, 133-34
Kennedy, Robert, 133-34
Kennedy, Stephen, 133-34
Kent, James, 9, 77n, 179n
Kentucky constitutional conventions,
  33, 40-42, 125
Kentucky constitutions (1792) (1799),
  180n
Kentucky Court of Appeals, 41, 124,
  178, 193
Kentucky District Court (United
  States Court for the District of
  Kentucky), 19-20, 22, 25, 28
Kentucky federal courts, Order Books,
  6. *See also* Kentucky District Court
  (1789-1801, 1802-1816); Sixth
  Circuit Court (1801-1802); Seventh
  Circuit Court (1807-1816)
Kentucky Resolutions, 24, 71, 195, 197
Knox, Henry, 40, 47

land companies, 167-68, 170
Landis, James M., 3-4

McClung, William, and Sixth Circuit
  Court, 22, 54, 56-57, 93; refuses
  appointment as U.S. attorney, 72,
  105
McDowell, Samuel, Jr., 63-64
McNairy, John, 54-56, 93, 152n
Madison, James, 46n, 49n, 118n,
  151-52
Mannen, John, 118-19, 136
Marshall, Humphrey, and McClung's
  appointment, 56; as ally of J. H.
  Daveiss, 46, 74, 117n; as
  "Coriolanus," 42; as litigant, 43; as
  surveyor, 173; characteristics of, 35n,

Library of Congress Cataloging in Publication Data

Tachau, Mary K   Bonsteel, 1926-
    Federal courts in the early Republic.
    Bibliography: p.
    Includes index.
    1. Courts—Kentucky—History.   2. Law—Kentucky—
History and criticism.   3. Law—United States—History
and criticism.   I. Title.
KFK1278.T3   347'.769'0109   78-51196
ISBN 0-691-04661-1